D1219338

IN THE NAME OF

ALLAH

THE ALL-COMPASSIONATE, ALL-MERCIFUL

SHAHÂDAH

(TESTIMONY OF FAITH)
&
ITS ESSENTIAL CONDITIONS

- Title: *Shahâdah (Testimony of Faith) &*
- *Its Essential Conditions*
- Author: Yahya M. A. Ondigo
- English Edition 1 (2014)
- Layout Design: IIPH, Egypt Branch
- Cover Design: Manal Khalifa

The Pillars of Islam Made Easy - I

SHAHÂDAH

(TESTIMONY OF FAITH)

&

ITS ESSENTIAL CONDITIONS

الشهادة وشروطها

Yahya M. A. Ondigo

الدار العالمية للكتاب الإسلامي

INTERNATIONAL ISLAMIC PUBLISHING HOUSE

Copyright © 2014 International Islamic Publishing House

King Fahd National Library Cataloging-in-Publication Data

Ondigo, Yahya M. A.

Shahâdah (Testimony of Faith) & Its Essential Conditions. / Yahya M. A. Ondigo. — Riyadh, 2014

208 pp ; 21 cm

ISBN Hardcover: 978-603-501-204-1

1- Pillars of Islamic worship 2- Islamic rulings

I- Title

240 dc

Legal Deposit no. **1434/3227**

ISBN Hardcover: 978-603-501-204-1

All rights reserved for the Publisher. No part of this book may be produced or transmitted in any form or by any means, electronic or mechanical, including photocopying, recording, or by any information storage and retrieval system, without written permission from the Publisher.

The scanning, uploading and distribution of this book via the Internet or via any other means without the written permission of the Publisher is illegal and punishable by law. Please purchase only authorized electronic editions, and do not participate in or encourage electronic piracy of copyrighted materials. Your support is appreciated.

International Islamic Publishing House (IIPH)
P.O. Box 55195 Riyadh 11534, Saudi Arabia
Tel: 966 11 4650818 / 4647213 — Fax: 966 11 4633489
E-mail: editorial@iiph.com — iiphsa@gmail.com
www.iiph.com | www.iiph.com.sa

Contents

Pronunciation and Transliteration Chart

Arabic script	Pronunciation	Trans-literated form
أ	short ‘a’, as in *cat*	a
آ — ى	longer ‘a’, as in *cab* (not as in *cake*)	â
ب	/b/ as in *bell*, *rubber* and *tab*	b
ت	/t/ as in *tap*, *mustard* and *sit*	t
ة	takes the sound of the preceding diacritical mark sometimes ending in h (when in pausal form): ah, ih or ooh; or atu(n), ati(n) or ata(n) when uninterrupted	h or t (when followed by another Arabic word)
ث	/th/ as in *thing*, *maths* and *wealth*	th
ج	/j/ as in *jam*, *ajar* and *age*	j
ح	a ‘harsher’ sound than the English initial /h/, and may occur medially and in word-final position as well	ḥ
خ	as in *Bach* (in German); may occur initially and medially as well	kh

Arabic script	Pronunciation	Trans-literated form
د	/d/ as in *do*, *muddy* and *red*	d
ذ	as in *this*, *father* and *smooth*	dh
ر	/r/ as in *raw*, *arid* and *war*; may also be a rolled 'r', as pronounced in Spanish	r
ز	/z/ as in *zoo*, *easy* and *gaze*	z
س	/s/ as in *so*, *messy* and *grass*	s
ش	as in *ship*, *ashes* and *rush*	sh
ص	no close equivalent in English, but may be approximated by pronouncing it as /sw/ or /s/ farther back in the mouth	ṣ
ض	no close equivalent in English, but may be approximated by pronouncing it as /d/ farther back in the mouth	ḍ
ط	no close equivalent in English, but may be approximated by pronouncing it as /t/ farther back in the mouth	ṭ
ظ	no close equivalent in English, but may be approximated by pronouncing 'the' farther back in the mouth	dh
ع	no close equivalent in English: a guttural sound in the back of the throat	'
غ	no close equivalent in English, but may be closely approximated by pronouncing it like the French /r/ in 'rouge'	gh

Arabic script	Pronunciation	Trans-literated form
ف	/f/ as in *fill*, *effort* and *muff*	f
ق	no close equivalent in English, but may be approximated by pronouncing it as /k/ farther back in the mouth	q
ك	/k/ as in *king*, *buckle* and *tack*	k
ل	/l/ as in *lap*, *halo*; in the word Allah, it becomes velarized as in *ball*	l
م	/m/ as in *men*, *simple* and *ram*	m
ن	/n/ as in *net*, *ant* and *can*	n
هـ — ه — ـه	/h/ as in *hat*; unlike /h/ in English, in Arabic /h/ is pronounced in medial and word-final positions as well	h
و	as in *wet* and *away*	w
و	long 'u', as in *boot* and *too*	oo
ي	as in *yard* and *mayo*	y
ي	long 'e', as in *eat*, *beef* and *see*	ee
ء	glottal stop: may be closely approximated by pronouncing it like 't' in the Cockney English pronunciation of *butter*: *bu'er*, or the stop sound in *uh-oh!*	' (omitted in initial position)

Diphthongs

Arabic script	Pronunciation	Trans-literated form
أو، ◌َو	long 'o', as in *owe*, *boat* and *go*	au, aw
أي، ◌َي	long 'a', as in *aid*, *rain* and *say*	ay, ai, ei

Diacritical marks (tashkeel)

Name of mark	Pronunciation	Trans-literated form
◌َ fatḥah	very short 'a' or schwa (unstressed vowel)	a
◌ِ kasrah	shorter version of ee or schwa (unstressed vowel)	i
◌ُ ḍammah	shorter version of oo	u
◌ّ shaddah	a doubled consonant is stressed in the word, and the length of the sound is also doubled	double letter
◌ْ sukoon	no vowel sound between consonants or at the end of a word	absence of vowel

Arabic honorific symbols used in this book

(سبحانه وتعالى): *Subḥânahu wa Ta'âlâ* — Glorified and Exalted is He

(ﷺ): *Ṣalla Allâhu 'alayhi wa sallam* — Blessings and peace be upon him

(عليه السلام): *'Alayhi as-salâm* — Peace be upon him

(رضي الله عنه): *Raḍiya Allâhu 'anhu* — May Allah be pleased with him

(رضي الله عنها): *Raḍiya Allâhu 'anhâ* — May Allah be pleased with her

Hadith grade terms in this book

Sound:	*ṣaḥeeḥ*
Reliable:	*ḥasan*
Weak:	*ḍa'eef*
Odd:	*ghareeb*
Authentic:	includes sound, reliable, or any grade in between
Acceptable:	*sakat 'anhu*; the grader of the hadith did not comment on it, meaning that he found nothing unacceptable in it

A Word about the Word *Lord*

The word *lord* in English has several related meanings. The original meaning is 'master' or 'ruler', and in this sense it is often used to refer to human beings: 'the lord of the mansion' or 'Lord So-and-So' (in the United Kingdom, for example). The word *Lord* with a capital L is used in the lexicon of Islam to refer to the One and Only God — Allah. In Islam, there is no ambiguity about the meaning of this word. While it is true that one may occasionally use the word *lord* (whether capitalized or not) to refer to a human being, in Islamic discourse the reference of this term is always clear from the context. Whereas for Christians, Hindus and other polytheists, the word *Lord* with a capital L may refer to Allah, to Jesus or to some imagined deity, for Muslims, there can be no plurality of meaning. Allah alone is the Lord, and the Lord is Allah — not Jesus, not Rama, not any other being.

The Editor

When 'jihad' refers to fighting

Although jihad is often translated into English as 'holy war', it must be noted that war has never been described as 'holy' in any of Islam's primary texts or even early Islamic literature. Linguistically speaking, jihad is an Islamic term that applies to a broad spectrum of activities, ranging from daily striving to meet the day's challenges, to the striving against one's desires and self, to the struggle to provide for one's family. Its basic definition is 'the act of striving or struggling in the way of Allah'. Therefore, jihad is not limited to war; it includes struggling with one's soul, speech, body and wealth so that the message of Allah reaches all humans willing to receive it.

Islamic scholars have referred to different types of jihad, such as jihad against the self (to understand Islam, act upon it, call others to it and be patient with the difficulties of making this call), jihad against the Devil (repelling Satanic whispers, doubts and lusts), jihad against the tongue (controlling it, using it to enjoin what is good, forbid what is wrong, spread the correct teachings of Islam and answer false ideologies), jihad against aggression with the purpose of protecting Islam and the lives, honour and property of Muslims) and other types of jihad like jihad against the hypocrites, jihad against oppressors and jihad against mischief makers.

Jihad — in the context of fighting — has specific rules and conditions that need to be met before jihad is initiated. The first rule is that people are not to be fought because of what they believe, or to coerce them to accept Islam. The second rule is to 'fight only those who fight you' and never initiate unprovoked aggression *(Qur'an 2: 190)*. That means that Muslims are only allowed to fight back, rather than initiating fighting; but 'fighting back' includes fighting against actual aggression as well as proactively addressing real threats of aggression. In both cases, Muslims are instructed to be prepared and ready to defend their nation before they actually engage in military conflict. There are additional conditions, but the above-mentioned conditions are vital for putting jihad in its broader meaning in the proper context.

Another condition of the sort of jihad which involves fighting is that it should take place only under an Islamic authority that 'raises the banner' for such jihad. It is not following the Sunnah at all for any individual or self-appointed group of Muslims to wage war on behalf of a nation. Instead, Muslims should be united under the single authority of an imam or khaleefah (caliph), except in the case where an individual needs to defend his own family and property, or to help his neighbour to do so. This is proved by the example of the early Muslims as well as texts in the Qur'an and the Sunnah:

﴾When there comes to them [the hypocrites] a matter related to [public] safety or fear, they spread it about; if only they had referred it to the Messenger and to such of them as are in authority, those among them who are able to think through the matter would have understood it.﴿ *(Qur'an 4: 83)*

> «Ḥudhayfah ibn Yaman asked the Prophet (*ṣalla Allâhu 'alayhi wa sallam* — blessings and peace be upon him): What if (the Muslims) have no single leader (they are divided into disputing groups)? The Prophet (ﷺ) answered:

If they have no single leader or unified group, then leave all these disputing groups, even if you have to bite on a tree until your death.» [part of a longer hadith recorded by Bukhari]

There are other conditions for jihad. In general, the rules laid out for war in Islam should be upheld unless there is some legitimate need or strategy when fighting occurs that would necessitate going against those rules. A Muslim should not kill himself or herself *(Qur'an 4: 29)* nor kill another Muslim, except by accident *(Qur'an 4: 92)*. Women, children, the elderly and other non-combatants should not be harmed. Land should not be destroyed, nor trees cut down. Corpses should not be mutilated. Islam should not be imposed upon non-believers. Rather, if combatant non-Muslims choose on their own to embrace Islam, even if only as a deceitful trick, it should be accepted by the Muslim leadership, and fighting should stop. Peace should be sought before lives are lost. Treaties and agreements should be upheld. Prisoners should be well-treated. Above all, justice must be done.

﴾Fight in the path [according to the rules set by Allah] of Allah only those who fight you, but do not commit aggression [transgress limits]. Allah does not love aggressors. ...And fight them until persecution is no more, and religion is [freely embraced] for [the individual's faith in] Allah. But if they desist, then let there be no aggression except against transgressors.﴿

(Qur'an 2: 190, 193)

﴾Allah does not forbid you from being good, kind, just, and fair to those who have not fought you because of religion nor driven you from your homeland. Allah loves those who are just. Allah forbids you from giving allegiance to those who have fought you because of religion and have driven you from your homeland, and those who supported your expulsion...﴿ *(Qur'an 60: 8-9)*

In addition, the Muslim nation is encouraged to maintain strong military capabilities to promote justice and to deter acts of war and aggression.

﴾And make ready for them [their potential aggression] all you can of power, including steeds of war, to deter the enemy of Allah and your enemy, and others besides, whom you may not know but whom Allah knows.﴿ *(Qur'an 8: 60)*

The Editor

Publisher's Note

All praise and thanks belong to Allah alone, the One, the Almighty, and All-Merciful. Blessings and peace be upon Prophet Muhammad, the last of His messengers and prophets, and upon his family, his Companions, and all those who follow in his footsteps until the end of time.

It is always very heartening to note that Islam is the fastest growing religion in the world. On a daily basis, many individuals enter the fold of Islam by testifying that there is no God other than Allah and that Prophet Muhammad (ﷺ) is His servant and messenger. However, it is also very disturbing to observe many Muslims straying from the true message of the testimony of faith.

In this book, the author has clearly outlined the seven conditions attached to the testimony of faith; he has invited all Muslims to take note of and implement these in their everyday life. Bereft of these conditions, the testimony of faith is nothing more than lip service. This is a commendable effort by the author to invite the readers' attention to an oft-neglected issue.

May Allah accept the efforts of all those who contributed to the production of this book, and may it be acceptable to Him, *âmeen.*

Muhammad Abdul Mohsin Al-Tuwaijri
Managing Director
International Islamic Publishing House
Riyadh, Saudi Arabia

Dedication

This work is dedicated to my beloved wives, Safiyyah and Rahmah, for their patience and moral and spiritual encouragement as well as their strong commitment to home management. May Allah (*Subḥânahu wa Ta'âlâ* — Glorified and Exalted is He) reward us abundantly with His boundless mercy both in this world and in the hereafter. May Allah also forgive our sins and grant us righteous children who strive to the best of their ability in the path of Allah and are a source of joy for us in this life and in the next. May Allah accept all our righteous deeds and grant us mansions in paradise to reward our best actions. Indeed, our best wishes and prayers are in accordance with the words of *ar-Raḥmân* (Allah, the Most Merciful):

﴿... رَبَّنَا هَبْ لَنَا مِنْ أَزْوَٰجِنَا وَذُرِّيَّٰتِنَا قُرَّةَ أَعْيُنٍ وَٱجْعَلْنَا لِلْمُتَّقِينَ إِمَامًا ﴿٧٤﴾﴾ (سورة الفرقان: ٧٤)

﴿...Our Lord, grant us from among our wives and offspring comfort to our eyes and make us an example for the righteous.﴾

(Qur'an 25: 74)[1]

---

[1] The translations of the meanings of the Qur'anic verses in this book have been taken from Saheeh International, *The Qur'an: Arabic Text with Corresponding English Meanings* (Jeddah: Abul-Qasim Publishing House, 1997). Some changes have been made for the sake of clarity.

Foreword

A person enters Islam simply through the recitation of a few words known as the *shahâdah*[2] — the testimony of faith. This is the first fundamental principle of Islam. Uttering the shahâdah means to say: *lâ ilâha illâ Allâh, Muḥammadun rasool Ullâh*; that is, there is no god but Allah and Muhammad is the Messenger of Allah (ﷺ).

Upon attesting to the aforementioned words, individuals are supposed to change radically. They were disbelievers before; now, they have become Muslims. Previously, they were impure and now, they are pure. They had been destined for hell; now the gates of paradise are open for them.

In our social life, the shahâdah becomes the basis of differentiating one individual from another. Those who recite it constitute one nation — the Muslim Ummah — while those who reject it form another. If a father recites it and his son refuses to do so, the relationship between the two changes drastically; for one thing, they are no longer eligible to inherit from each other. On the other hand, if a total stranger proclaims the shahâdah and marries into a Muslim family, he and his children become eligible for inheritance. The power of the shahâdah is, thus, so strong that it takes precedence

---

2 Wherever possible, Arabic terms have been translated into English. In cases where we have chosen to retain the Arabic, the transliterated word or phrase is shown in italics the first time it appears in the text; the term is also defined in the Glossary found at the end of this book. [Editor]

even over blood ties. It can join strangers together into a nation and it can cut members of the same family off from each other.

Although the shahâdah is very important, its mere utterance is not enough. Indeed, there are certain prerequisites for the testimony of faith; these have been presented in this book. The author has demonstrated that the effectiveness of the shahâdah lies in its meaning. If the meaning does not penetrate deep into the hearts and has no impact powerful enough to bring about a change in thoughts, morals, and actions, then mere utterance is meaningless.

Suppose one feels thirsty and starts shouting, "Water! Water! Water!" Will the thirst disappear even if one repeats these words a million times? Of course not! The same applies to the shahâdah. The mere declaration of the shahâdah — without a full understanding of its meaning, importance, conditions, and the implications of its implementation — can never bring about a radical change in an individual. Therefore, in turn, it cannot have any impact upon the society either.

In this magnificent book, the essential elements of the shahâdah — the first fundamental principle of Islam — have been presented in a clear and lucid manner. As a result, this book is a highly suitable teaching aid for all levels. I strongly recommend this work of Capt. (Rtd.) Yahya as a well-balanced and fitting tribute to our *da'wah.*[3] May Allah reward him for the time and effort he has spent in compiling this wonderful and much-needed book.

Sheikh Abdallah A. Kheir

Kenyatta University, Imam and lecturer

Department of Philosophy and Religious Studies

Nairobi, Kenya

---

3 Da'wah: disseminating the teachings of Islam and calling people to accept and embrace Islam.

Introduction

Islam is founded on the concept of *tawḥeed* (oneness of Allah); it is the monotheistic belief that Allah (ﷻ) is the One Absolute, Eternal God to the exclusion of any other deity. The public manifestation of tawḥeed is the shahâdah: that is, the 'testimony of faith' or the 'confession of faith'. It is: 'lâ ilâha illâ Allâh, Muḥammadun rasool Ullâh', the declaration that 'there is no God but Allah and Muhammad is His Messenger'. The shahâdah is the first 'pillar' or the fundamental principle of Islam.

Prophet Muhammad (ﷺ) spent thirteen long years inviting the people of Makkah, the Quraysh, to tawḥeed. In essence, he invited them to acknowledge the unity of Allah and to accept him as His Last messenger and prophet, entrusted with a universal message to all humankind. All his efforts were expended in instilling the full conviction of the shahâdah in the hearts of the new reverts. These were the Companions of the Prophet (ﷺ), radically transformed by their faith, who turned out to be the vanguard of the Islamic state in Madinah.

However, it is not enough to just pronounce the shahâdah — the declaration of faith — without a full understanding of:

- Its pillars,
- Its meaning,
- Its importance,
- Its implications,

- Its seven conditions, and
- The implementation of its seven conditions.

Millions of Muslims all over the world today have recited the declaration of faith and many more are proclaiming this shahâdah daily without understanding its requirements. This ignorance of the crucial significance of the shahâdah has seriously weakened the *eemân* (faith) of the Muslims; it has also contributed to their social, economic, moral, and marital decline. In fact, the ineffectuality of Muslims stems from the deficiency in their faith rather than a lack of material resources.

Muslims have abdicated their status as 'witnesses' over humankind, as stated in the Qur'an:

﴿ وَكَذَٰلِكَ جَعَلْنَٰكُمْ أُمَّةً وَسَطًا لِّتَكُونُوا۟ شُهَدَآءَ عَلَى ٱلنَّاسِ وَيَكُونَ ٱلرَّسُولُ عَلَيْكُمْ شَهِيدًا ... ﴿١٤٣﴾ ﴾ (سورة البقرة: ١٤٣)

﴾And thus we have made you a just community that you will be witnesses over the people and the Messenger will be a witness over you...﴿ *(Qur'an 2: 143)*

﴿ وَجَٰهِدُوا۟ فِى ٱللَّهِ حَقَّ جِهَادِهِۦ ۚ هُوَ ٱجْتَبَىٰكُمْ وَمَا جَعَلَ عَلَيْكُمْ فِى ٱلدِّينِ مِنْ حَرَجٍ ۚ مِّلَّةَ أَبِيكُمْ إِبْرَٰهِيمَ ۚ هُوَ سَمَّىٰكُمُ ٱلْمُسْلِمِينَ مِن قَبْلُ وَفِى هَٰذَا لِيَكُونَ ٱلرَّسُولُ شَهِيدًا عَلَيْكُمْ وَتَكُونُوا۟ شُهَدَآءَ عَلَى ٱلنَّاسِ ۚ فَأَقِيمُوا۟ ٱلصَّلَوٰةَ وَءَاتُوا۟ ٱلزَّكَوٰةَ وَٱعْتَصِمُوا۟ بِٱللَّهِ هُوَ مَوْلَىٰكُمْ ۖ فَنِعْمَ ٱلْمَوْلَىٰ وَنِعْمَ ٱلنَّصِيرُ ﴿٧٨﴾ ﴾ (سورة الحج: ٧٨)

﴾And strive for Allah with the striving due to Him. He has chosen you and has not placed upon you in the religion any difficulty. [It is] the religion of your father, Abraham. He [Allah] named you Muslims before [in former scriptures] and in this [revelation] that the Messenger may be a witness over you and you may be witnesses over the people. So establish prayer and give zakâh [compulsory charity] and hold fast to Allah. He is your Protector; excellent is the Protector, and excellent is the Helper.》 *(Qur'an 22: 78)*

It is very distressing that many Muslims are no longer able to set an exemplary standard for a just, righteous society. Instead of being witnesses to humankind, they have become a *fitnah* (a source of tribulation), even though the Prophet (ﷺ) supplicated to Allah to protect the believers from this condition.

﴿رَبَّنَا لَا تَجْعَلْنَا فِتْنَةً لِّلَّذِينَ كَفَرُوا وَاغْفِرْ لَنَا رَبَّنَا ۖ إِنَّكَ أَنتَ الْعَزِيزُ الْحَكِيمُ ﴿٥﴾﴾

(سورة الممتحنة: ٥)

《Our Lord, make us not [objects of] torment for the disbelievers and forgive us, our Lord. Indeed, it is You Who are the Exalted in Might, the Wise.》 *(Qur'an 60: 5)*

Once you have recited or declared the shahâdah, it becomes incumbent upon you to strive to grasp a profound understanding of what it means, and to act and shape your life in accordance with what it entails. This will enable you to grow in your faith to the extent that you are able to implement and establish the legislation of Allah in your life and ultimately deserve the inheritance of paradise by His grace.

I pray to Allah to accept this humble effort on the first fundamental principle of Islam; may He add it to our scales of good deeds on the Day of Judgement. I also pray for Allah to grant me His special favour and aid in accomplishing this task, and put His guidance and favour in the hearts of the readers in order to enable them to benefit from this small effort. Finally, I pray to Allah to reward all those who have contributed to the success of this humble publication in one way or another. In particular, my sincere gratitude and prayers are for Sheikh Abdallah A. Kheir, the imam and lecturer of Kenyatta University, who read through the manuscripts, gave his humble advice, and wrote the foreword.

May Allah reward him and his family abundantly, and give him strength and good health to continue serving Islam. May Allah also guide all of us onto the straight path, forgive all our shortcomings, and grant us paradise by His grace.

﴿ ... رَبَّنَا تَقَبَّلْ مِنَّآ إِنَّكَ أَنتَ ٱلسَّمِيعُ ٱلْعَلِيمُ ﴿١٢٧﴾ رَبَّنَا وَٱجْعَلْنَا مُسْلِمَيْنِ لَكَ وَمِن ذُرِّيَّتِنَآ أُمَّةً مُّسْلِمَةً لَّكَ وَأَرِنَا مَنَاسِكَنَا وَتُبْ عَلَيْنَآ إِنَّكَ أَنتَ ٱلتَّوَّابُ ٱلرَّحِيمُ ﴿١٢٨﴾ ﴾

(سورة البقرة: ١٢٧- ١٢٨)

﴾...Our Lord, accept [this] from us. Indeed You are the Hearing, the Knowing. Our Lord, and make us Muslims [in submission] to You and from our descendants a Muslim nation [in submission] to You. And show us our rites and accept our repentance. Indeed, You are the Accepting of Repentance, the Merciful.﴿

(Qur'an 2: 127-128)

Yahya M. A. Ondigo
Benadir University
Mogadishu, Somalia

Chapter One

The Meaning of *Shahâdah*

The meaning of *Lâ ilâha illâ Allâh*

The shahâdah, 'lâ ilâha illâ Allâh, Muḥammadun rasool Ullâh', constitutes two assertions. It is, in fact, a dual testimony; firstly, it is the declaration that there is no god worthy of worship in the whole universe except Allah, the only true God. Secondly, it is the attestation that Muhammad (ﷺ) is the final prophet and messenger of Allah, sent to the whole world.

The first part of the testimony comprises a negation and an affirmation. 'Lâ ilâha' is the negation of all false deities that are being worshipped by humanity today, whether they are humans, angels, jinn (non-human, rational beings created by Allah from fire and often referred to as 'devils'), heavenly bodies, wealth, power, false human ideologies, or man-made political, scientific, and economic systems.

The affirmation, 'illâ Allâh', is the attestation of the reality of the one and only true unique God: Allah (ﷻ).

'Lâ ilâha' — that is, the renunciation of all other gods, belief systems, and concepts — is the subject of a large number of verses in the Qur'an:

﴿وَإِلَٰهُكُمْ إِلَٰهٌ وَاحِدٌ ۖ لَّا إِلَٰهَ إِلَّا هُوَ الرَّحْمَٰنُ الرَّحِيمُ ﴿١٦٣﴾﴾ (سورة البقرة: ١٦٣)

﴿And your god is one God. There is no deity [worthy of worship] except Him, the Entirely Merciful, the Especially Merciful.﴾

(Qur'an 2: 163)

﴿إِلَٰهُكُمْ إِلَٰهٌ وَاحِدٌ ۚ فَالَّذِينَ لَا يُؤْمِنُونَ بِالْآخِرَةِ قُلُوبُهُم مُّنكِرَةٌ وَهُم مُّسْتَكْبِرُونَ
﴿٢٢﴾﴾ (سورة النحل: ٢٢)

﴿Your god is one God. But those who do not believe in the hereafter — their hearts are disapproving and they are arrogant.﴾

(Qur'an 16: 22)

﴿ذَٰلِكَ بِأَنَّ اللَّهَ هُوَ الْحَقُّ وَأَنَّ مَا يَدْعُونَ مِن دُونِهِ هُوَ الْبَاطِلُ وَأَنَّ
اللَّهَ هُوَ الْعَلِيُّ الْكَبِيرُ ﴿٦٢﴾﴾ (سورة الحج: ٦٢)

﴿That is because Allah is the Truth, and that which they call upon other than Him is falsehood, and because Allah is the Most High, the Grand.﴾

(Qur'an 22: 62)

Elsewhere, Allah has also affirmed:

﴿ذَٰلِكُمُ اللَّهُ رَبُّكُمْ ۖ لَا إِلَٰهَ إِلَّا هُوَ ۖ خَالِقُ كُلِّ شَيْءٍ فَاعْبُدُوهُ ۚ وَهُوَ عَلَىٰ كُلِّ
شَيْءٍ وَكِيلٌ ﴿١٠٢﴾﴾ (سورة الأنعام: ١٠٢)

﴿That is Allah, your Lord; there is no deity except Him, the Creator of all things, so worship Him. And He is Disposer of all things.﴾

(Qur'an 6: 102)

Indeed, the first advice Luqmân, a wise servant of Allah, gave to his beloved son was to negate the worship of all false deities. He said, as mentioned in the following verses:

﴿وَلَقَدْ آتَيْنَا لُقْمَانَ الْحِكْمَةَ أَنِ اشْكُرْ لِلَّهِ ۚ وَمَن يَشْكُرْ فَإِنَّمَا يَشْكُرُ لِنَفْسِهِ ۖ وَمَن
كَفَرَ فَإِنَّ اللَّهَ غَنِيٌّ حَمِيدٌ ﴿١٢﴾ وَإِذْ قَالَ لُقْمَانُ لِابْنِهِ وَهُوَ يَعِظُهُ يَا بُنَيَّ لَا تُشْرِكْ بِاللَّهِ ۖ
إِنَّ الشِّرْكَ لَظُلْمٌ عَظِيمٌ ﴿١٣﴾﴾ (سورة لقمان: ١٢-١٣)

﴾And We had certainly given Luqmân wisdom [and said]: Be grateful to Allah. And whoever is grateful is grateful for [the benefit of] himself. And whoever denies [His favour] — then indeed, Allah is Free of Need and Praiseworthy. And [mention, O Muhammad] when Luqmân said to his son while he was instructing him: O my dear son, do not associate [anything] with Allah. Indeed, association [with Him] is great injustice.﴿

(Qur'an 31: 12-13)

The affirmation, 'illâ Allâh', in proclaiming the reality of the one and only inimitable God, Allah, encompasses Allah's most beautiful and perfect names along with His attributes and His role as the Creator and Lawgiver; thus, He is the only one worthy of worship.

i) The most beautiful and perfect names belong to Allah (سُبْحَانَهُ وَتَعَالَىٰ)

Allah alone has the most beautiful and perfect names and attributes. No one in the whole universe shares His perfection and His characteristics. This has been elaborated in the following verses:

﴿ٱللَّهُ لَآ إِلَٰهَ إِلَّا هُوَ ۖ لَهُ ٱلۡأَسۡمَآءُ ٱلۡحُسۡنَىٰ ﴿٨﴾﴾ (سورة طه: ٨)

﴾Allah — there is no deity except Him. To Him belong the best names.﴿ *(Qur'an 20: 8)*

﴿هُوَ ٱللَّهُ ٱلَّذِي لَآ إِلَٰهَ إِلَّا هُوَ ۖ عَٰلِمُ ٱلۡغَيۡبِ وَٱلشَّهَٰدَةِ ۖ هُوَ ٱلرَّحۡمَٰنُ ٱلرَّحِيمُ ﴿٢٢﴾ هُوَ
ٱللَّهُ ٱلَّذِي لَآ إِلَٰهَ إِلَّا هُوَ ٱلۡمَلِكُ ٱلۡقُدُّوسُ ٱلسَّلَٰمُ ٱلۡمُؤۡمِنُ ٱلۡمُهَيۡمِنُ ٱلۡعَزِيزُ
ٱلۡجَبَّارُ ٱلۡمُتَكَبِّرُ ۚ سُبۡحَٰنَ ٱللَّهِ عَمَّا يُشۡرِكُونَ ﴿٢٣﴾ هُوَ ٱللَّهُ ٱلۡخَٰلِقُ
ٱلۡبَارِئُ ٱلۡمُصَوِّرُ ۖ لَهُ ٱلۡأَسۡمَآءُ ٱلۡحُسۡنَىٰ ۚ يُسَبِّحُ لَهُۥ مَا فِي ٱلسَّمَٰوَٰتِ وَٱلۡأَرۡضِ ۖ وَهُوَ ٱلۡعَزِيزُ
ٱلۡحَكِيمُ ﴿٢٤﴾﴾ (سورة الحشر: ٢٢-٢٤)

﴿He is Allah, other than Whom there is no deity, Knower of the unseen and the witnessed. He is the Entirely Merciful, the Especially Merciful. He is Allah, other than Whom there is no deity, the Sovereign, the Pure, the Perfection, the Bestower of Faith, the Overseer, the Exalted in Might, the Compeller, the Superior. Exalted is Allah above whatever they associate with Him. He is Allah, the Creator, the Inventor, the Fashioner; to Him belong the best names. Whatever is in the heavens and earth is exalting Him. And He is the Exalted in Might, the Most Wise.﴾ *(Qur'an 59: 22-24)*

﴿وَلِلَّهِ ٱلْأَسْمَآءُ ٱلْحُسْنَىٰ فَٱدْعُوهُ بِهَا ۖ وَذَرُوا۟ ٱلَّذِينَ يُلْحِدُونَ فِىٓ أَسْمَـٰٓئِهِۦ ۚ ... ﴿١٨٠﴾﴾

(سورة الأعراف: ١٨٠)

﴿And to Allah belong the best names, so invoke Him by them. And leave [the company of] those who practice deviation concerning His names…﴾ *(Qur'an 7: 180)*

On the subject of Allah's most beautiful names, Abu Hurayrah (*raḍiya Allâhu 'anhu* — may Allah be pleased with him) narrated that Prophet Muhammad (ﷺ) said:

> «Allah has ninety-nine names: that is, one hundred minus one. Whoever guards them (comprehends their meaning and acts accordingly) will enter paradise. Allah is *witr* (an odd number: one) and loves the witr (odd numbers).» (Bukhari)[4]

It is recommended to supplicate to Allah alone, associating no partners with Him, using His beautiful names and attributes

---

[4] All hadiths in this text have been checked and verified by IIPH's researchers. It is rare, but it does happen that a hadith is not verifiable within the timeframe of researching and editing the book. In that case, a decision is made by the editorial board whether or not to include the hadith. It is IIPH's policy not to include weak hadiths or fabricated (fake) hadiths in our publications. If a weak hadith is included in any text, it is only because the author of the book discusses it as a weak hadith. [Editor]

whenever one is in need. One should also refrain from uttering the beautiful names of Allah as magic spells, parroting them without understanding what they mean. Moreover, one should only describe Allah as He has described Himself in the glorious Qur'an, and as Prophet Muhammad (ﷺ) has described Him in his hadiths (statements or actions recorded by his Companions).

ii) Allah (سبحانه وتعالى) is the only Creator

Allah is the only true Creator, Cherisher, and Sustainer. He is the Omnipotent, the Omniscient, and the Omnipresent. The following verses confirm this:

﴿ٱلْحَمْدُ لِلَّهِ رَبِّ ٱلْعَٰلَمِينَ ﴿٢﴾﴾ (سورة الفاتحة: ٢)

﴾[All] praise is [due] to Allah, Lord of the worlds.﴿ *(Qur'an 1: 2)*[5]

﴿بَدِيعُ ٱلسَّمَٰوَٰتِ وَٱلْأَرْضِ ۖ وَإِذَا قَضَىٰٓ أَمْرًا فَإِنَّمَا يَقُولُ لَهُۥ كُن فَيَكُونُ ﴿١١٧﴾﴾

(سورة البقرة: ١١٧)

﴾Originator of the heavens and the earth. When He decrees a matter, He only says to it: Be, and it is.﴿ *(Qur'an 2: 117)*

﴿هُوَ ٱلَّذِى خَلَقَ لَكُم مَّا فِى ٱلْأَرْضِ جَمِيعًا ثُمَّ ٱسْتَوَىٰٓ إِلَى ٱلسَّمَآءِ فَسَوَّىٰهُنَّ سَبْعَ سَمَٰوَٰتٍ ۚ وَهُوَ بِكُلِّ شَىْءٍ عَلِيمٌ ﴿٢٩﴾﴾ (سورة البقرة: ٢٩)

﴾It is He Who created for you all of that which is on the earth. Then He directed Himself to the heaven [His being above all cre-

---

5 Lord: The actual word used in the Qur'an is *Rabb*. There is no equivalent word for Rabb in the English language. This word has a wide variety of meanings including: the One and only Lord for the whole universe, its Creator, Owner, Organizer, Provider, Master, Planner, Sustainer, Cherisher, Loving and Caring Guardian, and Giver of Security. Rabb is also one of the names of Allah.

ation] and made them seven heavens, and He is Knowing of all things.﴿ *(Qur'an 2: 29)*

﴿ٱللَّهُ خَٰلِقُ كُلِّ شَيۡءٖۖ وَهُوَ عَلَىٰ كُلِّ شَيۡءٖ وَكِيلٞ ٦٢﴾ (سورة الزُّمَر: ٦٢)

﴾Allah is the Creator of all things, and He is the Guardian and Disposer of all affairs.﴿ *(Qur'an 39: 62)*

iii) Allah (سبحانه وتعالى) is the best Sustainer

﴿قُلۡ أَغَيۡرَ ٱللَّهِ أَتَّخِذُ وَلِيّٗا فَاطِرِ ٱلسَّمَٰوَٰتِ وَٱلۡأَرۡضِ وَهُوَ يُطۡعِمُ وَلَا يُطۡعَمُۗ ... ١٤﴾

(سورة الأنعام: ١٤)

﴾Say: Is it other than Allah I should take as a protector, Creator of the heavens and the earth, while it is He Who feeds and is not fed?...﴿ *(Qur'an 6: 14)*

﴿وَكَأَيِّن مِّن دَآبَّةٖ لَّا تَحۡمِلُ رِزۡقَهَا ٱللَّهُ يَرۡزُقُهَا وَإِيَّاكُمۡۚ وَهُوَ ٱلسَّمِيعُ ٱلۡعَلِيمُ
٦٠ وَلَئِن سَأَلۡتَهُم مَّنۡ خَلَقَ ٱلسَّمَٰوَٰتِ وَٱلۡأَرۡضَ وَسَخَّرَ ٱلشَّمۡسَ وَٱلۡقَمَرَ لَيَقُولُنَّ ٱللَّهُۖ
فَأَنَّىٰ يُؤۡفَكُونَ ٦١ ٱللَّهُ يَبۡسُطُ ٱلرِّزۡقَ لِمَن يَشَآءُ مِنۡ عِبَادِهِۦ وَيَقۡدِرُ لَهُۥٓۚ إِنَّ ٱللَّهَ بِكُلِّ شَيۡءٍ
عَلِيمٞ ٦٢﴾ (سورة العنكبوت: ٦٠-٦٢)

﴾And how many a creature carries not its [own] provision. Allah provides for it and for you. And He is the Hearing, the Knowing. If you asked them: Who created the heavens and earth and subjected the sun and the moon? — they would surely say: Allah. Then how are they deluded? Allah extends provision for whom He wills of His servants and restricts for him. Indeed Allah is, of all things, Knowing.﴿ *(Qur'an 29: 60-62)*

﴿مَآ أُرِيدُ مِنۡهُم مِّن رِّزۡقٖ وَمَآ أُرِيدُ أَن يُطۡعِمُونِ ٥٧ إِنَّ ٱللَّهَ هُوَ ٱلرَّزَّاقُ ذُو ٱلۡقُوَّةِ ٱلۡمَتِينُ
٥٨﴾ (سورة الذاريات: ٥٨)

﴿I do not want from them any provision, nor do I want them to feed Me. Indeed, it is Allah Who is the [continual] Provider, the firm Possessor of Strength.﴾ *(Qur'an 51: 57-58)*

﴿ ... وَٱللَّهُ خَيۡرُ ٱلرَّٰزِقِينَ ﴿١١﴾ ﴾ (سورة الجمعة: ١١)

﴿...Allah is the best of providers.﴾ *(Qur'an 62: 11)*[6]

A lack of reliance on Allah as the true Sustainer and Provider of all that exists is one of the major reasons Muslims have a weak level of faith. Consequently, they express their readiness to compromise the Islamic principles and betray their fellow Muslims for paltry gain.

Prophet Muhammad (ﷺ) is reported to have stated that whatever sustenance has been written for the people will reach them, regardless of the situation in which they may be; likewise, the sustenance that was not meant for certain people can never be obtained, regardless of how hard they try to secure it. Prophet Muhammad (ﷺ) acknowledged this reality daily in his supplication after *ṣalâh* (formal prayer), and his Companions emulated his example. Warrâd (the freed slave of al-Mugheerah ibn Shu'bah) narrated:

> «Al-Mugheerah wrote to Mu'âwiyah ibn Abu Sufyân that Allah's Messenger (ﷺ) used to recite the following after ending his prayer with the *tasleem* (salutation):
>
> *Lâ ilâha illâ Allâh waḥdahu lâ shareeka lahu; lahul-mulku wa lahul-ḥamdu, wahuwa 'alâ kulli shay'in qadeer. Allâhumma lâ mâni'a limâ a'ṭayta wa lâ mu'ṭiya limâ mana'ta wa lâ yanfa'u dhal jaddi minkal-jadd.*
>
> None has the right to be worshipped except Allah alone, without a partner; to Him belongs sovereignty and all praise and He is over all things Omnipotent. O Allah, none can

---

6 See also *(Qur'an 11: 6)*, *(Qur'an 13: 26)*, and *(Qur'an 15: 21)*.

prevent what You have willed to bestow and none can bestow what You have willed to prevent; no wealth or majesty can benefit anyone as from You is all wealth and majesty.» (Bukhari)

iv) Allah (ﷻ) is the only One to be worshipped

Allah is the one and only Lord of the whole universe; He is its Creator, Sustainer, Provider, Cherisher, and Caring Guardian. Thus, He alone deserves to be worshipped by His creation, as He has proclaimed in the Qur'an:

﴿وَمَا خَلَقْتُ ٱلْجِنَّ وَٱلْإِنسَ إِلَّا لِيَعْبُدُونِ ۝٥٦﴾ (سورة الذاريات: ٥٦)

﴾And I did not create the jinn and humankind except to worship Me.﴿ *(Qur'an 51: 56)*

﴿يَٰٓأَيُّهَا ٱلنَّاسُ ٱعْبُدُوا۟ رَبَّكُمُ ٱلَّذِى خَلَقَكُمْ وَٱلَّذِينَ مِن قَبْلِكُمْ لَعَلَّكُمْ تَتَّقُونَ ۝٢١ ٱلَّذِى جَعَلَ لَكُمُ ٱلْأَرْضَ فِرَٰشًا وَٱلسَّمَآءَ بِنَآءً وَأَنزَلَ مِنَ ٱلسَّمَآءِ مَآءً فَأَخْرَجَ بِهِۦ مِنَ ٱلثَّمَرَٰتِ رِزْقًا لَّكُمْ ۖ فَلَا تَجْعَلُوا۟ لِلَّهِ أَندَادًا وَأَنتُمْ تَعْلَمُونَ ۝٢٢﴾

(سورة البقرة: ٢١-٢٢)

﴾O humankind, worship your Lord, who created you and those before you, that you may become righteous — [He] who made for you the earth a bed [spread out] and the sky a ceiling and sent down rain from the sky and brought forth thereby fruits as provision for you. So do not attribute to Allah equals while you know [that there is nothing similar to Him].﴿ *(Qur'an 2: 21-22)*

The aforementioned verses address all humankind. Their instructions are not restricted to the Muslims. Rather, they are very explicit in stating that the worship of Allah is the sole purpose of our existence. When humans deny the worship of Allah, their belief in Allah becomes questionable; the inevitable outcome of such a denial is an unrighteous life. Allah has mentioned:

﴿ وَٱعْبُدُوا۟ ٱللَّهَ وَلَا تُشْرِكُوا۟ بِهِۦ شَيْـًٔا ۖ وَبِٱلْوَٰلِدَيْنِ إِحْسَـٰنًا وَبِذِى ٱلْقُرْبَىٰ وَٱلْيَتَـٰمَىٰ وَٱلْمَسَـٰكِينِ وَٱلْجَارِ ذِى ٱلْقُرْبَىٰ وَٱلْجَارِ ٱلْجُنُبِ وَٱلصَّاحِبِ بِٱلْجَنۢبِ وَٱبْنِ ٱلسَّبِيلِ وَمَا مَلَكَتْ أَيْمَـٰنُكُمْ ۗ إِنَّ ٱللَّهَ لَا يُحِبُّ مَن كَانَ مُخْتَالًا فَخُورًا ﴿٣٦﴾ ﴾ (سورة النساء: ٣٦)

﴾Worship Allah and associate nothing with Him, and to parents do good, and to relatives, orphans, the needy, the near neighbour, the neighbour farther away, the companion at your side, the traveller, and those whom your right hands possess. Indeed, Allah does not like those who are self-deluding and boastful.﴿

(Qur'an 4: 36)

Furthermore, when humankind associates partners or sets up rivals with Allah in His worship then, according to the Messenger of Allah (ﷺ), it commits the greatest sin. This sin completely contradicts the shahâdah by negating the concept of tawḥeed and oneness of Allah.

«'Abdullâh narrated: I asked the Prophet (ﷺ): What is the greatest sin in the sight of Allah?

He replied: That you set up a rival unto Allah though He alone created you.

I said: That is indeed a great sin.

Then I asked: What is next?

He answered: To kill your son lest he should share your food with you.

I queried: What is next?

He said: To commit adultery with the wife of your neighbour.» (Bukhari)

v) Allah (ﷻ) is the only lawgiver

Implicit in the first assertion of the shahâdah is that Allah is the only lawgiver and the only true governor. This clearly indicates that sovereignty belongs to Allah alone. Human beings can govern and rule their fellow human beings only as vicegerents on behalf of Allah. Since Allah created humanity, it logically follows that only He knows what is best for His creation. Therefore, He is the only one who can legislate how to live, conduct one's life, and regulate all affairs — whether economic, social, moral, or political. Indeed, only Allah can be the wise, rational, and judicious guide for humankind, for He is the All-Knowing, the All-Seeing, the All-Hearing, and the All-Powerful; He is cognizant of the past, present, and future, fully aware of what is beneficial and what is harmful for humanity. He is the only One who is well-acquainted with all things.

Allah has sent messengers and prophets for this purpose since the time of Adam (*'alayhi as-salâm* — peace be upon him) and Eve. The reality, stated in the Qur'an in a number of verses, is clear-cut: the only way to lead a successful and happy life, both in this world and in the hereafter, is to live according to the law of Allah.

﴿قُلْنَا ٱهْبِطُوا۟ مِنْهَا جَمِيعًا ۖ فَإِمَّا يَأْتِيَنَّكُم مِّنِّى هُدًى فَمَن تَبِعَ هُدَاىَ فَلَا خَوْفٌ عَلَيْهِمْ وَلَا هُمْ يَحْزَنُونَ ﴿٣٨﴾ وَٱلَّذِينَ كَفَرُوا۟ وَكَذَّبُوا۟ بِـَٔايَـٰتِنَآ أُو۟لَـٰٓئِكَ أَصْحَـٰبُ ٱلنَّارِ ۖ هُمْ فِيهَا خَـٰلِدُونَ ﴿٣٩﴾﴾ (سورة البقرة: ٣٨-٣٩)

﴾We said: Go down from it, all of you. And when guidance comes to you from Me, whoever follows My guidance — there will be no fear concerning them, nor will they grieve. And those who disbelieve and deny Our signs — those will be companions of the fire; they will abide therein eternally.﴿ *(Qur'an 2: 38-39)*

﴿إِنَّ رَبَّكُمُ ٱللَّهُ ٱلَّذِى خَلَقَ ٱلسَّمَٰوَٰتِ وَٱلْأَرْضَ فِى سِتَّةِ أَيَّامٍ ثُمَّ ٱسْتَوَىٰ عَلَى ٱلْعَرْشِ يُغْشِى ٱلَّيْلَ ٱلنَّهَارَ يَطْلُبُهُۥ حَثِيثًا وَٱلشَّمْسَ وَٱلْقَمَرَ وَٱلنُّجُومَ مُسَخَّرَٰتٍۭ بِأَمْرِهِۦٓ ۗ أَلَا لَهُ ٱلْخَلْقُ وَٱلْأَمْرُ ۗ تَبَارَكَ ٱللَّهُ رَبُّ ٱلْعَٰلَمِينَ ٥٤﴾ (سورة الأعراف: ٥٤)

﴿Indeed, your Lord is Allah, who created the heavens and earth in six days and then established Himself above the throne. He covers the night with the day, [another night] chasing it rapidly; and [He created] the sun, the moon, and the stars, subjected by His command. Unquestionably, His is the creation and the command; blessed is Allah, Lord of the worlds.﴾ *(Qur'an 7: 54)*

﴿ثُمَّ رُدُّوٓا۟ إِلَى ٱللَّهِ مَوْلَىٰهُمُ ٱلْحَقِّ ۚ أَلَا لَهُ ٱلْحُكْمُ وَهُوَ أَسْرَعُ ٱلْحَٰسِبِينَ ٦٢﴾

(سورة الأنعام: ٦٢)

﴿Then they [His servants] are returned to Allah, their true Lord. Unquestionably, His is the judgement, and He is the swiftest of accountants.﴾ *(Qur'an 6: 62)*

﴿أَفَغَيْرَ ٱللَّهِ أَبْتَغِى حَكَمًا وَهُوَ ٱلَّذِىٓ أَنزَلَ إِلَيْكُمُ ٱلْكِتَٰبَ مُفَصَّلًا ۚ وَٱلَّذِينَ ءَاتَيْنَٰهُمُ ٱلْكِتَٰبَ يَعْلَمُونَ أَنَّهُۥ مُنَزَّلٌ مِّن رَّبِّكَ بِٱلْحَقِّ ۖ فَلَا تَكُونَنَّ مِنَ ٱلْمُمْتَرِينَ ١١٤﴾

(سورة الأنعام: ١١٤)

﴿[Say]: Then is it other than Allah I should seek as judge while it is He who has revealed to you the Book explained in detail? And those to whom We [previously] gave the scripture know that it is sent down from your Lord in truth, so never be among the doubters.﴾ *(Qur'an 6: 114)*

Chapter Two
Muhammad (ﷺ): The Last Prophet

The second part of the shahâdah, 'Muḥammadun rasool Ullâh', is to bear witness that Muhammad (ﷺ) is the messenger of Allah, affirming him as the last prophet, the greatest and best prophet, and the only universal messenger.

i) Muhammad (ﷺ) is the seal of prophethood

Inherent in the above proclamation is the acceptance of Muhammad (ﷺ) as the last prophet and messenger; he is the seal of prophethood. No prophet will come after him, and this is absolutely clear from Allah's proclamation in the Qur'an concerning Prophet Muhammad (ﷺ):

﴿مَّا كَانَ مُحَمَّدٌ أَبَآ أَحَدٍ مِّن رِّجَالِكُمْ وَلَٰكِن رَّسُولَ ٱللَّهِ وَخَاتَمَ ٱلنَّبِيِّـۧنَ ۗ وَكَانَ ٱللَّهُ بِكُلِّ شَىْءٍ عَلِيمًا ۝٤٠﴾ (سورة الأحزاب: ٤٠)

﴾Muhammad is not the father of [any] one of your men, but [he is] the Messenger of Allah and the last of the prophets. And ever is Allah, of all things, Knowing.﴿ *(Qur'an 33: 40)*

The Prophet (ﷺ) himself stated that he was the last prophet and messenger, unlike all the prophets who came before him; none of them was ever reported to have declared himself the seal of prophethood. Abu Hurayrah (رضي الله عنه) narrated that Allah's Messenger (ﷺ) said:

> «My similitude, in comparison with the other prophets before me, is that of a man who has built a house nicely and beautifully, except (that its beauty is marred by the absence of) one brick in a corner. People walk around it, wondering at its beauty, but say: If only this brick (that would perfect its beauty) were put into its place! I am that brick and I am the last of the prophets.» (Bukhari)

Abu Hurayrah (رضي الله عنه) also reported the Prophet (ﷺ) as saying:

> «The Israelis used to be ruled and guided by prophets. Whenever a prophet died, another would take his place. Verily, there will be no prophet after me, but there will be caliphs who will increase in number.
>
> People asked: O Allah's Messenger! What do you order us (to do)?
>
> He replied: Obey the one who is first given the pledge of allegiance. Fulfil their (the caliphs') rights, for Allah will ask them about (any shortcoming) in ruling those whom He has put under their guardianship.» (Bukhari)

ii) Muhammad (ﷺ) is the greatest prophet

Allah has honoured Prophet Muhammad (ﷺ) with the highest rank among His prophets and messengers. Indeed, all prophets were granted special favours; however, the status that Allah conferred on Prophet Muhammad (ﷺ) is the most exalted and the most sublime. Allah has stated the following in the Qur'an:

﴿ تِلْكَ ٱلرُّسُلُ فَضَّلْنَا بَعْضَهُمْ عَلَىٰ بَعْضٍ مِّنْهُم مَّن كَلَّمَ ٱللَّهُ وَرَفَعَ بَعْضَهُمْ دَرَجَٰتٍ
وَءَاتَيْنَا عِيسَى ٱبْنَ مَرْيَمَ ٱلْبَيِّنَٰتِ وَأَيَّدْنَٰهُ بِرُوحِ ٱلْقُدُسِ وَلَوْ شَآءَ ٱللَّهُ مَا
ٱقْتَتَلَ ٱلَّذِينَ مِنۢ بَعْدِهِم مِّنۢ بَعْدِ مَا جَآءَتْهُمُ ٱلْبَيِّنَٰتُ وَلَٰكِنِ ٱخْتَلَفُوا۟ فَمِنْهُم مَّنْ
ءَامَنَ وَمِنْهُم مَّن كَفَرَ وَلَوْ شَآءَ ٱللَّهُ مَا ٱقْتَتَلُوا۟ وَلَٰكِنَّ ٱللَّهَ يَفْعَلُ مَا يُرِيدُ ﴿٢٥٣﴾ ﴾

(سورة البقرة: ٢٥٣)

﴿Those messengers — some of them We caused to exceed others. Among them were those to whom Allah spoke, and He raised some of them in degree. And We gave Jesus, the son of Mary, clear proofs, and We supported him with the pure spirit. If Allah had willed, those [generations] succeeding them would not have fought each other after the clear proofs had come to them. But they differed, and some of them believed and some of them disbelieved. And if Allah had willed, they would not have fought each other, but Allah does what He intends.﴾ *(Qur'an 2: 253)*

Prophet Muhammad (ﷺ) also professed himself to be the noblest soul among the sons of Adam (عليه السلام), as per the following hadith:

Abu Hurayrah (رضي الله عنه) reported Allah's Messenger (ﷺ) as saying:

> «I shall be pre-eminent among the descendants of Adam on the Day of Resurrection. My grave will be the first to open up; I will be the first intercessor and the first whose intercession will be accepted (by Allah).» (Muslim)

Jâbir ibn 'Abdullâh (رضي الله عنه) reported that the Prophet (ﷺ) said:

> «I am the leader of the messengers, and this is no boast (I am not haughty). I am the last of the prophets, and this is no boast (I take no pride in it); I shall be the first intercessor

and the first whose intercession will be accepted, and this is no boast (I take no pride in it).» (Recorded by ad-Dârimi and authenticated by al-Albâni)

In the glorious Qur'an, Allah Himself has borne witness to the status given by Him to His beloved Prophet Muhammad (ﷺ). He has affirmed that among all the prophets and messengers, the Prophet (ﷺ) was the best in terms of character and conduct.

﴿وَإِنَّكَ لَعَلَىٰ خُلُقٍ عَظِيمٍ ۝٤﴾ (سورة القلم: ٤)

﴾And indeed, you are of a great moral character.﴿ *(Qur'an 68: 4)*

﴿لَّقَدْ كَانَ لَكُمْ فِي رَسُولِ ٱللَّهِ أُسْوَةٌ حَسَنَةٌ لِّمَن كَانَ يَرْجُوا۟ ٱللَّهَ وَٱلْيَوْمَ ٱلْـَٔاخِرَ وَذَكَرَ ٱللَّهَ كَثِيرًا ۝٢١﴾ (سورة الأحزاب: ٢١)

﴾There has certainly been for you in the Messenger of Allah an excellent pattern for anyone whose hope is in Allah and the last day and [who] remembers Allah often.﴿ *(Qur'an 33: 21)*

The Prophet (ﷺ) reiterated the words of Allah when he said:

«Surely, I was only sent to complete the most noble character traits.» (Recorded by al-Ḥâkim and al-Bayhaqi and authenticated by al-Albâni)

«Moreover, when the Prophet's wife, 'Â'ishah (*raḍiya Allâhu 'anhâ* — may Allah be pleased with her), was asked about the Prophet's character, she replied: His character was that of the Qur'an.» (Muslim and Abu Dâwood)

Thus, it is evident that the Prophet's character and behaviour exemplified Allah's guidance contained within the Qur'an. This undeniable fact is confirmed through the glowing tributes that have been bestowed upon him even by prominent non-Muslim thinkers and scholars over the centuries.

In the nineteenth century, Thomas Carlyle, a Scottish essayist and historian, endorsed Prophet Muhammad (ﷺ) as the emblematic hero-prophet in *On Heroes, Hero-Worship and the Heroic in History* (1841).

Alphonse de Lamartine, a French writer and poet, touches upon some aspects of Islam and its 'founder' in his *History of Turkey*. He conceives three objective standards for conferring greatness:

> If the grandeur of the design, the pettiness of the means, the immensity of the results be the three measures of human genius, who would dare to compare humanly the greatest men of modern history to Mahomet [Muhammad]? The most famous of them have agitated but armies, laws, empires; they have (when they founded any thing [*sic*]) but physical potencies, often crumbled to the earth before themselves. Mahomet has recast armies, legislations, empires, peoples, dynasties, with millions of men throughout a third of the inhabited globe. More than this, he recast altars, gods, religions, ideas, creeds, souls. He has founded upon a *book*, of which every letter is become a law, a spiritual nationality which embraces peoples of every tongue and race, and he has stamped as the indelible character of this Mussulman [Muslim] nationality, the hatred of false gods, and the passion of the one and true God. This patriotism, avengeful of the profanations of heaven, was the virtue of the children of Mahomet; the conquest of one third of the world to his doctrine was his miracle; or rather, it was not the miracle of a man, but that of reason. The idea of the unity of God, proclaimed in the lassitude of fabulous theogonies, had in itself such virtue, that in exploding upon his lips, it fired the temples of old idolatry, and kindled with their flames one third [of] the globe. ...
>
> ...his life, his mediations, his heroic [reviling] against the superstitions of his country, his daring in affronting the fury of the idolators, his constancy in enduring it for [thirteen] years at Mecca, his acceptation of the part of laughing-stock and

almost victim among his countrymen, his flight; in fine, his ceaseless preaching, his precarious wars, his confidence of success, his superhuman fortitude in reverses, his longanimity in victory, his ambition all of idea and none of empire, his prayers without end, his mystic converse with God, his death and his triumph after the tomb, attest more than an imposture — a conviction. It was this conviction that gave him the power of restoring a dogma. This dogma was twofold, the unity of God and the immateriality of God, — the one saying what is God, the other saying what [H]e is not; the one subverting with the sabre the divinities of falsehood, the other inaugurating with the word an idea.

Philosopher, orator, apostle, lawgiver, warrior, conqueror of ideas, restorer of rational dogmas, of a worship without images, founder of twenty terrestrial empires, and one spiritual empire — such was Mahomet!

What man was greater, by all the scales on which we measure human greatness?[7]

Reverend Bosworth Smith (in the mid-1870s) and George Bernard Shaw (in the early twentieth century) both paid glowing accolades to Prophet Muhammad (ﷺ):

By a fortune absolutely unique in history, Mohammed is a threefold founder — of a nation, of an empire, and of a religion.[8]

If any religion had the chance of ruling over England, nay Europe within the next hundred years, it could be Islam... I have always held the religion of Muhammad in high estimation because of its wonderful vitality. It is the only religion that ap-

---

[7] Alphonse de Lamartine, *History of Turkey* (New York: D. Appleton & Co., 1857), 1:155-156.

[8] R. Bosworth Smith, *Mohammed and Mohammedanism* (London: Smith, Elder & Co., 1876), 343.

> pears to me to possess that assimilating capacity to the changing phase of existence which can make it appeal to every age... I believe that if a man like him were to assume the dictatorship of the modern world, he would succeed in solving its problems in a way that would bring it much needed peace and happiness.[9]

In the more recent past, a US psychoanalyst has provided three criteria for the selection of the greatest leader of all time:

> Leaders must fulfill three functions: provide for the well being of the led, provide a social organization in which people feel relatively secure, and provide them with one set of beliefs. People like Pasteur and Salk are leaders in the first sense. People like Gandhi and Confucius, on the one hand, and Alexander, Caesar and Hitler on the other, are leaders in the second and perhaps the third sense. Jesus and Buddha belong to the third category alone. Perhaps the greatest leader of all times was Muhammad, who combined all the three functions.[10]

In his 1978 book (reprinted in 1992 and 1999), *The 100: A Ranking of the Most Influential Persons in History*, American astrophysicist and historian Michael Hart evaluated and analyzed individuals from the earliest times up to the late twentieth century, from all over the world and from all walks of life. He considered thinkers, philosophers, prophets, religious leaders, scientists, and others in terms of the degree of their influence and the order of their excellence. Then he compiled a list of the one hundred individuals who have had the greatest impact on humankind. He justifies his choice of the individual, whom he ranked the first among the hundred, as follows:

---

[9] George Bernard Shaw, *Genuine Islam* (Singapore, 1936), vol. I, no. 8.

[10] Jules Masserman, "Who were history's greatest leaders?" *Time Magazine*, 15 July 1974; quoted in Ahmed Deedat, *The Choice: Islam and Christianity* (Delhi, India: Millat Book Centre, 1997), 1:160.

> My choice of Muhammad to lead the list of the world's most influential persons may surprise some readers and may be questioned by others, but he was the only man in history who was supremely successful on both the religious and secular levels...[11]

Indeed, it is no exaggeration to proclaim that the greatest human soul who has ever lived on the earth is Prophet Muhammad (ﷺ).

iii) Muhammad (ﷺ) is the only universal messenger

Prophet Muhammad (ﷺ) was the only prophet and messenger who was sent with a universal, complete, and comprehensive message — Islam. This last guidance from Allah is the completion and culmination of His favour via Prophet Muhammad (ﷺ). It is a complete and comprehensive message,[12] fit to guide all humankind and jinn for all time until the Day of Judgement. Allah has asserted in the Qur'an:

﴿ وَمَآ أَرْسَلْنَـٰكَ إِلَّا رَحْمَةً لِّلْعَـٰلَمِينَ ﴿١٠٧﴾ ﴾ (سورة الأنبياء: ١٠٧)

﴾And We have not sent you [O Muhammad] except as a mercy to the worlds.﴿ *(Qur'an 21: 107)*

﴿ وَمَآ أَرْسَلْنَـٰكَ إِلَّا كَآفَّةً لِّلنَّاسِ بَشِيرًا وَنَذِيرًا وَلَـٰكِنَّ أَكْثَرَ ٱلنَّاسِ لَا يَعْلَمُونَ ﴿٢٨﴾ ﴾ (سورة سبأ: ٢٨)

---

[11] Michael H. Hart, *The 100: A Ranking of the Most Influential Persons in History* (Secaucus, NJ: Carol Publishing Group, 1992), 33.

[12] A message of peace, justice, honour, human dignity, and so on.

﴾And We have not sent you except comprehensively to humankind as a bringer of good tidings and a warner. But most of the people do not know.﴿ *(Qur'an 34: 28)*

﴿ قُلْ يَٰٓأَيُّهَا ٱلنَّاسُ إِنِّى رَسُولُ ٱللَّهِ إِلَيْكُمْ جَمِيعًا ٱلَّذِى لَهُۥ مُلْكُ ٱلسَّمَٰوَٰتِ وَٱلْأَرْضِ ۖ لَآ إِلَٰهَ إِلَّا هُوَ يُحْىِۦ وَيُمِيتُ ۖ فَـَٔامِنُوا۟ بِٱللَّهِ وَرَسُولِهِ ٱلنَّبِىِّ ٱلْأُمِّىِّ ٱلَّذِى يُؤْمِنُ بِٱللَّهِ وَكَلِمَٰتِهِۦ وَٱتَّبِعُوهُ لَعَلَّكُمْ تَهْتَدُونَ ﴿١٥٨﴾ ﴾

(سورة الأعراف: ١٥٨)

﴾Say [O Muhammad]: O humankind, indeed I am the Messenger of Allah to you all, [from Him] to whom belongs the dominion of the heavens and the earth. There is no deity except Him; He gives life and causes death. So believe in Allah and His Messenger, the unlettered prophet, who believes in Allah and His words, and follow him that you may be guided.﴿ *(Qur'an 7: 158)*

The Prophet (ﷺ) attested to his unique position of universality over all other prophets in the following hadith:

Jâbir ibn 'Abdullâh (رضي الله عنه) narrated that the Prophet (ﷺ) said: «I have been given five things which were not given to anyone else before me.

1. Allah made me victorious by awe (by frightening my enemies) for a distance of one month's journey.
2. The earth has been made for me (and for my followers) a place for praying and a thing to perform dry-earth ablution; therefore, any of my followers can pray wherever (they happen to be when) the time of a prayer is due.
3. War booty has been made lawful for me, yet it was not lawful for anyone else before me.
4. I have been given the right of intercession (on the Day of Resurrection).

5. Every prophet was sent to his nation only; however, I have been sent to all humankind.» (Bukhari and Muslim)

The implication of the second part of the shahâdah is that the only human being who should be obeyed absolutely, without question, is Prophet Muhammad (ﷺ). This is because obeying him actually constitutes obeying Allah and vice versa, as the Qur'an has confirmed:

﴿مَّن يُطِعِ ٱلرَّسُولَ فَقَدۡ أَطَاعَ ٱللَّهَ ... ﴿٨٠﴾﴾ (سورة النساء: ٨٠)

﴾He who obeys the Messenger has obeyed Allah...﴿

(Qur'an 4: 80)

Chapter Three

The Implications of *Shahâdah*

The most radical political statement

The shahâdah is, unquestionably, the most radical political statement one can declare in this troubled world. In fact, by pronouncing the shahâdah, one is explicitly proclaiming the following:

i. True allegiance belongs to Allah alone, the Almighty. He has total dominion, sovereignty, control, and governance of all affairs and of everything in the universe.
ii. Absolute trust, along with complete and full reliance, is exclusively for Allah, the All-Powerful.
iii. Dependence on any deities, ideologies, systems, and so-called superpowers and individuals is rejected.

A major implication of the shahâdah, therefore, is that one is absolutely liberated from any kind of subjugation, whether it is external (to other deities, world politics, ideologies, economic expedients, and so on) or internal (to greed, delusions of this worldly life, and so forth).

Another implication is that one grasps the correct world view and a true, incorruptible understanding of the fleeting and transitory life of this world. Consequently, those individuals who affirm such faith in Allah feel secure and tranquil; they witness harmony in everyday life, regardless of their physical conditions and material situations. Allah has avowed:

﴿لَآ إِكۡرَاهَ فِي ٱلدِّينِۖ قَد تَّبَيَّنَ ٱلرُّشۡدُ مِنَ ٱلۡغَيِّۚ فَمَن يَكۡفُرۡ بِٱلطَّٰغُوتِ وَيُؤۡمِنۢ بِٱللَّهِ فَقَدِ ٱسۡتَمۡسَكَ بِٱلۡعُرۡوَةِ ٱلۡوُثۡقَىٰ لَا ٱنفِصَامَ لَهَاۗ وَٱللَّهُ سَمِيعٌ عَلِيمٌ ٢٥٦﴾

(سورة البقرة: ٢٥٦)

﴿There shall be no compulsion in [acceptance of] the religion. The right course has become clear from the wrong. So whoever disbelieves in *ṭâghoot*[13] and believes in Allah has grasped the most trustworthy handhold with no break in it. And Allah is Hearing and Knowing.﴾ *(Qur'an 2: 256)*

﴿۞ وَمَن يُسۡلِمۡ وَجۡهَهُۥٓ إِلَى ٱللَّهِ وَهُوَ مُحۡسِنٞ فَقَدِ ٱسۡتَمۡسَكَ بِٱلۡعُرۡوَةِ ٱلۡوُثۡقَىٰۗ وَإِلَى ٱللَّهِ عَٰقِبَةُ ٱلۡأُمُورِ ٢٢﴾

(سورة لقمان: ٢٢)

﴿And whoever submits his face to Allah while he is a doer of good — then he has grasped the most trustworthy handhold. And to Allah will be the outcome of [all] matters.﴾ *(Qur'an 31: 22)*

Elsewhere, Allah has reiterated the implications of the utterance of the shahâdah in the daily life of a Muslim:

﴿وَإِن يَمۡسَسۡكَ ٱللَّهُ بِضُرّٖ فَلَا كَاشِفَ لَهُۥٓ إِلَّا هُوَۖ وَإِن يَمۡسَسۡكَ بِخَيۡرٖ فَهُوَ عَلَىٰ كُلِّ شَيۡءٖ قَدِيرٞ ١٧ وَهُوَ ٱلۡقَاهِرُ فَوۡقَ عِبَادِهِۦۚ وَهُوَ ٱلۡحَكِيمُ ٱلۡخَبِيرُ ١٨﴾

(سورة الأنعام: ١٧-١٨)

﴿And if Allah should touch you with adversity, there is no remover of it except Him; if He touches you with good — then He is over all things competent. He is the Subjugator over His serv-

[13] Ṭâghoot: idols; everything evil that is worshipped.

ants, and He is the Wise, the Acquainted [with all].❳

(Qur'an 6: 17-18)

«It was narrated on the authority of Ibn 'Abbâs (ﷺ), who said: One day I was (mounted) behind[14] the Prophet (ﷺ). He said to me: Young man, I shall teach you some words (of advice):

Be mindful of Allah, and you will find Him in front of you. If you ask, ask Allah; if you seek help, seek help from Allah. Know that if the whole nation were to gather together to benefit you with anything, it would not benefit you with anything except what Allah has already prescribed for you; if they gather together to harm you with anything, they will not be able to harm you except to the extent that Allah has already prescribed for you. The pens have been lifted and the pages have dried.» (A sound hadith recorded by at-Tirmidhi)[15]

Imam an-Nawawi and al-Haythami, in their clarification of the essence of the aforementioned hadith, state:

---

[14] He was riding behind the Prophet (ﷺ) on the same animal.

[15] Another valid translation of this hadith is: Narrated Ibn 'Abbâs (ﷺ): «Once I was behind the Prophet (ﷺ) and he said to me: Young man, I will teach you a few words: Be loyal to Allah (worship Him alone and fear wherever you may be); remember him always and obey His orders. He will save you from every evil and will take care of you in all spheres of life. Be loyal and obedient to Allah; you will find Him near (in front of you); that is, He will respond to your requests. If you ask, ask Allah. If you seek help, seek help from Allah. Know that if all the people get together in order to benefit you with something, they will not be able to benefit you in anything except what Allah has decreed for you; if they all get together in order to harm you with something, they will not be able to harm you in anything except what Allah has decreed for you.»

When you seek help for the affairs of the world and the hereafter, then seek help from Allah; especially in the affairs in which there is no power with anyone other than Allah, such as curing diseases, seeking provisions and guidance and this is exactly what Allah particularised for Himself alone in the preceding verse above.[16]

In effect, this complete and total reliance and absolute trust in Allah is a clear exposition of the implications of the shahâdah. For this reason, Allah is deemed to be more than sufficient for His slaves — His worshippers.

In the words of the wise: for those who desire proof and evidence, the Qur'an is sufficient; for those who seek help, Allah is sufficient; for those who desire an admonition, death is enough; to those who are not satisfied with all that, the fire will suffice, as Allah has stated:

﴿ أَلَيْسَ ٱللَّهُ بِكَافٍ عَبْدَهُۥ ۖ وَيُخَوِّفُونَكَ بِٱلَّذِينَ مِن دُونِهِۦ ۚ وَمَن يُضْلِلِ ٱللَّهُ فَمَا لَهُۥ مِنْ هَادٍ ﴿٣٦﴾ وَمَن يَهْدِ ٱللَّهُ فَمَا لَهُۥ مِن مُّضِلٍّ ۗ أَلَيْسَ ٱللَّهُ بِعَزِيزٍ ذِى ٱنتِقَامٍ ﴿٣٧﴾ ﴾ (سورة الزُّمَر: ٣٦-٣٧)

﴾Is not Allah sufficient for His servant [Prophet Muhammad]? And [yet] they threaten you with those [they worship] other than Him. Whomever Allah leaves astray — for him there is no guide, and whomever Allah guides — for him there is no misleader. Is not Allah Exalted in Might and Owner of Retribution?﴿

(Qur'an 39: 36-37)

Shaykh 'Abdul-Qâdir al-Jeelâni wrote the following in his *Fatḥ ar-Rabbâni* with regard to Allah being sufficient for His slaves:

---

[16] Muhammad ibn Jameel Zaynoo*, The Methodology of the Saved Sect* (London: Invitation to Islam, 2003), 41.

Ask Allah and do not ask other than Him. Seek help from Allah, and do not seek help from other than Him. Woe to you, with which face will you meet Him tomorrow? You contend with Him in the world, turning away from Him, and approaching His creation, thus associating partners with Him. You submit your needs to them and you rely upon them in your important matters. Increase the ways and means between yourself and Allah, for verily, if you stop that, then it is foolishness.[17]

The legislated form of seeking help is that one should seek help from Allah alone during all difficult affairs and circumstances. Doing otherwise would negate one's shahâdah. Thus, seeking help from anyone other than Allah, such as the prophets and the deceased, pious people, is a form of *shirk* — attribution of partners to Allah. From the preceding Qur'anic verse and hadith, it is absolutely clear that no one other than Allah has the ability to benefit or harm us. All others whose help may be sought can neither hear our supplications nor respond to them even if they did hear them. Allah has emphasized:

﴿... وَالَّذِينَ تَدْعُونَ مِن دُونِهِۦ مَا يَمْلِكُونَ مِن قِطْمِيرٍ ﴿١٣﴾ إِن تَدْعُوهُمْ لَا يَسْمَعُوا۟ دُعَآءَكُمْ وَلَوْ سَمِعُوا۟ مَا ٱسْتَجَابُوا۟ لَكُمْ ۖ وَيَوْمَ ٱلْقِيَـٰمَةِ يَكْفُرُونَ بِشِرْكِكُمْ ۚ وَلَا يُنَبِّئُكَ مِثْلُ خَبِيرٍ ﴿١٤﴾﴾ (سورة فاطر: ١٣-١٤)

﴿...And those whom you invoke other than Him do not possess [as much as] the membrane of a date seed. If you invoke them, they do not hear your supplication; and if they heard, they would not respond to you. On the Day of Resurrection, they will deny your association. None can inform you like [one] Acquainted [with all matters].﴾ *(Qur'an 35: 13-14)*

In another verse, Allah has clarified:

---

[17] Zaynoo, *The Methodology of the Saved Sect*, 42.

﴿لَهُۥ دَعۡوَةُ ٱلۡحَقِّۚ وَٱلَّذِينَ يَدۡعُونَ مِن دُونِهِۦ لَا يَسۡتَجِيبُونَ لَهُم بِشَيۡءٍ إِلَّا كَبَٰسِطِ كَفَّيۡهِ إِلَى ٱلۡمَآءِ لِيَبۡلُغَ فَاهُ وَمَا هُوَ بِبَٰلِغِهِۦۚ وَمَا دُعَآءُ ٱلۡكَٰفِرِينَ إِلَّا فِي ضَلَٰلٖ ۝١٤﴾ (سورة الرعد: ١٤)

﴿To Him [alone] is the supplication of truth. Those whom they call upon besides Him do not respond to them with anything, except as one who stretches his hands toward water [from afar, calling it] to reach his mouth, but it will not reach it [thus]. And the supplication of the disbelievers is not but in error [that is, futility].﴾

(Qur'an 13: 14)

Allah has informed us in the aforementioned verse that supplication (*du'â'*), a form of worship, must be directed to Him alone. He draws an analogy to show the futility of expecting any benefit or response to calls to anyone other than Him. Those who call upon others instead of Allah will find no benefit in those upon whom they call. This is because they cannot fulfil their needs. Their similitude is like the one who stands at the side of a well to draw water from it with his bare hands. Obviously, this is impossible!

Ibn Katheer mentions in the explanation of the aforementioned verse that Mujâhid said, "He calls for water with his tongue and he points to it, but it will never come to him."[18]

Indeed, Allah has passed the judgement of disbelief on those who call upon others besides Him. He has clearly warned:

﴿... وَمَا دُعَآءُ ٱلۡكَٰفِرِينَ إِلَّا فِي ضَلَٰلٖ ۝١٤﴾ (سورة الرعد: ١٤)

﴿...And the supplication of the disbelievers is not but in error [that is, futility].﴾ *(Qur'an 13: 14)*

The consequences of committing disbelief by calling upon others besides Allah are very severe, given that disbelief is a negation of the shahâdah. Therefore, Muslims have been strictly warned to

---

18 Ismâ'eel ibn Katheer, *Tafseer Ibn Katheer*.

supplicate to Allah alone, the All-Powerful, the Almighty, in order to attain the status of true believers who worship Him to the exclusion of all else.

In the words of Muhammad ibn Jameel Zaynoo:

> So be warned, O Muslim, if you call upon other than Allah then you have committed disbelief (kufr), thus, negating the shahâdah. Therefore call upon Allah alone...[19]

The permissible form of seeking help from others besides Allah (سُبْحَانَهُ وَتَعَالَىٰ)

Without doubt, Allah has the dominion and control over all the affairs of His creation. Therefore, He alone deserves our complete and total allegiance; He must be our first call for support and help.

Even so, seeking aid from those living in our midst — that is, other members of the community — is also permissible according to Islamic Sharia (law). In fact, Allah enjoins us to cooperate and help others in all righteous matters, such as the building of mosques, provision of vital social services, and attending to the needs of the community. Allah has confirmed this in the Qur'an:

﴿... وَلَا تَعَاوَنُوا۟ عَلَى ٱلْإِثْمِ وَٱلْعُدْوَٰنِ ۚ وَٱتَّقُوا۟ ٱللَّهَ ۖ إِنَّ ٱللَّهَ شَدِيدُ ٱلْعِقَابِ ﴿٢﴾﴾

(سورة المائدة: ٢)

﴾...And cooperate in righteousness and piety, but do not cooperate in sin and aggression. And fear Allah; indeed, Allah is severe in penalty.﴿ *(Qur'an 5: 2)*

﴿... فَٱسْتَغَٰثَهُ ٱلَّذِى مِن شِيعَتِهِۦ عَلَى ٱلَّذِى مِنْ عَدُوِّهِۦ فَوَكَزَهُۥ مُوسَىٰ ... ﴿١٥﴾﴾

(سورة القصص: ١٥)

---

19 Zaynoo, *The Methodology of the Saved Sect*, 94.

﴿...And the one from his faction called for help to him against the one from his enemy, so Moses struck him...﴾ *(Qur'an 28: 15)*

﴿... فَأَعِينُونِي بِقُوَّةٍ أَجْعَلْ بَيْنَكُمْ وَبَيْنَهُمْ رَدْمًا ﴿٩٥﴾﴾ (سورة الكهف: ٩٥)

﴿...but assist me with strength; I will make between you and them a dam.﴾ *(Qur'an 18: 95)*

This injunction is also reiterated in the traditions of Prophet Muhammad (ﷺ), who is reported to have said:

«Allah supports and helps his servant as long as the servant helps his brother.» (Muslim)

Frequent recitation of *shahâdah* renews *eemân*

Finally, one of the most significant implications of the shahâdah is that its frequent recitation renews one's eemân.

«The Messenger of Allah (ﷺ) said: Renew your faith!
He was asked: O Messenger of Allah, how do we renew our faith?
He replied: By saying many times: Lâ ilâha illâ Allâh (There is no god but Allah).» (Aḥmad and al-Ḥâkim; al-Haythami deemed its chain to be good)

In another hadith, the Messenger of Allah (ﷺ) is reported to have said:

«Faith becomes worn out inside you just as a garment becomes worn out, so ask Allah to renew the faith in your hearts.» (al-Ḥâkim and aṭ-Ṭabarâni; al-Haythami graded it as reliable)

Islamic scholars contend that eemân cannot be a static quality. It waxes and wanes, increasing with righteous submissiveness and worship, and decreasing through sins and deviance. In this context, eemân getting old and worn out means that it loses strength and radiance on account of sins.

This is why the Prophet (ﷺ) said in one of his statements that when individuals commit a sin, a black spot appears on their hearts. If they sincerely repent, this spot gets washed out; otherwise, it remains. When they commit another sin, another black spot appears on their hearts; thus, on account of further sins, these black spots increase until, ultimately, their entire hearts are blackened and rusted, as Allah has described in the Qur'an:

﴿كَلَّا بَلْ رَانَ عَلَىٰ قُلُوبِهِم مَّا كَانُوا يَكْسِبُونَ ﴿١٤﴾﴾ (سورة المطفّفين: ١٤)

﴿No! Rather, the stain has covered their hearts of that which they were earning.﴾ *(Qur'an 83: 14)*

In two other hadiths, the Prophet (ﷺ) is reported to have said:

«The comparison of the one who remembers Allah and the one who does not remember Allah is like that of the living and the dead.» (Bukhari)[20]

«Should I not inform you of the best and the most sanctifying deed before your Lord, which does more to raise your position (with Him) and is better for you than the disbursement of gold and money, or battle with the enemy?
They (the Companions) said: Inform us.
He said: Remembrance of Allah.» (Recorded by Ibn Mâjah and at-Tirmidhi; authenticated by al-Ḥâkim)[21]

The aforementioned hadith likens the condition of those who are heedless to Allah to the condition of the dead. This is confirmed in the following Qur'anic verse:

---

20 Quoted in Sa'eed ibn 'Ali ibn Wahf al-Qahtâni, *Hisnul Muslim: Arabic-English* (Gassim, Saudi Arabia: Foreign Guidance Center, 1996), 24.

21 al-Qahtâni, *Hisnul Muslim,* 25.

﴿أَوَمَن كَانَ مَيْتًا فَأَحْيَيْنَٰهُ وَجَعَلْنَا لَهُۥ نُورًا يَمْشِى بِهِۦ فِى ٱلنَّاسِ كَمَن مَّثَلُهُۥ فِى ٱلظُّلُمَٰتِ لَيْسَ بِخَارِجٍ مِّنْهَا ۚ كَذَٰلِكَ زُيِّنَ لِلْكَٰفِرِينَ مَا كَانُوا۟ يَعْمَلُونَ ﴿١٢٢﴾﴾

(سورة الأنعام: ١٢٢)

﴾And is one who was dead, and We gave him life and made for him light by which to walk among the people, like one who is in darkness, never to emerge therefrom? Thus it has been made pleasing to the disbelievers that which they were doing.﴿

(Qur'an 6: 122)

In this analogy, the living individuals are those who have been given the light of faith, knowledge, and insight; the dead are those who are in the darkness of disbelief, ignorance, and narrow-mindedness, unable to perceive or come out into the light of guidance.

Thus, the *kalimah*, the phrase 'lâ ilâha illâ Allâh', bestows faith along with a new life away from the darkness of disbelief in Allah. The latter has been likened to spiritual death or rather, in the material world, to being the 'living dead'.

Consider the ordeal inflicted upon Prophet Jonah (عليه السلام)! The description of his plight in the Qur'an is an admonition and a reminder of the implications of the shahâdah. Prophet Jonah disobeyed Allah, and hence, was punished. He lived inside the dark belly of a whale for three days and nights. Had he not proclaimed the shahâdah, he would have remained spiritually dead in the darkness of the whale's belly until the Day of Judgement. The Qur'an has described:

﴿وَذَا ٱلنُّونِ إِذ ذَّهَبَ مُغَٰضِبًا فَظَنَّ أَن لَّن نَّقْدِرَ عَلَيْهِ فَنَادَىٰ فِى ٱلظُّلُمَٰتِ أَن لَّآ إِلَٰهَ إِلَّآ أَنتَ سُبْحَٰنَكَ إِنِّى كُنتُ مِنَ ٱلظَّٰلِمِينَ ﴿٨٧﴾ فَٱسْتَجَبْنَا لَهُۥ وَنَجَّيْنَٰهُ مِنَ ٱلْغَمِّ ۚ وَكَذَٰلِكَ نُـۨجِى ٱلْمُؤْمِنِينَ ﴿٨٨﴾﴾

(سورة الأنبياء: ٨٧-٨٨)

﴿And [mention] the man of the fish [Jonah], when he went off in anger[22] and thought that We would not decree [anything] upon him.[23] He called out within the darknesses:[24] There is no deity except You; exalted are You. Indeed, I have been of the wrongdoers. So We responded to him and saved him from the distress; thus do We save the believers.﴾ *(Qur'an: 21: 87-88)*

In another verse, the story of Prophet Jonah has been elaborated further as guidance and a reprimand:

﴿ وَإِنَّ يُونُسَ لَمِنَ ٱلْمُرْسَلِينَ ﴿١٣٩﴾ إِذْ أَبَقَ إِلَى ٱلْفُلْكِ ٱلْمَشْحُونِ ﴿١٤٠﴾ فَسَاهَمَ فَكَانَ مِنَ
ٱلْمُدْحَضِينَ ﴿١٤١﴾ فَٱلْتَقَمَهُ ٱلْحُوتُ وَهُوَ مُلِيمٌ ﴿١٤٢﴾ فَلَوْلَآ أَنَّهُۥ كَانَ مِنَ ٱلْمُسَبِّحِينَ ﴿١٤٣﴾ لَلَبِثَ
فِى بَطْنِهِۦٓ إِلَىٰ يَوْمِ يُبْعَثُونَ ﴿١٤٤﴾ ۞ فَنَبَذْنَٰهُ بِٱلْعَرَآءِ وَهُوَ سَقِيمٌ ﴿١٤٥﴾ وَأَنۢبَتْنَا عَلَيْهِ
شَجَرَةً مِّن يَقْطِينٍ ﴿١٤٦﴾ وَأَرْسَلْنَٰهُ إِلَىٰ مِاْئَةِ أَلْفٍ أَوْ يَزِيدُونَ ﴿١٤٧﴾ فَـَٔامَنُوا۟ فَمَتَّعْنَٰهُمْ
إِلَىٰ حِينٍ ﴿١٤٨﴾ ﴾ (سورة الصافات: ١٣٩-١٤٨)

﴿And indeed, Jonah was among the messengers. [Mention] when he ran away to the laden ship. He drew lots and was among the losers. Then the fish swallowed him, while he was blameworthy. Had he not been of those who exalt Allah, He would have remained inside its belly until the day they were resurrected. But We threw him onto the open shore while he was ill, and We caused to grow over him a gourd vine. We sent him to [his people of] one hundred thousand or more, and they believed, so We gave them enjoyment [of life] for a time.﴾ *(Qur'an: 37: 139-148)*

This passage clearly illustrates the power and effectiveness of the remembrance of the shahâdah — 'lâ ilâha illâ Allâh' — especially when one is in dire straits.

---

[22] At the disbelief of his people.

[23] Or 'would not restrict him' inside the belly of the fish.

[24] Of the night, of the sea, and of the fish's interior.

Chapter Four

The Importance of *Shahâdah*

Shahâdah is the vital key that opens the doors of Islam. It is the passport without which one cannot enter the abode of Islam. It is the pivotal concept that Prophet Muhammad (ﷺ) struggled to instil in the hearts of his disbelieving countrymen, the Quraysh. He spent thirteen long years suffering hardship, trials, and persecution while trying to convince people to embrace the concept of tawḥeed and affirm it in their hearts and deeds in order to free themselves from all false deities — including the 360 idols that were in the *Kaaba* (the House of Allah in Makkah).

All the prophets were sent to establish *lâ ilâha illâ Allâh*

Prophet Muhammad (ﷺ) was not the only one who struggled to establish the oneness of Allah. All the prophets and messengers were sent with the sole purpose of inviting their people to the same concept. Many prophets and messengers — nay, all prophets and messengers — spent their lives only to expound and establish this very important creed of tawḥeed in people's lives. Allah has proclaimed:

﴿وَمَآ أَرۡسَلۡنَا مِن قَبۡلِكَ مِن رَّسُولٍ إِلَّا نُوحِيٓ إِلَيۡهِ أَنَّهُۥ لَآ إِلَٰهَ إِلَّآ أَنَا۠ فَٱعۡبُدُونِ ٢٥﴾ (سورة الأنبياء: ٢٥)

﴿And We sent not before you any messenger except that We revealed to him that: There is no deity except Me, so worship Me.﴾ *(Qur'an 21: 25)*

The fact that all prophets and messengers were sent for the same purpose — that is, to proclaim the shahâdah and establish it as the driving force in people's lives — clearly signifies this concept. Prophets Noah, Abraham, Moses, Hood, Ṣâliḥ, and Jesus (peace be upon them) all invited their people to accept the principle of tawḥeed, as demonstrated in the following verses:

﴿لَقَدۡ أَرۡسَلۡنَا نُوحًا إِلَىٰ قَوۡمِهِۦ فَقَالَ يَٰقَوۡمِ ٱعۡبُدُواْ ٱللَّهَ مَا لَكُم مِّنۡ إِلَٰهٍ غَيۡرُهُۥٓ إِنِّيٓ أَخَافُ عَلَيۡكُمۡ عَذَابَ يَوۡمٍ عَظِيمٖ ٥٩﴾ (سورة الأعراف: ٥٩)

﴿We had certainly sent Noah to his people, and he said: O my people, worship Allah; you have no deity other than Him. Indeed, I fear for you the punishment of a tremendous day.﴾ *(Qur'an 7: 59)*[25]

﴿وَلَقَدۡ بَعَثۡنَا فِي كُلِّ أُمَّةٖ رَّسُولًا أَنِ ٱعۡبُدُواْ ٱللَّهَ وَٱجۡتَنِبُواْ ٱلطَّٰغُوتَۖ فَمِنۡهُم مَّنۡ هَدَى ٱللَّهُ وَمِنۡهُم مَّنۡ حَقَّتۡ عَلَيۡهِ ٱلضَّلَٰلَةُۚ فَسِيرُواْ فِي ٱلۡأَرۡضِ فَٱنظُرُواْ كَيۡفَ كَانَ عَٰقِبَةُ ٱلۡمُكَذِّبِينَ ٣٦﴾ (سورة النحل: ٣٦)

﴿And We certainly sent into every nation a messenger, [saying]: Worship Allah and avoid ṭâghoot. Among them were those whom Allah guided, and among them were those upon whom error was [deservedly] decreed. So proceed through the earth and observe how was the end of the deniers.﴾ *(Qur'an 16: 36)*

---

[25] See also *(Qur'an 21: 51-70)*, *(Qur'an 20: 9-15)*, *(Qur'an 20: 47-56)*, and *(Qur'an 3: 45-53)*.

The status of *lâ ilâha illâ Allâh*

In his book *The Declaration of Faith,* Shaykh Saalih ibn Fawzaan al-Fawzaan clearly outlines the unparalleled and exalted status of the testimony of faith, while clarifying the essence of the shahâdah. He indicates that it is a declaration the Muslims pronounce repeatedly in their daily lives: in the calls to prayer, in speeches, and in sermons.

He goes on to say that the shahâdah is an assertion upon which the earth and heavens are built and for which everything was created; it is the reason Allah sent messengers, revealed books, and prescribed laws. He emphasizes that it is on the basis of the testimony of faith that humans and jinn are categorized into believers and disbelievers, righteous and evil. It is the reason Allah set up the scales and register for the Day of Judgement, and defined the cause of injunctions, rewards, and punishments. He comments:

> It is the right for which the creation was created and about it and its rights will they be questioned and brought to account. Because of it there is punishment and reward; due to it the direction of Prayer (qiblah) was set-up; upon it rests the very foundation of the Religion; and because of it swords are drawn for striving and fighting (jihaad). It is the Right of Allaah over His slaves; the Declaration (kalimah) of Islaam; and the key to Paradise; about it both the earlier and later people will be questioned. Indeed, no person will stand before Allaah without being asked two questions: What did you worship? And how did you respond to the Messengers?[26]

---

[26] Ibn al-Qayyim, *Zâd al-Ma'âd*, 1:34, quoted in Saalih ibn Fawzaan al-Fawzaan, *The Declaration of Faith.* (United Kingdom: Message of Islam, 1998), 9.

The shaykh affirms that the answer to the first question is to understand the doctrine of 'lâ ilâha illâ Allâh', establish it, and act upon it. The reply to the second question is to recognize that Muhammad (ﷺ) is the Messenger of Allah, affirm his role in the spreading Allah's message, and obey that message.

While mentioning the virtues of the shahâdah, Shaykh ibn Fawzaan al-Fawzaan goes on to explain that:

> It has great virtues and has a great place with Allaah. Whoever says it with truthfulness will enter the Gardens of Paradise and whoever did not utter it truthfully, his property and blood will be safeguarded in this world, but his reckoning will be with Allaah the Mighty and Majestic.[27]

He eloquently indicates that it is a succinct statement that is light upon the tongue but heavy on the scales of judgement.

The shaykh quotes the following hadiths to indicate that 'lâ ilâha illâ Allâh' is the best form of remembrance of Allah:[28]

Abu Sa'eed al-Khudri (رضي الله عنه) narrated that Allah's Messenger (ﷺ) said:

> «Moses requested: O my Lord, teach me something by which I can remember You and supplicate to You.
> Allah instructed: Moses, say 'lâ ilâha illâ Allâh'.
> Moses responded: O my Lord, all Your slaves say this.
> Allah said: O Moses! If the seven heavens and all that they contain — other than Me — and the seven earths were placed in one scale, and 'lâ ilâha illâ Allâh' were put in the other, then 'lâ ilâha illâ Allâh' would outweigh them all.» (A sound hadith recorded by Ibn Ḥibbân and al-Ḥâkim)

---

[27] al-Fawzaan, *The Declaration of Faith*, 15-18.

[28] al-Fawzaan, *The Declaration of Faith*, 15-18.

'Abdullâh ibn 'Umar (ﷺ) narrated that the Prophet (ﷺ) said: «The best supplication is the supplication on the day of *'Arafah.*[29] The best that I, or any other prophet sent before me, has said is: None has the right to be worshipped except Allah, alone, having no partner. To Him belongs the sovereignty, and to Him belongs all praise, and He has power over everything…» (Recorded by at-Tirmidhi and authenticated by al-Albâni)

Some of the virtues of the kalimah have been mentioned by Ḥâfidh Ibn Rajab in his book titled *Kalimatul-Ikhlâṣ*, quoted by Shaykh Saalih ibn Fawzaan.[30] These include:

- The one whose final words are 'lâ ilâha illâ Allâh' will enter the gardens of paradise.
- It is a means of salvation from the hellfire.
- It necessitates being forgiven.
- It is the best of all good actions; it wipes away sins.
- It renews faith in one's heart.
- On the Day of Judgement, it will outweigh the record of sins on the scales.
- It traverses all barriers until it reaches Allah, the Majestic.
- It is an attestation whose proclaimer is declared truthful by Allah.
- It is the best of what the prophets have affirmed.
- It is the best form of remembrance, the best of all actions, and the one that is multiplied the most (in earning rewards).

---

[29] 'Arafah: the plain outside of Makkah where pilgrims gather at the climax of the Hajj pilgrimage.

[30] Ibn Rajab, *Kalimatul-Ikhlâṣ*, 54-66, quoted in al-Fawzaan, *The Declaration of Faith*.

- It is equivalent to freeing slaves.
- It is a protection against Satan.
- It is a means of security against the darkness in the grave and against the terror of the final gathering.
- It will be a distinguishing sign for the believers when they emerge from their graves.
- All the eight gates of paradise will be opened to its testifiers and they may enter it through any one of their choosing. Even if its testifiers enter the hellfire due to falling short in fulfilling some of their rights, they will, eventually but most definitely, be taken out from it.

Therefore, after reciting the shahâdah, one should strive to understand its meaning, implications, importance, pillars, and seven conditions. One should exert oneself to lead a life according to these conditions. Without the fulfilment of these conditions, one cannot truly imbibe firm faith; rather, one's faith will waver all the time. However, if one has full and comprehensive knowledge of the shahâdah and all that it entails, and one makes every effort to live by it, there is no doubt that one's faith will remain steadfast. Since one will constantly strive to please one's Lord, Allah, the shahâdah will ensure success both in this world and the hereafter:

﴿ يُثَبِّتُ ٱللَّهُ ٱلَّذِينَ ءَامَنُوا۟ بِٱلْقَوْلِ ٱلثَّابِتِ فِى ٱلْحَيَوٰةِ ٱلدُّنْيَا وَفِى ٱلْـَٔاخِرَةِ ۖ وَيُضِلُّ ٱللَّهُ ٱلظَّـٰلِمِينَ ۚ وَيَفْعَلُ ٱللَّهُ مَا يَشَآءُ ﴿٢٧﴾ ﴾ (سورة إبراهيم: ٢٧)

﴾Allah keeps firm those who believe, with the firm word, in worldly life and in the hereafter. Allah sends astray the wrongdoers, and Allah does what He wills.﴿ *(Qur'an 14: 27)*

The Quraysh came to negotiate with the Messenger of Allah (ﷺ) in order to persuade him to stop preaching the message of Islam, which was gaining ground in Makkah. The Messenger of Allah (ﷺ) turned to them, saying (according to his biographers),

"Do you not see that I will guide you to the means by which you will gain sovereignty over both the Arabs and non-Arabs?"

In another version, the Prophet (ﷺ) asked Abu Ṭâlib, "O Uncle, why do you not call them unto something better?"

Abu Ṭâlib asked him, "What is it that to which you invite them?"

The Prophet (ﷺ) replied, "I invite them to hold fast to a message that is bound to give them access to kingship over the Arabs and the non-Arabs."

According to Ibn Is-ḥâq's version, "Just one word will give you supremacy over the Arabs and the non-Arabs."

In his biography of Prophet Muhammad (ﷺ), titled *The Sealed Nectar*, Safi-ur-Rahman Mubarakpuri explains:

> The Makkan deputies were taken by incredible surprise and began to wonder what sort of word was that which would benefit them to that extent. Abu Jahl asked: What is that word? I swear by your father that we will surely grant you your wish followed by ten times as much. The Prophet (ﷺ) responded: I want you to testify that there is no god worthy to be worshipped but Allah (lâ ilâha illâ Allâh), and then divest yourselves of any sort of worship you harbor for any deities other than Allah.[31]

Those who implement the seven conditions of the shahâdah will, Allah willing, inherit paradise. This is the reward for those who have been true to their declaration of faith, as confirmed in the words of Allah:

﴿وَالَّذِينَ هُم بِشَهَادَاتِهِمْ قَائِمُونَ (٣٣) وَالَّذِينَ هُمْ عَلَىٰ صَلَاتِهِمْ يُحَافِظُونَ (٣٤) أُولَٰئِكَ فِي جَنَّاتٍ مُّكْرَمُونَ (٣٥)﴾

(سورة المعارج: ٣٣-٣٥)

---

31 Safi-ur-Rahman al-Mubarakpuri, *Ar-Raheeq Al-Makhtum (The Sealed Nectar)* (Riyadh: Darussalam Publishers and Distributors, 1995), 121.

﴾And those who are in their testimonies upright, and those who [carefully] maintain their prayer — they will be in gardens, honoured.﴿ *(Qur'an 70: 33-35)*

A true understanding of the shahâdah and the implementation of its seven conditions will safeguard one from the pitfalls and the imperfect and false ideologies in this world such as secularism, democracy, capitalism, communism, atheism, and so forth. This is because firm adherence to the shahâdah enables one to hold onto something that can never break.

Moreover, the Prophet (ﷺ) has said:

«Urge those of you who are on their deathbeds to say: lâ ilâha illâ Allâh; for verily, whoever's final words are 'lâ ilâha illâ Allâh' will eventually enter paradise even if he has to go through whatever (punishment) he has to go through.» (Recorded by Ibn Ḥibbân and authenticated by al-Albâni)[32]

It has been narrated on the authority of 'Uthmân (رضي الله عنه) that the Messenger of Allah (ﷺ) said:

«He who died knowing (full well) that there is no god worthy of worship but Allah entered paradise.» (Muslim)

Seven conditions of *shahâdah* — prerequisites for entry into paradise

The following seven chapters will elaborate on the seven conditions of the shahâdah. These conditions constitute the fundamentals of a number of treatises on this subject by established reputable and traditional Islamic scholars. Our success, both in this world and in the hereafter, depends upon a complete and thorough

---

32 As quoted in Zaynoo, *The Methodology of The Saved Sect*, 35.

knowledge of, as well as compliance with, these conditions. They have been traditionally referred to as the teeth or notches of the key that will open the door to paradise. A word of caution: the shahâdah is nullified by the association of partners with Allah in any shape or form, just as the state of ritual purity is invalidated by urination, defecation, and so on.

Indeed, our final redemption is contingent upon the shahâdah, given the following words of the Prophet (ﷺ):

> «Whoever says 'lâ ilâha illâ Allâh', it will be his salvation someday, no matter what befalls him before that.» (Recorded by al-Bayhaqi and authenticated by al-Albâni)[33]

Even so, it must be understood that merely pronouncing the shahâdah without the fulfilment of the seven conditions is of no benefit. Ibn Rajab, in his commentary on hadiths collated in *Ṣaḥeeḥ Bukhâri* and *Ṣaḥeeḥ Muslim*, asserts that the recitation of the shahâdah is sufficient grounds for entry into paradise; however, that is dependent upon a few conditions. He writes that scholars explain these hadiths to mean that pronouncing the shahâdah "is a cause for entering the gardens of paradise and being saved from the hellfire, and that it is deserving of this outcome."

He emphasizes, however, that such results will not be attained unless the conditions of the shahâdah are fulfilled and any impediments are removed. Indeed, if there is a deficiency in one of its conditions, or the presence of an obstruction to its fulfilment, rewards may be withheld.

He cites the following as clarification:

> Al-Ḥasan said to al-Farazdaq, who was burying his wife: What have you prepared for this day?

---

[33] As quoted in Zaynoo, *The Methodology of The Saved Sect*, 35.

He replied: Testifying to 'lâ ilâha illâ Allâh' for the last seventy years.

Al-Ḥasan said: What wonderful preparation. However, 'lâ ilâha illâ Allâh' has certain conditions, so beware of defaming chaste women.

It was once said to al-Ḥasan: Some people think that whoever says 'lâ ilâha illâ Allâh' will enter the gardens of paradise.

He replied: Whoever says 'lâ ilâha illâ Allâh', and fulfils its right and obligations will enter the gardens of paradise.

Wahb ibn Munabbih was once asked: Is not 'lâ ilâha illâ Allâh' the key to paradise?

He answered: Indeed, but every key has certain ridges and teeth. If one possesses that key, with the ridges and the teeth, the doors will be opened for him. If not, they will not [open]![34]

---

[34] 'Abdur-Raḥmân ibn Aḥmad ibn Rajab, *Kalimatul-Ikhlâṣ wa Taḥqeeq Ma'nâhâ* (Damascus: al-Maktab al-Islâmi, 1961).

Chapter Five
The First Condition: Knowledge that Negates Ignorance

﴿وَإِذۡ قَالَ رَبُّكَ لِلۡمَلَٰٓئِكَةِ إِنِّي جَاعِلٞ فِي ٱلۡأَرۡضِ خَلِيفَةٗۖ قَالُوٓاْ أَتَجۡعَلُ فِيهَا
مَن يُفۡسِدُ فِيهَا وَيَسۡفِكُ ٱلدِّمَآءَ وَنَحۡنُ نُسَبِّحُ بِحَمۡدِكَ وَنُقَدِّسُ لَكَۖ قَالَ إِنِّيٓ
أَعۡلَمُ مَا لَا تَعۡلَمُونَ ﴿٣٠﴾ وَعَلَّمَ ءَادَمَ ٱلۡأَسۡمَآءَ كُلَّهَا ثُمَّ عَرَضَهُمۡ عَلَى ٱلۡمَلَٰٓئِكَةِ
فَقَالَ أَنۢبِـُٔونِي بِأَسۡمَآءِ هَٰٓؤُلَآءِ إِن كُنتُمۡ صَٰدِقِينَ ﴿٣١﴾ قَالُواْ سُبۡحَٰنَكَ لَا عِلۡمَ لَنَآ إِلَّا
مَا عَلَّمۡتَنَآۖ إِنَّكَ أَنتَ ٱلۡعَلِيمُ ٱلۡحَكِيمُ ﴿٣٢﴾﴾ (سورة البقرة: ٣٠-٣٢)

﴾And [mention, O Muhammad] when your Lord said to the angels: Indeed, I will make upon the earth a successive authority. They said: Will You place upon it one who causes corruption therein and sheds blood, while we declare Your praise and sanctify You? Allah said: Indeed, I know that which you do not know. And He taught Adam the names — all of them. Then He showed them to the angels and said: Inform Me of the names of these, if you are truthful. They said: Exalted are You; we have no knowledge except what You have taught us. Indeed, it is You Who are the Knowing, the Wise.﴿ *(Qur'an 2: 30-32)*

﴿ٱقۡرَأۡ بِٱسۡمِ رَبِّكَ ٱلَّذِي خَلَقَ ﴿١﴾ خَلَقَ ٱلۡإِنسَٰنَ مِنۡ عَلَقٍ ﴿٢﴾ ٱقۡرَأۡ وَرَبُّكَ ٱلۡأَكۡرَمُ ﴿٣﴾ ٱلَّذِي عَلَّمَ
بِٱلۡقَلَمِ ﴿٤﴾ عَلَّمَ ٱلۡإِنسَٰنَ مَا لَمۡ يَعۡلَمۡ ﴿٥﴾﴾ (سورة العلق: ١-٥)

﴿Recite in the name of your Lord, Who created — created man from a clinging substance. Recite, and your Lord is the most Generous — Who taught by the pen — taught man that which he knew not.﴾ *(Qur'an 96: 1-5)*

﴿ فَٱعْلَمْ أَنَّهُۥ لَآ إِلَٰهَ إِلَّا ٱللَّهُ ... ﴿١٩﴾ ﴾ (سورة محمد: ١٩)

﴿So know [O Muhammad] that there is no deity except Allah…﴾ *(Qur'an 47: 19)*

﴿ شَهِدَ ٱللَّهُ أَنَّهُۥ لَآ إِلَٰهَ إِلَّا هُوَ وَٱلْمَلَٰٓئِكَةُ وَأُوْلُواْ ٱلْعِلْمِ قَآئِمًۢا بِٱلْقِسْطِ ۚ لَآ إِلَٰهَ إِلَّا هُوَ ٱلْعَزِيزُ ٱلْحَكِيمُ ﴿١٨﴾ ﴾ (سورة آل عمران: ١٨)

﴿Allah witnesses that there is no deity except Him, and [so do] the angels and those of knowledge — [that He is] maintaining [creation] in justice. There is no deity except Him, the Exalted in Might, the Wise.﴾ *(Qur'an 3: 18)*

﴿ ... إِلَّا مَن شَهِدَ بِٱلْحَقِّ وَهُمْ يَعْلَمُونَ ﴿٨٦﴾ ﴾ (سورة الزُّخرُف: ٨٦)

﴿…but only those who testify to the truth [can benefit], and they know.﴾ *(Qur'an 43: 86)*

The aforementioned verses from the Qur'an undeniably demonstrate that the most important and crucial obligation on a Muslim is the acquisition of knowledge. This is because correct knowledge precedes correct action. The opposite is also true, partial or false knowledge can and does lead to disastrous conduct.[35] Witness the condition of the contemporary Muslim community!

For this reason, the first prophet of God, our great-grandfather Adam, was endowed foremost with knowledge. Likewise, the final prophet and messenger and a mercy to all creatures, Muhammad (ﷺ), was also commanded to seek knowledge. This

---

35 Abdul Wahid Hamid, *Islam The Natural Way* (London: MELS Publishing and Distributing, 1989), 26-27.

divine injunction has been reiterated in a significant number of traditions of the Prophet (ﷺ).

On the authority of Abu Hurayrah (ﷺ), the Prophet (ﷺ) said:

«For he who treads the path in search of knowledge, Allah will make that path easy, leading to paradise.» (Muslim and at-Tirmidhi)

Ibn 'Abdur-Raḥmân narrated that he heard Mu'âwiyah giving a sermon in which he said:

«I heard the Prophet (ﷺ) saying: For whomever Allah wishes good, He gives him a true understanding of the religion (of Islam).» (Bukhari)

«Katheer ibn Qays said: I was sitting with Abu ad-Dardâ' (ﷺ) in a mosque in Damascus when a man came and said: O Abu ad-Dardâ'! I have come to you from Madinah, the city of the Prophet (ﷺ), only to verify a single hadith which I have been given to understand that you are narrating from Allah's Messenger (ﷺ).

Abu ad-Dardâ' (ﷺ) said: I heard Allah's Messenger (ﷺ) saying: Whoever takes a path in search of knowledge, Allah facilitates a path for him among the paths to paradise. Indeed, the angels lower their wings for the seeker of knowledge out of pleasure in what he seeks; those in the heavens and the earth and even the fishes in water seek forgiveness for a person endowed with knowledge. Verily, the superiority of a scholar over a worshipper is like the brightness of the full moon over all the stars in the night; verily, the Muslim scholars are the inheritors of the prophets. Verily, the prophets do not bequeath *dinars* or *dirhams* (gold or silver coins), but they bequeath knowledge. Therefore, whoever takes it (knowledge) has taken a great portion.» (A sound hadith recorded by Abu Dâwood)

'Uthmân (ﷺ) narrated that the Prophet (ﷺ) said:

«The best among you (Muslims) are those who learn the Qur'an and teach it.» (Bukhari)

This shows that the value of knowledge and the obligation to seek it are the very cornerstones of Islam. Both have been repeatedly and strongly emphasized in the Qur'an and in the traditions of Prophet Muhammad (ﷺ). This implies that actions should not be based on blind imitation; this does not befit a right-thinking, sensible human being. Indeed, logical action based on sound fundamental knowledge is so crucial for a Muslim that Imam Bukhari, in his *Ṣaḥeeḥ al-Bukhâri,* has a whole chapter called 'Chapter of knowledge before speech and action'.

Another implication of the first condition of the shahâdah is that it is almost impossible for one to be a good Muslim and to conduct one's life in accordance with Islam while remaining ignorant and barbaric. How well we understand Islam, and how well we fulfil our roles and duties as human beings and Muslims, will depend upon the type of knowledge we strive to acquire and the sources utilized to gain that knowledge along with the purpose and use of the acquired knowledge. In this manner, one's shahâdah can be successfully implemented.

Categories of knowledge

Knowledge is such a vast ocean that we need help in deciding what type of knowledge is most crucial and important to acquire. Otherwise, we will end up wasting a lot of our limited time in this world in unproductive and useless pursuits. Towards that end, it is imperative to know how reputable Islamic scholars have classified knowledge.

Knowledge can be broadly categorized in two ways: firstly, true vs. false knowledge and secondly, beneficial vs. non-beneficial knowledge.

1) True vs. false knowledge

All true knowledge comes from Allah, as affirmed in the Qur'an:

﴿ وَعَلَّمَ ءَادَمَ ٱلْأَسْمَآءَ كُلَّهَا ... ﴿٣١﴾ ﴾ (سورة البقرة: ٣١)

﴿And He taught Adam the names — all of them...﴾ *(Qur'an 2: 31)*

﴿عَلَّمَ ٱلْإِنسَٰنَ مَا لَمْ يَعْلَمْ ﴿٥﴾ ﴾ (سورة العلق: ٥)

﴿Taught man that which he knew not.﴾ *(Qur'an 96: 5)*

On the other hand, the knowledge taught by Satan and his henchmen is false knowledge. This includes witchcraft, magic, astrology, and some aspects of Western philosophy and psychology, clearly exemplified in the following verses:

﴿ وَلَمَّا جَآءَهُمْ رَسُولٌ مِّنْ عِندِ ٱللَّهِ مُصَدِّقٌ لِّمَا مَعَهُمْ نَبَذَ فَرِيقٌ مِّنَ ٱلَّذِينَ
أُوتُوا۟ ٱلْكِتَٰبَ كِتَٰبَ ٱللَّهِ وَرَآءَ ظُهُورِهِمْ كَأَنَّهُمْ لَا يَعْلَمُونَ ﴿١٠١﴾ وَٱتَّبَعُوا۟ مَا
تَتْلُوا۟ ٱلشَّيَٰطِينُ عَلَىٰ مُلْكِ سُلَيْمَٰنَ ۖ وَمَا كَفَرَ سُلَيْمَٰنُ وَلَٰكِنَّ ٱلشَّيَٰطِينَ
كَفَرُوا۟ يُعَلِّمُونَ ٱلنَّاسَ ٱلسِّحْرَ وَمَآ أُنزِلَ عَلَى ٱلْمَلَكَيْنِ بِبَابِلَ هَٰرُوتَ وَمَٰرُوتَ ۚ
... ﴿١٠٢﴾ ﴾ (سورة البقرة: ١٠٢)

﴿And when a messenger from Allah came to them confirming that which was with them, a party of those who had been given the scripture threw the scripture of Allah behind their backs as if they did not know [what it contained]. They followed [instead] what the devils had recited during the reign of Solomon. It was not Solomon who disbelieved, but the devils disbelieved, teaching people magic and that which was revealed to the two angels at Babylon, Hâroot and Mâroot…❵ *(Qur'an 2: 101-102)*

It is futile to waste time seeking false knowledge. However, if one intends to use this information to guide those who have been led astray, an exception can be made for one to learn the nature of these falsehoods. Extreme caution should be taken to ground oneself in the true knowledge of tawḥeed before such an undertaking, though, to ensure that one does not deviate from the right path and get lost!

2) Beneficial vs. non-beneficial knowledge

Knowledge that is useful for the well-being of humanity, society, and the environment is classified as beneficial knowledge. This category includes knowledge about:

- Tawḥeed (about the Creator)
- The role of angels and jinn
- The roles of prophets, especially the final prophet
- The divine revelations
- The purpose of creation
- Human nature and what brings one nearer to Allah
- How to establish an Islamic state
- What has been made subservient to humans: physical sciences along with the use of reason, observation, and experimentation. For example, knowledge of certain fields such as astronomy and navigation, agriculture, medical sciences, oceanography and marine engineering, history, geography, physics, chemistry, biology, and so on.

Knowledge that is not useful and does not improve the well-being of humanity and the environment is considered to be non-beneficial. The distinction between the two types, along with the dangers of non-beneficial knowledge, was affirmed by Prophet Muhammad (ﷺ) in the following supplication:

> «'Abdullâh ibn 'Amr (رضي الله عنه) narrated that the Prophet (ﷺ) used to seek Allah's refuge from four things: Knowledge that is of no benefit, a heart that does not fear Allah, a supplication that is not heard (not answered), and a soul that is never satisfied.» (Recorded by Abu Dâwood and Aḥmad, and authenticated by al-Ḥakim)

The Prophet (ﷺ) also used to recite the following supplication after the tasleem:

> «*Allâhuma inni as'aluka 'ilman nâfi'an wa rizqan ṭâyyiban wa 'amalan mutaqâbalan.*
>
> O Allah, I ask You for knowledge which is beneficial and sustenance which is good and deeds which are acceptable.» (Recorded by an-Nasâ'i and Ibn Mâjah; a sound hadith according to al-Albâni)[36]

Knowledge needed by the individual and the community

In order to clarify the first condition of the shahâdah, along with its purpose, scholars have divided all beneficial knowledge into two general categories. Knowledge that is required for an individual to discharge personal mandatory duties is considered to be *farḍ 'ayn* — an individual duty. The knowledge that is required by the community as a whole, for the execution of communal compulsory responsibilities, is referred to as *farḍ kifâyah* — collective duty.

---

[36] As quoted in al-Qahtâni, *Hisnul Muslim*, 103-104.

Knowledge required by each individual (*farḍ 'ayn*)

This is the knowledge that each person is obligated to acquire in order to fulfil his or her natural function as a human being and as a Muslim. Given that Allah has created human beings solely for His worship, a Muslim has certain individual, obligatory duties — the farḍ 'ayn. Those who perform these duties will be rewarded, while those who neglect them will be punished. This category of knowledge, essential for the discharge of personal obligations, includes the knowledge of:

◊ The five pillars of Islam,
◊ The six pillars of eemân,
◊ The Qur'an,
◊ The traditions of the Prophet (ﷺ) — the Sunnah, regarded as his way of life
◊ The biography of Prophet Muhammad (ﷺ),
◊ The history of Islam,
◊ Sharia,
◊ The Arabic language, and so on.

There is a well-known hadith that relates how angel Gabriel (عليه السلام) came to teach religion to the early Muslims, the Companions of Prophet Muhammad (ﷺ):

On the authority of 'Umar ibn al-Khaṭṭâb (رضي الله عنه) who said:

«One day, while we were sitting with the Messenger of Allah (ﷺ), a man appeared before us; his clothes were exceedingly white and his hair was exceedingly black. No signs of journeying were visible on him and none of us knew him. He walked up and sat down by the Prophet (ﷺ). Resting his knees against his and placing the palms of his hands on his thighs, he said:

O Muhammad, tell me about Islam.

The Messenger of Allah (ﷺ) responded: Islam means to testify that there is no god but Allah and that Muhammad is the Messenger of Allah, to perform ṣalâh, to pay zakâh (compulsory charity), to fast in Ramadan, and to make Hajj (pilgrimage) to the House if you are able to do so.

He said: You have spoken rightly.

We were amazed at him asking a question and then saying that the Prophet (ﷺ) had answered correctly.

The man said: Tell me about eemân.

The Prophet (ﷺ) answered: It is to believe in Allah, His angels, His books, His messengers, and the Last Day, and to believe in the divine destiny, both the good and the evil thereof.

He said: You have spoken correctly.

Then he said: Tell me about *iḥsân* (excellence).

The Prophet (ﷺ) replied: It means to worship Allah as though you are seeing Him, for even if you do not see Him, He sees you.

The man said: Tell me about the hour (of the Day of Judgement).

The Prophet (ﷺ) said: The one questioned about it knows no better than the questioner.

The man said: Tell me about its signs.

The Prophet (ﷺ) said: A slave girl will give birth to her mistress and you will see barefooted, naked, destitute herdsmen competing in constructing lofty buildings.

The man left and I stayed for some time. A while later, the Prophet (ﷺ) asked: O 'Umar! Do you know who the questioner was?

I replied: Allah and His Messenger know best.

The Prophet (ﷺ) said: It was Gabriel, who came to teach you your religion.» (Bukhari and Muslim)[37]

Obligatory knowledge, incumbent on every Muslim, constitutes knowledge of the following:

i. The first pillar of Islam: the shahâdah, or testimony of faith: its meaning, importance and implications, and its seven conditions which must be implemented in one's daily life. Unfortunately, many Muslims today are ignorant about this first pillar of Islam to the extent that the shahâdah comprises only a verbal mumbling of the Arabic words: lâ ilâha illâ Allâh, Muḥammadun rasool Ullâh.
In fact, quite a large number are barely familiar with the first condition, let alone the remaining six. Truly, this is one of the sources of our weakness today. Logically, if the foundation of a building is weak the whole building will be weak. It is in this spirit, given that the shahâdah is the focal point of belief, that the present work is dedicated to expounding this first principle of Islam.

ii. The second pillar: the obligatory ṣalâh, or the prayers. Every Muslim must learn how to perform the ṣalâh as it was performed by Prophet Muhammad (ﷺ). There are many works by Muslim scholars on how to perform ṣalâh correctly. Among the best of these works is a book by the scholar of Hadith Muhammad Nâṣiruddin al-Albâni titled *Ṣiffât uṣ-Ṣalât an-Nabi*.[38] Its English translation is also available.

iii. The third pillar: obligatory fasting in Ramadan. It is essential for every Muslim to know all about fasting in the month of

---

[37] Ezzeddin Ibrahim and Denys Johnson-Davies, *An-Nawawi's Forty Hadith* (UAE: Dar el-Shorouk, 2003), 28-33.

[38] Shaykh Muhammad Naasiru-Deen al-Albaani, *The Prophet's Prayer Described*, trans. Usama ibn Suhaib Hasan, accessed March 27, 2012, http://www.qss.org/articles/salah/toc.html.

Ramadan, including the actions that invalidate the fast, the special communal prayers performed after the night prayer in Ramadan, and the virtues of fasting. A Muslim must also be familiar with the righteous deeds that may be performed in this month — such as *'umrah* (minor pilgrimage to Makkah), giving charity (including *zakât al-fiṭr*),[39] recitation of the Qur'an, and seclusion in the mosque for spiritual purification. Such knowledge is part and parcel of what is necessary to discharge this mandatory duty.

iv. The fourth pillar: zakâh — the obligatory alms/charity. Every Muslim must know how to calculate the amount due for zakâh (2.5 percent of annual savings and certain percentages of other assets over the minimum value, which many prefer to distribute during Ramadan) in order to purify one's wealth and perform this obligatory duty.

v. The fifth pillar: Hajj — obligatory pilgrimage to Makkah. Information about how to perform Hajj and 'umrah, along with all the essential and recommended rituals for these processes, is a pre-requisite for performing these actions.

vi. Knowledge of the recitation of the Qur'an according to the rules of *tajweed.*[40] The Qur'an is our most important link to reality. Hence, a Muslim should strive to acquire a substantial knowledge of the Qur'an and its essential guidance.

vii. A knowledge of the Sunnah — the way and the traditions of Prophet Muhammad (ﷺ). The Qur'an is the first source of knowledge in Islam, and the Sunnah is the second. Therefore, a Muslim needs to have a good working knowledge of the Sunnah, for one cannot fully understand the Qur'an in

---

[39] Zakât al-fiṭr: obligatory charity at the end of the fast of Ramadan, payable in kind.

[40] Tajweed: rules of pronunciation and intonation for reciting the Qur'an.

isolation from it. Indeed, Prophet Muhammad (ﷺ) was given the duty to expound the Qur'an for humankind as well as show by example how to perform all the acts of worship. Allah has affirmed:

﴿ بِالْبَيِّنَاتِ وَالزُّبُرِ ۗ وَأَنزَلْنَا إِلَيْكَ الذِّكْرَ لِتُبَيِّنَ لِلنَّاسِ مَا نُزِّلَ إِلَيْهِمْ وَلَعَلَّهُمْ يَتَفَكَّرُونَ ﴿٤٤﴾ ﴾ (سورة النحل: ٤٤)

﴾[We sent them] with clear proofs and written ordinances. And We revealed to you the message that you may make clear to the people what was sent down to them and that they might give thought.﴿ *(Qur'an 16: 44)*

Prophet Muhammad's Sunnah is the practical implementation of Islam and the second source of the Sharia. The Sunnah encompasses his statements, actions, and approvals, transmitted via the Hadith collections. Every Muslim should be aware of the acts that are obligatory and the ones that are recommended, such as the supererogatory acts of worship.

viii. The knowledge of the Sharia is part of the fundamental knowledge that regulates our everyday life. We need the necessary information to execute our mandatory obligations. This includes an understanding of:

- The sources of the Sharia
- The purpose of the Sharia
- How the Sharia regulates and categorizes life's transactions, that is:
  - ◊ what is lawful
  - ◊ what is unlawful
  - ◊ what is disliked
  - ◊ what is neutral; neither forbidden nor recommended

ix. A Muslim also needs a working knowledge of classical Arabic in order to understand the Qur'an and the Sunnah of the Prophet (ﷺ). This is the key to a proper and complete comprehension of Islam. One does not have to speak Arabic fluently like an Arab; however, one must have a good grasp and working knowledge of the language. Many people do not speak English as fluently as native speakers, yet they have a good understanding of the English language.

The purpose of acquiring knowledge

The primary purpose of knowledge is to know Allah. Hence, by seeking knowledge one should aim to get closer to Allah and imbibe God-consciousness. One's purpose should not be to brag or to boast, showing off how much one has learned. Allah has qualified in the Qur'an:

﴿...إِنَّمَا يَخْشَى ٱللَّهَ مِنْ عِبَادِهِ ٱلْعُلَمَٰٓؤُا۟ ... ﴿٢٨﴾﴾ (سورة فاطر: ٢٨)

﴿...Only those fear Allah, from among His servants, who have knowledge...﴾ *(Qur'an 35: 28)*

When one strives to attain knowledge about Allah, His most beautiful names, His unique attributes, and His unparalleled characteristics, one learns to acknowledge one's insignificance and powerlessness. To reject our lowly status in comparison to Allah indicates our arrogance, a very grave sin in His sight. In reality, among the first people to be severely punished by Allah on the Day of Judgement will be those who sought knowledge for the purpose of being praised or considered very knowledgeable, as per the following *hadith qudsi* (sacred hadith):

On the authority of Abu Hurayrah (رضي الله عنه) who said:

«I heard the Messenger of Allah (ﷺ) saying: The first person against whom judgement will be pronounced on the

Day of Resurrection will be a man who died a martyr; he will be brought, and Allah will make known to him His favours and he will recognize them.

(The Almighty) will ask: And what did you do about them?

He will reply: I fought for You until I died a martyr.

He will say: You have lied — you fought only so that it might be said (of you): He is courageous. And so it was said. Then he will be ordered to be dragged on his face until he is cast into the hellfire.

(Another) will be a man who had studied (religious) knowledge and taught it and who used to recite the Qur'an. He will be brought, and Allah will make known to him His favours and he will recognize them. (The Almighty) will ask: And what did you do about them?

He will answer: I studied (religious) knowledge and taught it and recited the Qur'an for Your sake.

He will say: You have lied — you studied (religious) knowledge only so that it might be said (of you): He is learned, and you recited the Qur'an only so that it might be said (of you): He is a reciter. And so it was said.

Then he will be ordered to be dragged on his face until he is cast into the hellfire.

(Another) will be a man whom Allah had made rich and to whom He had given all kinds of wealth. He will be brought, and Allah will make known to him His favours and he will recognize them. (The Almighty) will ask: And what did you do about them?

He will respond: I left no path (untrodden) in which you like money to be spent without spending on it for Your sake.

Allah will say: You have lied — you did that only so that it might be said (of you): He is open-handed. And so it was said.

Then he will be ordered to be dragged on his face until he is cast into the hellfire.» (Muslim)

A secondary purpose of acquiring knowledge is to gain the good of this worldly life as well as the hereafter. Allah has described:

﴿... فَمِنَ ٱلنَّاسِ مَن يَقُولُ رَبَّنَآ ءَاتِنَا فِى ٱلدُّنْيَا وَمَا لَهُۥ فِى ٱلْـَٔاخِرَةِ مِنْ خَلَـٰقٍ ﴿٢٠٠﴾﴾ (سورة البقرة: ٢٠٠)

﴾...And among the people is he who says: Our Lord, give us in this world — and he will have in the hereafter no share.﴿ *(Qur'an 2: 200)*

This verse refers to those who ask for all that they desire in this world, without paying heed to whether it is good or evil. Such people view this world as an end in itself, not expecting anything in the hereafter. Their knowledge is limited to the physical aspects of this worldly life.[41] The believers, on the other hand, who seek knowledge as God-fearing individuals, pray both for the good of this world and for the good of the hereafter; they beseech Allah for protection from the hellfire as well. This has been expressed in the following verse:

﴿وَمِنْهُم مَّن يَقُولُ رَبَّنَآ ءَاتِنَا فِى ٱلدُّنْيَا حَسَنَةً وَفِى ٱلْـَٔاخِرَةِ حَسَنَةً وَقِنَا عَذَابَ ٱلنَّارِ ﴿٢٠١﴾ أُو۟لَـٰٓئِكَ لَهُمْ نَصِيبٌ مِّمَّا كَسَبُوا۟ ۚ وَٱللَّهُ سَرِيعُ ٱلْحِسَابِ ﴿٢٠٢﴾﴾

(سورة البقرة: ٢٠١-٢٠٢)

﴾But among them is he who says: Our Lord, give us in this world [that which is] good and in the hereafter [that which is] good and protect us from the punishment of the fire. Those will have a share of what they have earned, and Allah is swift in account.﴿

(Qur'an 2: 201-202)

---

[41] ﴾They know what is apparent of the worldly life, but they, of the hereafter, are unaware.﴿ *(Qur'an 30: 7)*

Yet another secondary purpose of seeking knowledge is to spread freedom, human dignity, truth, and justice on this earth through preaching the values of Islam. In reality, people are urgently in need of Islamic teachings if they hope to live a prosperous and happy life in this world and succeed on the Day of Judgement. Surely, the one who is knowledgeable and acts according to his or her natural instincts, in line with the guidance from the Qur'an and Sunnah, will be humble, polite, tolerant, and well-mannered. In contrast, the one who has little knowledge will not act according to natural instincts. Such a person will defy Allah's guidance and act arrogantly, causing tyranny and injustice in the land. This is exemplified in the advice that Luqmân, a wise servant of Allah, gave to his son while instructing and teaching him:

﴿ وَإِذْ قَالَ لُقْمَٰنُ لِٱبْنِهِۦ وَهُوَ يَعِظُهُۥ يَٰبُنَيَّ لَا تُشْرِكْ بِٱللَّهِ ۖ إِنَّ ٱلشِّرْكَ لَظُلْمٌ عَظِيمٌ
﴿١٣﴾ وَوَصَّيْنَا ٱلْإِنسَٰنَ بِوَٰلِدَيْهِ حَمَلَتْهُ أُمُّهُۥ وَهْنًا عَلَىٰ وَهْنٍ وَفِصَٰلُهُۥ فِى عَامَيْنِ أَنِ
ٱشْكُرْ لِى وَلِوَٰلِدَيْكَ إِلَىَّ ٱلْمَصِيرُ ﴿١٤﴾ وَإِن جَٰهَدَاكَ عَلَىٰٓ أَن تُشْرِكَ بِى مَا لَيْسَ
لَكَ بِهِۦ عِلْمٌ فَلَا تُطِعْهُمَا ۖ وَصَاحِبْهُمَا فِى ٱلدُّنْيَا مَعْرُوفًا ۖ وَٱتَّبِعْ سَبِيلَ مَنْ أَنَابَ
إِلَىَّ ۚ ثُمَّ إِلَىَّ مَرْجِعُكُمْ فَأُنَبِّئُكُم بِمَا كُنتُمْ تَعْمَلُونَ ﴿١٥﴾ يَٰبُنَىَّ إِنَّهَآ إِن تَكُ
مِثْقَالَ حَبَّةٍ مِّنْ خَرْدَلٍ فَتَكُن فِى صَخْرَةٍ أَوْ فِى ٱلسَّمَٰوَٰتِ أَوْ فِى ٱلْأَرْضِ يَأْتِ بِهَا ٱللَّهُ
ۚ إِنَّ ٱللَّهَ لَطِيفٌ خَبِيرٌ ﴿١٦﴾ يَٰبُنَىَّ أَقِمِ ٱلصَّلَوٰةَ وَأْمُرْ بِٱلْمَعْرُوفِ وَٱنْهَ عَنِ ٱلْمُنكَرِ
وَٱصْبِرْ عَلَىٰ مَآ أَصَابَكَ ۖ إِنَّ ذَٰلِكَ مِنْ عَزْمِ ٱلْأُمُورِ ﴿١٧﴾ وَلَا تُصَعِّرْ خَدَّكَ لِلنَّاسِ وَلَا تَمْشِ
فِى ٱلْأَرْضِ مَرَحًا ۖ إِنَّ ٱللَّهَ لَا يُحِبُّ كُلَّ مُخْتَالٍ فَخُورٍ ﴿١٨﴾ وَٱقْصِدْ فِى مَشْيِكَ وَٱغْضُضْ مِن
صَوْتِكَ ۚ إِنَّ أَنكَرَ ٱلْأَصْوَٰتِ لَصَوْتُ ٱلْحَمِيرِ ﴿١٩﴾ ﴾ (سورة لقمان: ١٣-١٩)

﴾And [mention, O Muhammad] when Luqmân said to his son while he was instructing him: O my son, do not associate [anything] with Allah. Indeed, association [with him] is great injustice. And We have enjoined upon man [care] for his parents. His mother carried him, [increasing her] in weakness upon weakness, and his weaning is in two years. Be grateful to Me and to your parents; to Me is the [final] destination. But if they endeavour to make you associate with Me that of which you have no knowledge, do not obey them but accompany them in [this] world with appropriate kindness and follow the way of those who turn back to Me [in repentance]. Then to Me will be your return, and I will inform you about what you used to do. [And Luqmân said:] O my son, indeed if wrong should be the weight of a mustard seed and should be within a rock or [anywhere] in the heavens or in the earth, Allah will bring it forth. Indeed, Allah is Subtle and Acquainted. O my son, establish prayer, enjoin what is right, forbid what is wrong, and be patient over what befalls you. Indeed, [all] that is of the matters [requiring] determination. And do not turn your cheek [in contempt] toward people and do not walk through the earth exultantly. Indeed, Allah does not like everyone self-deluded and boastful. And be moderate in your pace and lower your voice; indeed, the most disagreeable of sounds is the voice of donkeys.》 *(Qur'an 31: 13-19)*

From the advice that Luqmân gave to his beloved son, we can conclude that knowledge that is pursued and practiced with modesty and humility leads to beauty, dignity, freedom, and justice. It is also rewarded accordingly as Allah has mentioned:

﴿ ... يَرْفَعِ ٱللَّهُ ٱلَّذِينَ ءَامَنُوا۟ مِنكُمْ وَٱلَّذِينَ أُوتُوا۟ ٱلْعِلْمَ دَرَجَٰتٍ ۚ وَٱللَّهُ بِمَا تَعْمَلُونَ خَبِيرٌ ﴿١١﴾﴾ (سورة المجادلة: ١١)

《...Allah will raise those who have believed among you and those who were given knowledge, by degrees. And Allah is Acquainted with what you do.》 *(Qur'an 58: 11)*

Obviously, what is called the reservoir of knowledge is deep and unfathomable. It is a vast and open field that is not limited to the world of nature and observation. Therefore, it is virtually impossible for anyone to gain anything more than a fraction of what there is to know in the short life span granted here on the earth. Even the most learned individuals have only scratched the surface; this knowledge has been bestowed upon them through Allah's beneficence and generosity. This ultimate truth is clearly illustrated in the story of Moses (عليه السلام) and al-Khiḍr, given in some detail in Soorat *al-Kahf* (Chapter 18) in the Qur'an. It is also the subject of a long hadith narrated by Sa'eed ibn Jubayr (رضي الله عنه) and recorded by Imam Bukhari. The story serves as an admonition to Moses (عليه السلام), who had claimed to be the most learned among his people. Allah showed him, through his encounter with al-Khiḍr, how insignificant his knowledge actually was and how al-Khiḍr had been granted what appeared to be knowledge of the future only through Allah's munificence and bounty.

Allah has also revealed the following about this vast ocean of knowledge that none can encompass, except for the little that Allah wills for His servants:

﴿ ... وَلَا يُحِيطُونَ بِشَيْءٍ مِّنْ عِلْمِهِۦٓ إِلَّا بِمَا شَآءَ ... ﴿٢٥٥﴾ ﴾ (سورة البقرة: ٢٥٥)

﴾...and they encompass not a thing of His knowledge except for what He wills...﴿ *(Qur'an 2: 255)*

﴿ ...وَفَوْقَ كُلِّ ذِى عِلْمٍ عَلِيمٌ ﴿٧٦﴾ ﴾ (سورة يوسف: ٧٦)

﴾...but over every possessor of knowledge is one [more] knowing.﴿ *(Qur'an 12: 76)*

Since we can take in only the little knowledge that Allah wills, it becomes imperative to decide right from the beginning what sort of knowledge is most important and how to go about acquiring it.

Knowledge required by the community as a whole (*farḍ kifâyah*)

This is the knowledge that is incumbent on any society in order to discharge a communal mandatory obligation. A farḍ kifâyah is an act that is obligatory for the Muslim community collectively. If it is carried out by some members of the Muslim community, then other Muslims do not have to perform it; but if nobody takes it upon himself or herself to perform the act on behalf of the community, then all Muslims are considered to have failed and will be punished. It is the knowledge that a person may acquire as a means of earning a living in a lawful way. As much as we believe that our sustenance is decreed and written down while we are in our mother's wombs, that decreed sustenance might either be earned in a lawful or an unlawful manner. Therefore, professional knowledge is one means of getting our livelihood in a lawful way that pleases Allah. One may choose whatever profession one likes depending upon:

- An individual's talents
- An individual's interests
- The needs of the community
- The marketability of a particular profession

Obviously, the choice of a profession and the manner in which it is pursued must be guided and shaped by aspects of the obligatory individual knowledge, in response to the needs of the community (farḍ kifâyah).

Sources of knowledge

All the types of knowledge that we have discussed very briefly have been stressed in the Qur'an and the Sunnah; some types may be gained through the exercise of Allah-given intellect or, rather, reasoning. However, a major part of knowledge comes from true revelation given to the prophets.

No doubt, the foundation of the main categories of knowledge is the Qur'an and the Sunnah. However, all the knowledge known as farḍ 'ayn comprises knowledge of:

- The purpose of creation
- Belief in heaven and hell
- Belief and understanding of God
- Belief in angels as servants of God
- Punishment or happiness in the grave
- Belief in prophethood and prophecy
- How to establish and run an Islamic state
- Belief in resurrection, life in the hereafter, and so on

However, whenever our reasoning capacity, which admittedly is very limited, comes into conflict with the true revelation, we have to put aside our intellect and abide by the revelation of Allah along with the glorious Qur'an and the traditions (authentic sayings) of Prophet Muhammad (ﷺ).

Chapter Six
The Second Condition: Certainty that Negates Doubt

﴿ وَكَذَٰلِكَ نُرِيٓ إِبْرَٰهِيمَ مَلَكُوتَ ٱلسَّمَٰوَٰتِ وَٱلْأَرْضِ وَلِيَكُونَ مِنَ ٱلْمُوقِنِينَ ﴿٧٥﴾ ﴾ (سورة الأنعام: ٧٥)

﴾And thus did We show Abraham the realm of the heavens and the earth so that he would be among the certain [in faith].﴿

(Qur'an 6: 75)

﴿ إِنَّمَا ٱلْمُؤْمِنُونَ ٱلَّذِينَ ءَامَنُوا۟ بِٱللَّهِ وَرَسُولِهِۦ ثُمَّ لَمْ يَرْتَابُوا۟ وَجَٰهَدُوا۟ بِأَمْوَٰلِهِمْ وَأَنفُسِهِمْ فِى سَبِيلِ ٱللَّهِ ۚ أُو۟لَٰٓئِكَ هُمُ ٱلصَّٰدِقُونَ ﴿١٥﴾ ﴾ (سورة الحُجُرات: ١٥)

﴾The believers are only the ones who have believed in Allah and His Messenger and then doubt not but strive with their properties and their lives in the cause of Allah. It is those who are the truthful.﴿ *(Qur'an 49: 15)*

The second condition of the shahâdah stipulates that we should have complete certainty in it. In other words, our testimony of faith should be uttered without the slightest shred of doubt in our hearts.

Since Islam is the religion of *fiṭrah* (innate human disposition), there is no room for harbouring doubts and suspicions in our hearts concerning the basic fundamental principles of Islam. In reality, a steadfast and firm conviction in the five pillars of Islam, the six articles of faith, belief in the jinn, paradise and hellfire, resurrection, and so on is the only way to achieve peace and tranquillity in our hearts and minds in this troubled world.

For this reason, Allah has made 'certainty without doubt' a condition of true belief. Not only does unwavering belief result in a quiet and calm life in this world, but the rewards for it will also be immense in the hereafter. For the believers who are certain and firm in their shahâdah, Allah has promised paradise.

Abu Hurayrah (رضي الله عنه) narrated a hadith concerning an incident that occurred during the Tabook expedition. Provisions for the marching army were almost depleted, when 'Umar ibn al-Khaṭṭâb (رضي الله عنه) suggested for Prophet Muhammad (ﷺ) to gather the meagre remains and invoke Allah's blessings. During this event, there was a miraculous increase in the provisions. In this context, the Prophet (ﷺ) is reported to have said:

> «...I bear witness that there is no god but Allah and that I am His Messenger. The bondsman who would meet Allah without entertaining any doubt about these (two fundamentals) would enter heaven.» (Muslim)

This generous reward for those who fulfil the second condition of the shahâdah has been reiterated in another long hadith also ascribed to Abu Hurayrah (رضي الله عنه). Prophet Muhammad (ﷺ) concluded with the following words:

> «...Whoever you meet behind this wall, testifying to the fact that there is no deity worthy of worship except Allah and having certainty in his heart, give him glad tidings of paradise.» (Muslim)

Today, however, it is a very sad fact that although many of us have proclaimed the shahâdah and we repeat it more than ten times in our daily prayers, we are still afflicted with doubts. In particular, in the modern era in which science and technology are the new gods, belief in Allah is increasingly questioned and scrutinized, not only by the Orientalists but also by Muslims at the height of ignorance. Grave doubts concerning the significance and relevance of Islam have been cast into the minds of such Muslims. As a result, they are under the false notion that they can have happy and successful lives using concepts such as democracy or secularism rather than the implementation of the Sharia.

Today, a majority of Muslims are also inflicted with multiple diseases of the hearts due to the absence of the second condition of shahâdah: certainty in their lives. The most serious ailments of the heart include:

- hypocrisy
- showing off
- hatred
- backbiting
- disbelief in Allah
- envy and jealousy
- greed and miserliness
- arrogance and boastfulness
- nationalism and tribalism
- associating partners with Allah

A separate work is needed to discuss each of these ailments, which have become like a cancer in the body of the Muslim community. In this chapter, we will only discuss disbelief and hypocrisy. Towards the beginning of Soorat *al-Baqarah*, Allah has classified humankind into three categories: true believers, disbelievers, and hypocrites. He has described true believers, who have no doubts in their hearts, in the following words:

﴿ ذَٰلِكَ ٱلْكِتَٰبُ لَا رَيْبَ ۛ فِيهِ ۛ هُدًى لِّلْمُتَّقِينَ ﴿٢﴾ ٱلَّذِينَ يُؤْمِنُونَ بِٱلْغَيْبِ وَيُقِيمُونَ ٱلصَّلَوٰةَ وَمِمَّا رَزَقْنَٰهُمْ يُنفِقُونَ ﴿٣﴾ وَٱلَّذِينَ يُؤْمِنُونَ بِمَآ أُنزِلَ إِلَيْكَ وَمَآ أُنزِلَ مِن قَبْلِكَ وَبِٱلْءَاخِرَةِ هُمْ يُوقِنُونَ ﴿٤﴾ أُوْلَٰٓئِكَ عَلَىٰ هُدًى مِّن رَّبِّهِمْ ۖ وَأُوْلَٰٓئِكَ هُمُ ٱلْمُفْلِحُونَ ﴿٥﴾ ﴾ (سورة البقرة: ٢-٥)

﴾This is the book about which there is no doubt, a guidance for those conscious of Allah, who believe in the unseen, establish prayer, and spend out of what We have provided for them, and who believe in what has been revealed to you [O Muhammad] and what was revealed before you, and of the hereafter they are certain [in faith]. Those are upon [right] guidance from their Lord, and it is those who are the successful.﴿ *(Qur'an 2: 2-5)*

Disbelief in Allah (سُبْحَانَهُ وَتَعَالَىٰ)

When a heart lacks (certainty), it becomes doubtful and is subsequently led towards disbelief. There are two types of disbelief:

(a) Rejection of Allah (سُبْحَانَهُ وَتَعَالَىٰ) and His law

Those who are beset by the first type of disbelief — that is, those who deny Allah and His law — have been characterized as follows in Soorat *al-Baqarah*:

﴿ إِنَّ ٱلَّذِينَ كَفَرُوا۟ سَوَآءٌ عَلَيْهِمْ ءَأَنذَرْتَهُمْ أَمْ لَمْ تُنذِرْهُمْ لَا يُؤْمِنُونَ ﴿٦﴾ خَتَمَ ٱللَّهُ عَلَىٰ قُلُوبِهِمْ وَعَلَىٰ سَمْعِهِمْ ۖ وَعَلَىٰٓ أَبْصَٰرِهِمْ غِشَٰوَةٌ ۖ وَلَهُمْ عَذَابٌ عَظِيمٌ ﴿٧﴾ ﴾

(سورة البقرة: ٦-٧)

﴾Indeed, those who disbelieve — it is all the same for them whether you warn them or do not warn them; they will not believe. Allah has set a seal upon their hearts and upon their hearing, and over their vision is a veil. And for them is a great punishment.﴿

(Qur'an 2: 6-7)

Unfortunately, a large majority of people today fall into this category.

(b) Ingratitude towards Allah's blessings

The second type of disbelief — being ungrateful for the countless blessings of Allah — leads to the disobedience of Allah in many ways. This form of disbelief oppresses a significant number of Muslims today. We pray to Allah to remove this affliction from our hearts, make us recognize His blessings, and be constantly thankful to Him.

Allah will severely punish us from the moment we take His blessings for granted, stop acknowledging them, and fail to express our appreciation to Allah. Allah has warned in the Qur'an:

﴿وَإِذْ تَأَذَّنَ رَبُّكُمْ لَئِن شَكَرْتُمْ لَأَزِيدَنَّكُمْ ۖ وَلَئِن كَفَرْتُمْ إِنَّ عَذَابِي لَشَدِيدٌ ﴿٧﴾﴾ (سورة إبراهيم: ٧)

﴾And [remember] when your Lord proclaimed: If you are grateful, I will surely increase you [in favour]; but if you deny, indeed My punishment is severe.﴿ *(Qur'an 14: 7)*

Allah has reminded us in a number of places in the glorious Qur'an to be always appreciative of His countless blessings:

﴿فَاذْكُرُونِي أَذْكُرْكُمْ وَاشْكُرُوا لِي وَلَا تَكْفُرُونِ ﴿١٥٢﴾﴾ (سورة البقرة: ١٥٢)

﴾So remember Me; I will remember you. Be grateful to Me and do not deny Me.﴿ *(Qur'an 2: 152)*

﴿وَاللَّهُ أَخْرَجَكُم مِّن بُطُونِ أُمَّهَاتِكُمْ لَا تَعْلَمُونَ شَيْئًا وَجَعَلَ لَكُمُ السَّمْعَ وَالْأَبْصَارَ وَالْأَفْئِدَةَ ۙ لَعَلَّكُمْ تَشْكُرُونَ ﴿٧٨﴾﴾ (سورة النحل: ٧٨)

﴾And Allah has extracted you from the wombs of your mothers not knowing a thing, and He made for you hearing and vision and intellect that perhaps you would be grateful.﴿ *(Qur'an 16: 78)*

﴿ يَعْرِفُونَ نِعْمَتَ ٱللَّهِ ثُمَّ يُنكِرُونَهَا وَأَكْثَرُهُمُ ٱلْكَٰفِرُونَ ﴿٨٣﴾ ﴾

(سورة النحل: ٨٣)

﴿They recognize the favour of Allah; then they deny it. And most of them are disbelievers.﴾ *(Qur'an 16: 83)*

Allah has punished a number of Muslim communities in recent times by natural calamities, civil wars, subjugation, ethnic cleansing, and humiliation by other nations. These countries include Bosnia, Chechnya, Kashmir, Palestine, Kuwait, Iraq, Iran, Afghanistan, and Somalia. This is all because of their ingratitude for His blessings. Allah has emphasized:

﴿ وَمَآ أَصَٰبَكُم مِّن مُّصِيبَةٍ فَبِمَا كَسَبَتْ أَيْدِيكُمْ وَيَعْفُوا۟ عَن كَثِيرٍ ﴿٣٠﴾ ﴾

(سورة الشورىٰ: ٣٠)

﴿And whatever strikes you of disaster — it is for what your hands have earned; but He pardons much.﴾ *(Qur'an 42: 30)*

﴿ مَّا يَفْعَلُ ٱللَّهُ بِعَذَابِكُمْ إِن شَكَرْتُمْ وَءَامَنتُمْ ۚ وَكَانَ ٱللَّهُ شَاكِرًا عَلِيمًا ﴿١٤٧﴾ ﴾

(سورة النساء: ١٤٧)

﴿What would Allah do with your punishment if you are grateful and believe? And ever is Allah Appreciative and Knowing.﴾ *(Qur'an 4: 147)*

It is therefore essential that we remain thankful to Allah for His countless blessings by spreading the concept of gratitude among our fellow human beings who are less fortunate, by sharing with them the blessings that Allah has bestowed upon us.

Hypocrisy

In the Qur'an, human beings have been classified into three categories:

◊ True believers — those who have a firm faith in Allah as the Creator;

◊ Disbelievers — those who deny Allah and His laws;

◊ Hypocrites — those who profess belief with their tongues but harbour disbelief in their hearts.

In Soorat *al-Baqarah*, Allah has given a full description of those who are plagued with the disease of hypocrisy. He has also described the effects of this ailment:

﴿وَمِنَ النَّاسِ مَن يَقُولُ ءَامَنَّا بِاللَّهِ وَبِالْيَوْمِ الْآخِرِ وَمَا هُم بِمُؤْمِنِينَ (٨) يُخَادِعُونَ اللَّهَ
وَالَّذِينَ ءَامَنُوا وَمَا يَخْدَعُونَ إِلَّا أَنفُسَهُمْ وَمَا يَشْعُرُونَ (٩) فِي قُلُوبِهِم مَّرَضٌ فَزَادَهُمُ
اللَّهُ مَرَضًا وَلَهُمْ عَذَابٌ أَلِيمٌ بِمَا كَانُوا يَكْذِبُونَ (١٠) وَإِذَا قِيلَ لَهُمْ لَا تُفْسِدُوا فِي
الْأَرْضِ قَالُوا إِنَّمَا نَحْنُ مُصْلِحُونَ (١١) أَلَا إِنَّهُمْ هُمُ الْمُفْسِدُونَ وَلَٰكِن لَّا يَشْعُرُونَ
(١٢) وَإِذَا قِيلَ لَهُمْ ءَامِنُوا كَمَا ءَامَنَ النَّاسُ قَالُوا أَنُؤْمِنُ كَمَا ءَامَنَ السُّفَهَاءُ أَلَا إِنَّهُمْ هُمُ
السُّفَهَاءُ وَلَٰكِن لَّا يَعْلَمُونَ (١٣) وَإِذَا لَقُوا الَّذِينَ ءَامَنُوا قَالُوا ءَامَنَّا وَإِذَا خَلَوْا إِلَىٰ
شَيَاطِينِهِمْ قَالُوا إِنَّا مَعَكُمْ إِنَّمَا نَحْنُ مُسْتَهْزِءُونَ (١٤) اللَّهُ يَسْتَهْزِئُ بِهِمْ وَيَمُدُّهُمْ فِي طُغْيَانِهِمْ
يَعْمَهُونَ (١٥) أُولَٰئِكَ الَّذِينَ اشْتَرَوُا الضَّلَالَةَ بِالْهُدَىٰ فَمَا رَبِحَت تِّجَارَتُهُمْ وَمَا كَانُوا
مُهْتَدِينَ (١٦) مَثَلُهُمْ كَمَثَلِ الَّذِي اسْتَوْقَدَ نَارًا فَلَمَّا أَضَاءَتْ مَا حَوْلَهُ ذَهَبَ
اللَّهُ بِنُورِهِمْ وَتَرَكَهُمْ فِي ظُلُمَاتٍ لَّا يُبْصِرُونَ (١٧) صُمٌّ بُكْمٌ عُمْيٌ فَهُمْ لَا يَرْجِعُونَ (١٨) أَوْ
كَصَيِّبٍ مِّنَ السَّمَاءِ فِيهِ ظُلُمَاتٌ وَرَعْدٌ وَبَرْقٌ يَجْعَلُونَ أَصَابِعَهُمْ فِي ءَاذَانِهِم مِّنَ الصَّوَاعِقِ حَذَرَ
الْمَوْتِ وَاللَّهُ مُحِيطٌ بِالْكَافِرِينَ (١٩) يَكَادُ الْبَرْقُ يَخْطَفُ أَبْصَارَهُمْ كُلَّمَا أَضَاءَ لَهُم مَّشَوْا
فِيهِ وَإِذَا أَظْلَمَ عَلَيْهِمْ قَامُوا وَلَوْ شَاءَ اللَّهُ لَذَهَبَ بِسَمْعِهِمْ وَأَبْصَارِهِمْ إِنَّ اللَّهَ عَلَىٰ كُلِّ
شَيْءٍ قَدِيرٌ (٢٠)﴾ (سورة البقرة: ٨-٢٠)

﴿And of the people are some who say: We believe in Allah and the last day, but they are not believers. They [think to] deceive Allah and those who believe, but they deceive not except themselves and perceive [it] not. In their hearts is disease, so Allah has increased their disease; for them is a painful punishment because they [habitually] used to lie. When it is said to them: Do not cause corruption on the earth, they say: We are but reformers. Unquestionably, it is they who are the corrupters, but they perceive [it] not. When it is said to them: Believe as the people have believed, they say: Should we believe as the foolish have believed? Unquestionably, it is they who are the foolish, but they know [it] not. When they meet those who believe, they say: We believe; but when they are alone with their evil ones, they say: Indeed, we are with you; we were only mockers. [But] Allah mocks them and prolongs them in their transgression [while] they wander blindly. Those are the ones who have purchased error [in exchange] for guidance, so their transaction has brought no profit, nor were they guided. Their example is that of one who kindled a fire, but when it illuminated what was around him, Allah took away their light and left them in darkness [so] they could not see. Deaf, dumb, and blind — so they will not return [to the right path]. Or [their situation is] like a rainstorm from the sky within which is darkness, thunder, and lightning. They put their fingers in their ears against the thunderclaps in dread of death. But Allah is encompassing of the disbelievers. The lightning almost snatches away their sight. Every time it lights [the way] for them, they walk therein; but when darkness comes over them, they stand [still]. If Allah had willed, He could have taken away their hearing and their sight. Indeed, Allah is over all things competent.»

(Qur'an 2: 8-20)

Hypocrites are considered to be the worst people in the Muslim community and the most difficult people to deal with. Allah has described their characteristics in various passages of the glorious Qur'an.[42] There is even a specific chapter titled Soorat *al-*

---

[42] Refer to *Qur'an 3: 119; 4: 38; 4: 81; 4: 137-146; 8: 47*; and *9: 8*.

Munâfiqoon (the Hypocrites), which explains the behaviour of the people who have this disease, the 'two-faced' Muslims, as Prophet Muhammad (ﷺ) nicknamed them.

Abu Hurayrah (رضي الله عنه) narrated that the Prophet (ﷺ) said:

«The worst people in the sight of Allah on the Day of Resurrection will be the two-faced people who appear to some people with one face and to other people with another face.» (Bukhari)

Hypocrisy, just like disbelief, can also be classified into two categories:

(a) Hypocrisy in belief

There are six aspects of this form of hypocrisy:

- To hate or oppose the Messenger (ﷺ):

﴿ أَلَمْ يَعْلَمُوٓا۟ أَنَّهُۥ مَن يُحَادِدِ ٱللَّهَ وَرَسُولَهُۥ فَأَنَّ لَهُۥ نَارَ جَهَنَّمَ خَـٰلِدًا فِيهَا ۚ ذَٰلِكَ ٱلْخِزْىُ ٱلْعَظِيمُ ﴿٦٣﴾ يَحْذَرُ ٱلْمُنَـٰفِقُونَ أَن تُنَزَّلَ عَلَيْهِمْ سُورَةٌ تُنَبِّئُهُم بِمَا فِى قُلُوبِهِمْ ۚ قُلِ ٱسْتَهْزِءُوٓا۟ إِنَّ ٱللَّهَ مُخْرِجٌ مَّا تَحْذَرُونَ ﴿٦٤﴾ ﴾

(سورة التوبة: ٦٣-٦٤)

﴿Do they not know that whoever opposes Allah and His Messenger — that for him is the fire of hell, wherein he will abide eternally? That is the great disgrace. They hypocrites are apprehensive lest a soorah be revealed about them, informing them of what is in their hearts. Say: Mock [as you wish]; indeed, Allah will expose that which you fear.﴾ *(Qur'an 9: 63-64)*

- To belie Prophet Muhammad (ﷺ)
- To hate some or all of what was brought by the Messenger (ﷺ):

﴿ وَلَئِن سَأَلْتَهُمْ لَيَقُولُنَّ إِنَّمَا كُنَّا نَخُوضُ وَنَلْعَبُ ۚ قُلْ أَبِاللَّهِ وَآيَاتِهِ وَرَسُولِهِ كُنتُمْ تَسْتَهْزِئُونَ ﴿٦٥﴾ لَا تَعْتَذِرُوا قَدْ كَفَرْتُم بَعْدَ إِيمَانِكُمْ ۚ إِن نَّعْفُ عَن طَائِفَةٍ مِّنكُمْ نُعَذِّبْ طَائِفَةً بِأَنَّهُمْ كَانُوا مُجْرِمِينَ ﴿٦٦﴾ ﴾

(سورة التوبة: ٦٥-٦٦)

﴿And if you ask them, they will surely say: We were only conversing and playing. Say: Is it Allah and His verses and His Messenger that you were mocking? Make no excuse; you have disbelieved after your belief. If We pardon one faction of you, We will punish another faction because they were criminals.﴾

(Qur'an 9: 65-66)

- To belie some or all of what was brought by the messengers (peace be upon them all):

﴿ إِنَّ الَّذِينَ يَكْفُرُونَ بِاللَّهِ وَرُسُلِهِ وَيُرِيدُونَ أَن يُفَرِّقُوا بَيْنَ اللَّهِ وَرُسُلِهِ وَيَقُولُونَ نُؤْمِنُ بِبَعْضٍ وَنَكْفُرُ بِبَعْضٍ وَيُرِيدُونَ أَن يَتَّخِذُوا بَيْنَ ذَٰلِكَ سَبِيلًا ﴿١٥٠﴾ أُولَٰئِكَ هُمُ الْكَافِرُونَ حَقًّا ۚ وَأَعْتَدْنَا لِلْكَافِرِينَ عَذَابًا مُّهِينًا ﴿١٥١﴾ ﴾

(سورة النساء: ١٥٠-١٥١)

﴿Indeed, those who disbelieve in Allah and His messengers and wish to discriminate between Allah and His messengers and say: We believe in some and disbelieve in others, and wish to adopt a way in between — those are the disbelievers, truly. We have prepared for the disbelievers a humiliating punishment.﴾

(Qur'an 4: 150-151)

- To dislike the religion of Allah becoming victorious:

﴿ الَّذِينَ يَتَرَبَّصُونَ بِكُمْ فَإِن كَانَ لَكُمْ فَتْحٌ مِّنَ اللَّهِ قَالُوا أَلَمْ نَكُن مَّعَكُمْ وَإِن كَانَ لِلْكَافِرِينَ نَصِيبٌ قَالُوا أَلَمْ نَسْتَحْوِذْ عَلَيْكُمْ وَنَمْنَعْكُم مِّنَ الْمُؤْمِنِينَ ۚ فَاللَّهُ يَحْكُمُ بَيْنَكُمْ يَوْمَ الْقِيَامَةِ ۗ وَلَن يَجْعَلَ اللَّهُ لِلْكَافِرِينَ عَلَى الْمُؤْمِنِينَ سَبِيلًا ﴿١٤١﴾ ﴾

(سورة النساء: ١٤١)

﴾Those who wait [and watch] you. Then if you gain a victory from Allah, they say: Were we not with you? But if the disbelievers have a success, they say [to them]: Did we not gain the advantage over you, but we protected you from the believers? Allah will judge between [all of] you on the Day of Resurrection, and never will Allah give the disbelievers over the believers a way [to overcome them].﴿ *(Qur'an 4: 141)*

- To rejoice at the disgrace or humiliation of the religion

A person possessing all these qualities is indeed a supreme hypocrite and as such, is destined for the lowest depths of the hellfire:

﴿إِنَّ ٱلْمُنَٰفِقِينَ فِى ٱلدَّرْكِ ٱلْأَسْفَلِ مِنَ ٱلنَّارِ وَلَن تَجِدَ لَهُمْ نَصِيرًا ﴿١٤٥﴾ إِلَّا ٱلَّذِينَ تَابُوا۟ وَأَصْلَحُوا۟ وَٱعْتَصَمُوا۟ بِٱللَّهِ وَأَخْلَصُوا۟ دِينَهُمْ لِلَّهِ فَأُو۟لَٰٓئِكَ مَعَ ٱلْمُؤْمِنِينَ ۖ وَسَوْفَ يُؤْتِ ٱللَّهُ ٱلْمُؤْمِنِينَ أَجْرًا عَظِيمًا ﴿١٤٦﴾﴾

(سورة النساء: ١٤٥-١٤٦)

﴾Indeed, the hypocrites will be in the lowest depths of the fire — and never will you find for them a helper — except for those who repent, correct themselves, hold fast to Allah, and are sincere in their religion for Allah, for those will be with the believers. And Allah is going to give the believers a great reward.﴿

(Qur'an 4: 145-146)

(b) Hypocrisy in deeds and actions

The five aspects of hypocrisy in deeds and actions have been characterized and enumerated in a number of hadiths of Prophet Muhammad (ﷺ).

Abu Hurayrah (رضي الله عنه) narrated that the Prophet (ﷺ) said:

«The signs of a hypocrite are three: whenever he speaks, he lies. Whenever he promises, he breaks it (his promise). If you trust him, he proves to be dishonest (if you entrust him with something, he will not return it).» (Bukhari)

'Abdullâh ibn 'Amr (ﷺ) narrated that the Prophet (ﷺ) said:

«Whoever has the following four (characteristics) will be a pure hypocrite, and whoever has one of the following four characteristics will have one characteristic of hypocrisy unless and until he gives it up. Whenever he is entrusted, he betrays. Whenever he speaks, he lies. Whenever he makes a covenant, he proves to be treacherous. Whenever he quarrels, he behaves in a very impudent, evil, and insulting manner.» (Bukhari)

The hypocrites will fall off the bridge called the *ṣirâṭ*

On the Day of Judgement, everyone will have to go through the last test, which is the crossing over the hellfire on the bridge-called the *ṣirâṭ*, as Allah has mentioned in the Qur'an:

﴿ وَإِن مِّنكُمْ إِلَّا وَارِدُهَا كَانَ عَلَىٰ رَبِّكَ حَتْمًا مَّقْضِيًّا ﴿٧١﴾ ﴾ (سورة مريم: ٧١)

﴿And there is none of you except he will come to it. This is upon your Lord an inevitability decreed.﴾ *(Qur'an 19: 71)*

The manner and the ease of crossing this bridge will depend upon the depth and steadfastness of our belief and conviction in Allah, the extent of our adherence to His commands and injunctions, and the quality and quantity of our good deeds and actions.

In a long hadith, the Prophet (ﷺ) informed us about this last test of crossing the bridge placed over the hellfire and how people will fare:

Abu Sa'eed al-Khudri (ﷺ) narrated:

«We asked: O Allah's Messenger! Shall we see our Lord on the Day of Resurrection?

He replied: Do you have any difficulty in seeing the sun and the moon when the sky is clear?

We answered: No.

He said: So you will have no difficulty in seeing your Lord on that day as you have no difficulty in seeing the sun and the moon (in a clear sky).

The Prophet (ﷺ) said: Somebody will then announce: Let every nation follow what they used to worship. So the companions of the cross will go with their cross, and the idolaters (will go) with their idols, and the companions of every god (false deity) with their god, until there remain only those who used to worship Allah, both the obedient ones and the mischievous ones, and some of the People of the Scripture. Then hell will be presented to them as if it were a mirage.

It will be said to the Jews: What did you worship?

They will reply: We used to worship Ezra, son of Allah.

It will be said to them: You are liars, for Allah has neither a wife nor a son. What do you want (now)?

They will answer: We want You to provide us with water.

It will be said to them: Drink — and they will fall down into hell (instead).

It will be said to the Christians: What did you worship?

They will respond: We used to worship the Messiah, son of Allah.

It will be said: You are liars, for Allah has neither a wife nor a son. What do you want (now)?

They will answer: We want You to provide us with water.

It will be said to them: Drink — and they will fall down into hell (instead).

When there remain only those who used to worship Allah (alone), both the obedient ones and the mischievous ones, it will be said to them: What keeps you here when all the people have gone?

They will respond: We parted with them (in the world) when we were in greater need of them than we are today; we heard the call of one proclaiming: Let every nation follow what they used to worship, and now we are waiting for our Lord.

The Almighty will come to them in a shape other than the one which they saw the first time, and He will say: I am your Lord. They will say: You are not our Lord.

None will speak to Him then but the prophets. It will be said to them: Do you know any sign by which you can recognize Him?

They will say: His shin. So Allah will uncover His shin, whereupon every believer will prostrate before Him and there will remain those who used to prostrate before Him just for showing off and for gaining good reputation. These people will try to prostrate, but their backs will become as rigid as pieces of wood (and they will not be able to prostrate). Then the bridge will be laid across hell.

We, the Companions of the Prophet (ﷺ) asked: O Allah's Messenger! What is the bridge?

He replied: It is a slippery (bridge) on which there are clamps and (hooks like) thorny seeds that is wide at one side and narrow at the other and has thorns with bent ends. Such a thorny seed is found in Najd and is called *as-sa'dân*. Some of the believers will cross the bridge as quickly as the blink of an eye; others as quick as lightning, a strong wind, fast horses, or she-camels. Some will be safe without any harm, some will be safe after receiving some scratches, and some will fall down into hell (fire). The last person will cross by being dragged (over the bridge).

The Prophet (ﷺ) said: You (Muslims) cannot be more pressing in claiming from me a right that has clearly proved to be yours than the believers in interceding with the Almighty for their (Muslim) brothers on that day, when they see themselves safe.

They will say: O Allah! (Save) our brothers (for they) used to pray with us, fast with us, and also do good deeds with us.

Allah will say: Go and take out (of hell) anyone in whose heart you find faith equal to the weight of one (gold) dinar. Allah will forbid the fire from burning the faces of those sinners.

They will go to them and find some of them in hell (fire) up to their feet, and some up to the middle of their legs. So they will take out those whom they recognize; then they will return, and Allah will say (to them): Go and take out (of hell) anyone in whose heart you find faith equal to the weight of half a dinar.

They will take out whomever they recognize and then return, and Allah will say: Go and take out (of hell) anyone in whose heart you find faith equal to the weight of an atom (or the smallest ant). So they will take out all those whom they recognize.

Abu Sa'eed (رضي الله عنه) said: If you do not believe me, then read the following Qur'anic verse:

﴿إِنَّ ٱللَّهَ لَا يَظْلِمُ مِثْقَالَ ذَرَّةٍ ۖ وَإِن تَكُ حَسَنَةً يُضَٰعِفْهَا وَيُؤْتِ مِن لَّدُنْهُ أَجْرًا عَظِيمًا ﴿٤٠﴾﴾ (سورة النساء: ٤٠)

﴿Indeed, Allah does not do injustice, [even] as much as an atom's weight; while if there is a good deed, He multiplies it and gives from Himself a great reward.﴾ *(Qur'an 4: 40)*

The Prophet (ﷺ) added: Then the prophets, the angels and the believers will intercede, and (last of all) Almighty (Allah) will say: Now remains My intercession. He will hold a handful of the fire, from which He will take out some people whose bodies have been burnt, and they will be thrown into a river at the entrance of paradise called the River of Life. They will grow on its banks as a seed carried by the torrent grows. You have noticed how it grows beside a rock or beside a tree, and how the side facing the sun is usually green while the side facing the shade is white. Those people will come out (of the River of Life) like pearls, and they will have (golden) necklaces. Then they will enter paradise, whereupon the people of paradise will say: These are the people emancipated by the Beneficent. He has admitted them into paradise without their having done any good deeds or having sent forth any good (for themselves).

Then it will be said to them: For you is what you have seen, and its equivalent as well.» (Bukhari)

In this moving statement of the Messenger of Allah (ﷺ) we have seen that:

- Some of the believers will cross the bridge as quickly as the blink of an eye.
- Others will cross it as fast as lightning.
- Others will cross it as fast as horses.
- Some will be safe without any harm.
- Some will be safe after receiving scratches.
- The hypocrites will fall into hellfire.
- The last person will be dragged across the bridge.

Strong, unwavering, unshakeable belief, which is the fulfilment of the second condition of the shahâdah, is the passport that will facilitate our last test — the passage over the ṣirâṭ. The way over the narrow bridge will be very dark, but it will be illuminated by Allah to facilitate its crossing, according to the strength of our faith and how we conducted our lives in the world. Also consider the following:

- A good Muslim who adhered to the Sharia and always struggled to please Allah throughout his or her life will be given light as bright as that of a flashlight:

﴿يَوْمَ تَرَى ٱلْمُؤْمِنِينَ وَٱلْمُؤْمِنَٰتِ يَسْعَىٰ نُورُهُم بَيْنَ أَيْدِيهِمْ وَبِأَيْمَٰنِهِم بُشْرَىٰكُمُ ٱلْيَوْمَ جَنَّٰتٌ تَجْرِى مِن تَحْتِهَا ٱلْأَنْهَٰرُ خَٰلِدِينَ فِيهَا ۚ ذَٰلِكَ هُوَ ٱلْفَوْزُ ٱلْعَظِيمُ ۝١٢﴾ (سورة الحديد: ١٢)

﴿On the day you see the believing men and believing women, their light proceeding before them and on their right, [it will be said]: Your good tidings today are [of] gardens beneath which rivers flow, wherein you will abide eternally. That is what the great attainment is.﴾ *(Qur'an 57: 12)*

﴿... يَوْمَ لَا يُخْزِى ٱللَّهُ ٱلنَّبِىَّ وَٱلَّذِينَ ءَامَنُوا۟ مَعَهُۥ ۖ نُورُهُمْ يَسْعَىٰ بَيْنَ أَيْدِيهِمْ وَبِأَيْمَٰنِهِمْ يَقُولُونَ رَبَّنَآ أَتْمِمْ لَنَا نُورَنَا وَٱغْفِرْ لَنَآ ۖ إِنَّكَ عَلَىٰ كُلِّ شَىْءٍ قَدِيرٌ ۝٨﴾

(سورة التحريم: ٨)

﴿...the day when Allah will not disgrace the Prophet and those who believed with him. Their light will proceed before them and on their right; they will say: Our Lord, perfect for us our light and forgive us. Indeed, You are over all things competent.﴾ *(Qur'an 66: 8)*

- For a weak Muslim, the light will be correspondingly dim. In such a light, one will be unable to see properly and will be more likely to stumble.

  Abu Hurayrah (ﷺ) reported Allah's Messenger (ﷺ) as saying: «A strong believer is better and is more lovable to Allah than a weak believer. There is good in everyone, (but) cherish what will benefit you (in the hereafter) and seek help from

Allah and do not lose heart. If anything (in the form of trouble) comes to you, do not say: If I had not done that, such-and-such would not have happened. Instead, say: Allah did what He had ordained to do. This is because your (saying of the word) 'if' opens the (gate) for Satan.» (Muslim)

- To those whose belief in and practice of Islam is indecisive and unsteady, wavering back and forth, the light granted will be irregular and sporadic. This will make their way across the bridge very hazardous and their condition will resemble that of the hypocrites. Allah has warned:

﴿إِنَّ ٱلَّذِينَ ءَامَنُواْ ثُمَّ كَفَرُواْ ثُمَّ ءَامَنُواْ ثُمَّ كَفَرُواْ ثُمَّ ٱزۡدَادُواْ كُفۡرٗا لَّمۡ يَكُنِ ٱللَّهُ لِيَغۡفِرَ لَهُمۡ وَلَا لِيَهۡدِيَهُمۡ سَبِيلَۢا ١٣٧﴾ (سورة النساء: ١٣٧)

﴿Indeed, those who have believed then disbelieved, then believed then disbelieved, and then increased in disbelief — never will Allah forgive them, nor will He guide them to a way.﴾ *(Qur'an 4: 137)*

﴿وَمِنَ ٱلنَّاسِ مَن يَعۡبُدُ ٱللَّهَ عَلَىٰ حَرۡفٖۖ فَإِنۡ أَصَابَهُۥ خَيۡرٌ ٱطۡمَأَنَّ بِهِۦۖ وَإِنۡ أَصَابَتۡهُ فِتۡنَةٌ ٱنقَلَبَ عَلَىٰ وَجۡهِهِۦ خَسِرَ ٱلدُّنۡيَا وَٱلۡأٓخِرَةَۚ ذَٰلِكَ هُوَ ٱلۡخُسۡرَانُ ٱلۡمُبِينُ ١١﴾

(سورة الحج: ١١)

﴿And of the people is he who worships Allah on an edge.[43] If he is touched by good, he is reassured by it; but if he is struck by trial, he turns on his face [to the other direction]. He has lost [this] world and the hereafter. That is what the manifest loss is.﴾ *(Qur'an 22: 11)*

- The hypocrites — who have certainly abandoned the second condition of the shahâdah and are sitting on the fence, conforming to the disbelievers and pretending to be with the believers — will be in total darkness. There will be no light at

---

43 At the edge of his or her religion, so to speak, with uncertainty, hypocrisy, or heedlessness.

all for them and they will fall over the bridge directly into the lowest pits of hellfire.

﴿ يَوْمَ يَقُولُ ٱلْمُنَٰفِقُونَ وَٱلْمُنَٰفِقَٰتُ لِلَّذِينَ ءَامَنُوا۟ ٱنظُرُونَا نَقْتَبِسْ مِن نُّورِكُمْ قِيلَ ٱرْجِعُوا۟ وَرَآءَكُمْ
فَٱلْتَمِسُوا۟ نُورًا فَضُرِبَ بَيْنَهُم بِسُورٍ لَّهُۥ بَابٌۢ بَاطِنُهُۥ فِيهِ ٱلرَّحْمَةُ وَظَٰهِرُهُۥ مِن قِبَلِهِ ٱلْعَذَابُ ﴿١٣﴾
يُنَادُونَهُمْ أَلَمْ نَكُن مَّعَكُمْ ۖ قَالُوا۟ بَلَىٰ وَلَٰكِنَّكُمْ فَتَنتُمْ أَنفُسَكُمْ وَتَرَبَّصْتُمْ وَٱرْتَبْتُمْ وَغَرَّتْكُمُ
ٱلْأَمَانِىُّ حَتَّىٰ جَآءَ أَمْرُ ٱللَّهِ وَغَرَّكُم بِٱللَّهِ ٱلْغَرُورُ ﴿١٤﴾ فَٱلْيَوْمَ لَا يُؤْخَذُ مِنكُمْ فِدْيَةٌ وَلَا مِنَ
ٱلَّذِينَ كَفَرُوا۟ ۚ مَأْوَىٰكُمُ ٱلنَّارُ ۖ هِىَ مَوْلَىٰكُمْ ۖ وَبِئْسَ ٱلْمَصِيرُ ﴿١٥﴾ ﴾ (سورة الحديد: ١٣-١٥)

﴾On the [same] day the hypocrite men and hypocrite women will say to those who believed: Wait for us that we may acquire some of your light. It will be said: Go back behind you[44] and seek light. A wall will be placed between them with a door, its interior containing mercy, but on the outside of it is torment. The hypocrites will call to the believers: Were we not with you? They will say: Yes, but you afflicted yourselves[45] and awaited [misfortune for us] and doubted, and wishful thinking deluded you until there came the command of Allah. And the deceiver [Satan] deceived you concerning Allah. So today no ransom will be taken from you or from those who disbelieved. Your refuge is the fire. It is most worthy of you, and wretched is the destination.﴿ *(Qur'an 57: 13-15)*

In several other places in the glorious Qur'an, Allah has related the delusions and misconceptions of the hypocrites, giving clear-cut warnings of dire consequences to those who harbour this disease of deceit and duplicity in their hearts:

﴿ بَشِّرِ ٱلْمُنَٰفِقِينَ بِأَنَّ لَهُمْ عَذَابًا أَلِيمًا ﴿١٣٨﴾ ٱلَّذِينَ يَتَّخِذُونَ ٱلْكَٰفِرِينَ أَوْلِيَآءَ مِن
دُونِ ٱلْمُؤْمِنِينَ ۚ أَيَبْتَغُونَ عِندَهُمُ ٱلْعِزَّةَ فَإِنَّ ٱلْعِزَّةَ لِلَّهِ جَمِيعًا ﴿١٣٩﴾ وَقَدْ نَزَّلَ عَلَيْكُمْ

---

44 To where light was acquired: that is, in the worldly life.

45 By hypocrisy or by falling into temptations.

فِي ٱلْكِتَٰبِ أَنْ إِذَا سَمِعْتُمْ ءَايَٰتِ ٱللَّهِ يُكْفَرُ بِهَا وَيُسْتَهْزَأُ بِهَا فَلَا تَقْعُدُوا۟ مَعَهُمْ حَتَّىٰ
يَخُوضُوا۟ فِى حَدِيثٍ غَيْرِهِۦٓ ۚ إِنَّكُمْ إِذًا مِّثْلُهُمْ ۗ إِنَّ ٱللَّهَ جَامِعُ ٱلْمُنَٰفِقِينَ وَٱلْكَٰفِرِينَ فِى
جَهَنَّمَ جَمِيعًا ﴿١٤٠﴾ ﴾ (سورة النساء: ١٣٨-١٤٠)

﴿Give tidings to the hypocrites that there is for them a painful punishment — those who take disbelievers as allies instead of the believers. Do they seek with them honour [through power]? But indeed, honour belongs to Allah entirely. It has already come down to you in the Book that when you hear the verses of Allah [recited] they are denied [by them] and ridiculed; so do not sit with them until they enter into another conversation. Indeed, you would then be like them. Indeed, Allah will gather the hypocrites and disbelievers in hell all together.﴾ *(Qur'an 4: 138-140)*

﴿إِنَّ ٱلْمُنَٰفِقِينَ يُخَٰدِعُونَ ٱللَّهَ وَهُوَ خَٰدِعُهُمْ وَإِذَا قَامُوٓا۟ إِلَى ٱلصَّلَوٰةِ قَامُوا۟ كُسَالَىٰ
يُرَآءُونَ ٱلنَّاسَ وَلَا يَذْكُرُونَ ٱللَّهَ إِلَّا قَلِيلًا ﴿١٤٢﴾ مُّذَبْذَبِينَ بَيْنَ ذَٰلِكَ لَآ إِلَىٰ هَٰٓؤُلَآءِ وَلَآ
إِلَىٰ هَٰٓؤُلَآءِ ۚ وَمَن يُضْلِلِ ٱللَّهُ فَلَن تَجِدَ لَهُۥ سَبِيلًا ﴿١٤٣﴾ ﴾ (سورة النساء: ١٤٢-١٤٣)

﴿Indeed, the hypocrites [think to] deceive Allah, but He is deceiving them. And when they stand for prayer, they stand lazily, showing [themselves to] the people and not remembering Allah except a little, wavering between them, [belonging] neither to the believers nor to the disbelievers. And whoever Allah leaves astray — never will you find for him a way.﴾ *(Qur'an 4: 142-143)*

This means to believe truthfully in the shahâdah, such that the inward conviction is reflected in outward action.

Chapter Seven
The Third Condition: Truthfulness

﴿يَٰٓأَيُّهَا ٱلَّذِينَ ءَامَنُوٓاْ ءَامِنُواْ بِٱللَّهِ وَرَسُولِهِۦ وَٱلۡكِتَٰبِ ٱلَّذِي نَزَّلَ عَلَىٰ رَسُولِهِۦ
وَٱلۡكِتَٰبِ ٱلَّذِيٓ أَنزَلَ مِن قَبۡلُۚ وَمَن يَكۡفُرۡ بِٱللَّهِ وَمَلَٰٓئِكَتِهِۦ وَكُتُبِهِۦ وَرُسُلِهِۦ
وَٱلۡيَوۡمِ ٱلۡأٓخِرِ فَقَدۡ ضَلَّ ضَلَٰلَۢا بَعِيدًا ﴿١٣٦﴾﴾ (سورة النساء: ١٣٦)

﴿O you who have believed, believe[46] in Allah and His Messenger and the Book that He sent down upon His Messenger and the scripture which He sent down before. Whoever disbelieves in Allah, His angels, His books, His messengers, and the last day has certainly gone far astray.﴾ *(Qur'an 4: 136)*

﴿قَدۡ أَفۡلَحَ ٱلۡمُؤۡمِنُونَ ﴿١﴾ ٱلَّذِينَ هُمۡ فِي صَلَاتِهِمۡ خَٰشِعُونَ ﴿٢﴾ وَٱلَّذِينَ هُمۡ عَنِ ٱللَّغۡوِ
مُعۡرِضُونَ ﴿٣﴾ وَٱلَّذِينَ هُمۡ لِلزَّكَوٰةِ فَٰعِلُونَ ﴿٤﴾ وَٱلَّذِينَ هُمۡ لِفُرُوجِهِمۡ حَٰفِظُونَ
﴿٥﴾ إِلَّا عَلَىٰٓ أَزۡوَٰجِهِمۡ أَوۡ مَا مَلَكَتۡ أَيۡمَٰنُهُمۡ فَإِنَّهُمۡ غَيۡرُ مَلُومِينَ ﴿٦﴾ فَمَنِ
ٱبۡتَغَىٰ وَرَآءَ ذَٰلِكَ فَأُوْلَٰٓئِكَ هُمُ ٱلۡعَادُونَ ﴿٧﴾ وَٱلَّذِينَ هُمۡ لِأَمَٰنَٰتِهِمۡ وَعَهۡدِهِمۡ رَٰعُونَ
﴿٨﴾ وَٱلَّذِينَ هُمۡ عَلَىٰ صَلَوَٰتِهِمۡ يُحَافِظُونَ ﴿٩﴾ أُوْلَٰٓئِكَ هُمُ ٱلۡوَٰرِثُونَ ﴿١٠﴾ ٱلَّذِينَ
يَرِثُونَ ٱلۡفِرۡدَوۡسَ هُمۡ فِيهَا خَٰلِدُونَ ﴿١١﴾﴾ (سورة المؤمنون: ١-١١)

---

[46] That is: renew, confirm, and adhere to your belief.

﴾Certainly will the believers have succeeded: they who are during their prayer humbly submissive, and they who turn away from ill speech, and they who are observant of zakâh, and they who guard their private parts except from their wives or those their right hands possess — for indeed, they will not be blamed — but whoever seeks beyond that, then those are the transgressors — and they who are to their trusts and their promises attentive, and they who carefully maintain their prayers — those are the inheritors who will inherit the highest level of paradise. They will abide therein eternally.﴿ *(Qur'an 23: 1-11)*

Definition of *eemân*

It is only when a person has knowledge about the shahâdah and is certain about it that Allah blesses him or her with true faith (eemân). Eemân is a conviction of the heart, a declaration by the tongue, and an implementation by the limbs. Faith is not a mere claim of belief. Rather, it is coupled with righteous deeds to please Allah. As the great student of the Companions of the Prophet (ﷺ), al-Ḥasan al-Baṣri, has said:

> Eemân is not a matter of wishful thinking (desires) but it is that which has settled in the heart and is confirmed by good deeds. (Bukhari)[47]

Eemân is separate and distinct from Islam; it is the quality that distinguishes the one who submits — the Muslim — from the one who truly believes and is fully committed to Islam — the *mu'min*. In his exegesis of the Qur'an, Ibn Katheer draws attention to this difference, referring to the Muslim and the mu'min as separate entities. For example, consider the following verse where both have been mentioned:

---

[47] As quoted in Muhammad ibn Jameel Zaynoo, *al-Aqeedah al-Islamiyah* (Dubai: Masjid Ibraheem Al-Khalil, 1404 AH), 32.

﴿إِنَّ ٱلْمُسْلِمِينَ وَٱلْمُسْلِمَٰتِ وَٱلْمُؤْمِنِينَ وَٱلْمُؤْمِنَٰتِ ... ﴿٣٥﴾﴾

(سورة الأحزاب: ٣٥)

﴿Indeed, the Muslim men and Muslim women, the believing men and believing women...﴾ *(Qur'an 33: 35)*

Eemân is certainly something other than Islam. In fact, the two concepts have been clarified quite explicitly in the following verse:

﴿۞ قَالَتِ ٱلْأَعْرَابُ ءَامَنَّا ۖ قُل لَّمْ تُؤْمِنُوا۟ وَلَٰكِن قُولُوٓا۟ أَسْلَمْنَا وَلَمَّا يَدْخُلِ ٱلْإِيمَٰنُ فِى قُلُوبِكُمْ ۖ ... ﴿١٤﴾﴾

(سورة الحُجُرات: ١٤)

﴿The Bedouins say: We have believed. Say: You have not [yet] believed; but say [instead]: We have submitted, for faith has not yet entered your hearts…﴾ *(Qur'an 49: 14)*

Furthermore, in the hadith in which the angel Gabriel (عليه السلام) came to teach the Companions (see Chapter 5), Islam, eemân, and iḥsân have been unambiguously defined as distinct concepts. There are important implications in recognizing the difference between Islam and eemân.

The two most sound collections of hadiths (Bukhari and Muslim) have reported that the Prophet (ﷺ) said:

> «The adulterer only commits adultery when he is not a believer. This is because it snatches away his eemân, although that does not mean he is a disbeliever,[48] according to the consensus of the Muslims.»

This indicates that there is a marked difference between Islam and eemân or, rather, between Muslims and *mu'mineen*. The difference between the two is that Muslims pray, fast, give zakâh, and might go for Hajj. Yet, at times, they indulge in major sins

---

[48] Meaning that his faith goes out just as he begins the act of adultery and returns after he has finished.

such as usury, alcohol, adultery, backbiting, racism, and so on. Hence, their character has many shortcomings.

On the other hand, the mu'mineen shun and stay away from all forms of major sins. This indicates their fear and consciousness of Allah, which remains all the time and is not restricted to the month of Ramadan like it is for many Muslims. They also strive daily to improve the level of their eemân. These are the people whom Allah has described and praised in a number of places in His glorious Book. To elaborate the third condition of shahâdah, let us consider only two passages as follows:

Characteristics of true believers

﴿قَدْ أَفْلَحَ ٱلْمُؤْمِنُونَ ﴿١﴾ ٱلَّذِينَ هُمْ فِى صَلَاتِهِمْ خَٰشِعُونَ ﴿٢﴾ وَٱلَّذِينَ هُمْ عَنِ ٱللَّغْوِ
مُعْرِضُونَ ﴿٣﴾ وَٱلَّذِينَ هُمْ لِلزَّكَوٰةِ فَٰعِلُونَ ﴿٤﴾ وَٱلَّذِينَ هُمْ لِفُرُوجِهِمْ حَٰفِظُونَ
﴿٥﴾ إِلَّا عَلَىٰٓ أَزْوَٰجِهِمْ أَوْ مَا مَلَكَتْ أَيْمَٰنُهُمْ فَإِنَّهُمْ غَيْرُ مَلُومِينَ ﴿٦﴾ فَمَنِ
ٱبْتَغَىٰ وَرَآءَ ذَٰلِكَ فَأُو۟لَٰٓئِكَ هُمُ ٱلْعَادُونَ ﴿٧﴾ وَٱلَّذِينَ هُمْ لِأَمَٰنَٰتِهِمْ وَعَهْدِهِمْ رَٰعُونَ
﴿٨﴾ وَٱلَّذِينَ هُمْ عَلَىٰ صَلَوَٰتِهِمْ يُحَافِظُونَ ﴿٩﴾ أُو۟لَٰٓئِكَ هُمُ ٱلْوَٰرِثُونَ ﴿١٠﴾ ٱلَّذِينَ
يَرِثُونَ ٱلْفِرْدَوْسَ هُمْ فِيهَا خَٰلِدُونَ ﴿١١﴾﴾ (سورة المؤمنون: ١-١١)

﴿Certainly will the believers have succeeded: they who are during their prayer humbly submissive, and they who turn away from ill speech, and they who are observant of zakâh, and they who guard their private parts except from their wives or those their right hands possess — for indeed, they will not be blamed — but whoever seeks beyond that, then those are the transgressors — and they who are to their trusts and their promises attentive, and they who carefully maintain their prayers — those are the inheritors who will inherit the highest level of paradise. They will abide therein eternally.﴾ *(Qur'an 23: 1-11)*

In another chapter, the believers have been referred to as servants or, rather, as worshippers of Allah having the following attributes:

﴿ وَعِبَادُ ٱلرَّحْمَٰنِ ٱلَّذِينَ يَمْشُونَ عَلَى ٱلْأَرْضِ هَوْنًا وَإِذَا خَاطَبَهُمُ ٱلْجَٰهِلُونَ قَالُوا۟
سَلَٰمًا ﴿٦٣﴾ وَٱلَّذِينَ يَبِيتُونَ لِرَبِّهِمْ سُجَّدًا وَقِيَٰمًا ﴿٦٤﴾ وَٱلَّذِينَ يَقُولُونَ رَبَّنَا
ٱصْرِفْ عَنَّا عَذَابَ جَهَنَّمَ إِنَّ عَذَابَهَا كَانَ غَرَامًا ﴿٦٥﴾ إِنَّهَا سَآءَتْ مُسْتَقَرًّا
وَمُقَامًا ﴿٦٦﴾ وَٱلَّذِينَ إِذَآ أَنفَقُوا۟ لَمْ يُسْرِفُوا۟ وَلَمْ يَقْتُرُوا۟ وَكَانَ بَيْنَ ذَٰلِكَ قَوَامًا
﴿٦٧﴾ وَٱلَّذِينَ لَا يَدْعُونَ مَعَ ٱللَّهِ إِلَٰهًا ءَاخَرَ وَلَا يَقْتُلُونَ ٱلنَّفْسَ ٱلَّتِى حَرَّمَ ٱللَّهُ إِلَّا
بِٱلْحَقِّ وَلَا يَزْنُونَ ۚ وَمَن يَفْعَلْ ذَٰلِكَ يَلْقَ أَثَامًا ﴿٦٨﴾ ﴾ (سورة الفرقان: ٦٣-٦٨)

﴿And the servants of the Most Merciful are those who walk upon the earth easily, and when the ignorant address them [harshly], they say [words of] peace and those who spend [part of] the night to their Lord prostrating and standing [in prayer] and those who say: Our Lord, avert from us the punishment of hell. Indeed, its punishment is ever adhering; indeed, it is evil as a settlement and residence. And [they are] those who, when they spend, do so not excessively or sparingly but are ever, between that, [justly] moderate and those who do not invoke with Allah another deity or kill the soul which Allah has forbidden [to be killed], except by right, and do not commit unlawful sexual intercourse. And whoever should do that will meet a penalty.﴾ *(Qur'an 25: 63-68)*

The result of truthfulness — the third stipulation of the shahâdah — is the elevation of a Muslim to the status of a mu'min.

The Prophet (ﷺ) has also described the believers and mentioned that they would be among the seven types of people who will be under the shade of Allah on the day when the earth will be turned into metal, when people will be scared, sweating, and roaming about as if they are drunk. This will be due to the scorching heat of the sun, only one or two miles above their heads. (Aḥmad and Muslim)

Abu Hurayrah (ﷺ) narrated that the Prophet (ﷺ) said:

«Seven will be shaded by Allah under His shade on the day when there will be no shade except His. They are:

1. A just ruler;
2. A young man who has been brought up in the worship of Allah (he has worshipped Allah [ﷻ] sincerely from his childhood);
3. A man whose heart is attached to the mosque (who offers the five compulsory congregational prayers in the mosque);
4. Two people who love each other only for Allah's sake; they meet and part in Allah's cause only;
5. A man who turns down the call of a charming woman of noble birth and refuses to commit adultery with her and says: I am afraid of Allah;
6. A person who practices charity so secretly that his left hand does not know what his right hand has given (nobody knows how much charity he has given);
7. A person who remembers Allah in seclusion and his eyes become flooded with tears.» (Bukhari)

Truthfulness is a sign of faith, just as lying is a sign of hypocrisy. Indeed, this quality is crucial for one's eternal salvation and is noted to have been a distinguishing trait of some of the Companions (may Allah be pleased with them) of Prophet Muhammad (ﷺ). They were known to have always spoken the truth, both during the time of ignorance and after entering the fold of Islam.

The Prophet (ﷺ) expounded the consequences of this sign of eemân in the following words:

«You must be truthful, for truthfulness leads to righteousness and righteousness leads to paradise. And beware of lying, for lying leads to immorality and immorality leads to hell. A man will keep telling the truth and striving to do so until he is recorded by Allah as a perpetually truthful person, and a man will keep telling lies and will persist in doing so until he is recorded by Allah as a perpetual liar.» (Muslim)

Therefore, our righteous deeds are an indication and reflection of our faith. If one claims to be a believer but fails to perform the prescribed mandatory obligations, such as ṣalâh and zakâh, this means the level of faith is very weak and the testimony of faith lacks the condition of truthfulness.

On the authority of Abu Hurayrah (رضي الله عنه), who said that Allah's Messenger (ﷺ) said:

«Verily, Allah does not look to your bodies or to your faces but He looks to your hearts.

The Prophet (ﷺ) then pointed towards his chest with his fingers.» (Muslim)

In another narration, Abu Hurayrah (رضي الله عنه) reported Allah's Messenger (ﷺ) as saying:

«Verily, Allah does not look to your faces and your wealth but He looks to your hearts and to your deeds.» (Muslim)

Levels of faith

Eemân is not an all-or-nothing characteristic. Rather, there are gradations and levels in it. The degree or rank of one's faith depends upon the level of one's knowledge, God-consciousness, and conviction in the shahâdah — lâ ilâha illâ Allâh. For instance, consider the following hadith.

It is narrated on the authority of Abu Hurayrah (ﷺ) that the Messenger of Allah (ﷺ) said:

«Faith has over seventy branches (or over sixty branches), the most excellent of which is the declaration that there is no god but Allah, and the humblest of which is the removal of what is injurious from the path, and modesty is a branch of faith.» (Muslim)

Prophet Muhammad (ﷺ) specified the relationship between the rank of one's faith and one's character.

'Â'ishah (ﷺ) narrated that Allah's Messenger (ﷺ) said, "Verily, the most perfect believers in faith have the best character and are the most caring towards their families." (A weak hadith recorded by at-Tirmidhi)

Faith, righteousness, and good character

Good character is the most dominant reflection of our faith. This is because eemân calms the soul and leads to a consistent effort to please Allah through righteous conduct. Wrongdoing and sin, on the other hand, lead to restiveness, agitation, and distress, just as the Prophet (ﷺ) said:

«An-Nawwâs ibn Sim'ân al-Anṣâri said: I asked Allah's Messenger (ﷺ) about righteousness and sin. He responded: Righteousness is good character, and sin is what bothers you and about which you do not want people to know.» (Muslim)

This hadith points to the fact that the consequence of faith is righteousness, which in turn leads to good character. Such character is distinguished by, among other things: kindness, honesty, humility, politeness, and truthfulness along with performing ṣalâh, paying zakâh, fasting in Ramadan and on other days, and giving charity. Therefore, it is not possible for a person who has faith and is considered to be righteous to have a bad character. Moreover, righteousness is not the mere performance of religious acts such as prayer, charity, fasting, and other outward deeds. Rather, these acts of worship, when coupled with true faith, are meant to naturally build good character.

﴿...وَأَقِمِ ٱلصَّلَوٰةَۖ إِنَّ ٱلصَّلَوٰةَ تَنْهَىٰ عَنِ ٱلْفَحْشَآءِ وَٱلْمُنكَرِۗ... ﴿٤٥﴾﴾

(سورة العنكبوت: ٤٥)

﴿...and establish prayer. Indeed, prayer prohibits immorality and wrongdoing...﴾ *(Qur'an 29: 45)*

Clearly faith, righteousness, and good character go together. As implied in the aforementioned verse, the establishment of prayer leads to virtuous deeds, justice, and decency. For this reason, ṣalâh, the prayer prescribed for the worship of Allah, is the foremost imperative obligation of a mu'min. The duty next in importance is respect and obedience to one's parents:

﴿ ۞ وَقَضَىٰ رَبُّكَ أَلَّا تَعْبُدُوٓا۟ إِلَّآ إِيَّاهُ وَبِٱلْوَٰلِدَيْنِ إِحْسَـٰنًا ۚ إِمَّا يَبْلُغَنَّ عِندَكَ ٱلْكِبَرَ أَحَدُهُمَآ أَوْ كِلَاهُمَا فَلَا تَقُل لَّهُمَآ أُفٍّ وَلَا تَنْهَرْهُمَا وَقُل لَّهُمَا قَوْلًا كَرِيمًا ﴿٢٣﴾ وَٱخْفِضْ لَهُمَا جَنَاحَ ٱلذُّلِّ مِنَ ٱلرَّحْمَةِ وَقُل رَّبِّ ٱرْحَمْهُمَا كَمَا رَبَّيَانِى صَغِيرًا ﴿٢٤﴾ رَّبُّكُمْ أَعْلَمُ بِمَا فِى نُفُوسِكُمْ ۚ إِن تَكُونُوا۟ صَـٰلِحِينَ فَإِنَّهُۥ كَانَ لِلْأَوَّٰبِينَ غَفُورًا ﴿٢٥﴾﴾

(سورة الإسراء: ٢٣-٢٥)

﴿And your Lord has decreed that you not worship except Him, and to parents, good treatment. Whether one or both of them reach old age [while] with you, say not to them [so much as]: uff,[49] and do not repel them but speak to them a noble word. And lower to them the wing of humility out of mercy and say: My Lord, have mercy upon them as they brought me up [when I was] small. Your Lord is most knowing of what is within yourselves. If you should

---

49 Uff: An expression of disapproval or irritation.

be righteous [in intention] — then indeed He is ever, to the often returning [to Him], Forgiving.﴿ *(Qur'an 17: 23-25)*[50]

﴾ وَوَصَّيْنَا ٱلْإِنسَـٰنَ بِوَٰلِدَيْهِ حَمَلَتْهُ أُمُّهُۥ وَهْنًا عَلَىٰ وَهْنٍ وَفِصَـٰلُهُۥ فِى عَامَيْنِ أَنِ ٱشْكُرْ لِى وَلِوَٰلِدَيْكَ إِلَىَّ ٱلْمَصِيرُ ﴿١٤﴾ وَإِن جَـٰهَدَاكَ عَلَىٰٓ أَن تُشْرِكَ بِى مَا لَيْسَ لَكَ بِهِۦ عِلْمٌ فَلَا تُطِعْهُمَا ۖ وَصَاحِبْهُمَا فِى ٱلدُّنْيَا مَعْرُوفًا ... ﴿١٥﴾ ﴿

(سورة لقمان: ١٤-١٥)

﴾And We have enjoined upon man [care] for his parents. His mother carried him, [increasing her] in weakness upon weakness, and his weaning is in two years. Be grateful to Me and to your parents; to Me is the [final] destination. But if they endeavour to make you associate with Me that of which you have no knowledge, do not obey them but accompany them in [this] world with appropriate kindness...﴿ *(Qur'an 31: 14-15)*

The Prophet (ﷺ) said:

«Whoever is not kind to our young ones and respectful to our elders is not one of us.» (Recorded by at-Tirmidhi and authenticated by al-Albâni)

A Muslim's duties to his or her parents

From the aforementioned Qur'anic and hadith evidence, it is obvious that to be a good Muslim, one has to treat parents and elders well.

One cannot truly be a good Muslim unless one treats his or her parents and elders well and properly by obeying them. Some of the duties that Muslims with true faith owe to their parents are:

- To express love and gratitude to them

[50] For those who intend righteousness, hastening to repent from sins and errors committed through human weakness, Allah has promised forgiveness.

- To speak to them kindly and respectfully
- To strive to do everything that will please them, within the limits of Sharia, in order to be a source of joy and happiness for them both in this world and the hereafter
- To offer them sound advice and guidance when it is needed, especially if they are not Muslims or they do not discharge some of the acts of worship like ṣalâh
- To avoid angry or exasperated expressions or negative reactions when they say or do something of which one does not approve
- To refrain from disobeying them unless they command you to do something that involves the disobedience of Allah
- To take care of their needs, especially when they have grown old and are unable to take care of themselves; this includes not showing any signs of displeasure or discomfort whenever they become sick. Rather, one should supplicate for them consistently.
- To continue praying for them even after their death, since the Prophet (ﷺ) clarified that when a son of Adam (a Muslim) dies, all good deeds are cut off from him except three: continuous charity, knowledge that benefits people, and righteous children who remember their parents in supplication.
- To fulfil, after their death, any contracts or debts that they may have left behind and to maintain good relationships with their friends
- To refrain, according to the Prophet (ﷺ), from condemning them or abusing them by denouncing and abusing the parents of others (who might, in turn, abuse one's own parents)

Essentially, the third condition of the shahâdah, truthfulness, stipulates that our words and actions should corroborate and be a mirror image of our faith in order to motivate us towards righteousness. Otherwise, our faith will be only lip service and empty talk, totally in contradiction to the third prerequisite of the shahâdah. Allah has strongly reprimanded such people:

﴿يَٰٓأَيُّهَا ٱلَّذِينَ ءَامَنُواْ لِمَ تَقُولُونَ مَا لَا تَفۡعَلُونَ ﴿٢﴾﴾ (سورة الصف: ٢-٣)

﴾O you who have believed, why do you say what you do not do? Great is hatred in the sight of Allah that you say what you do not do.﴿ *(Qur'an 61: 2-3)*

It is very significant that the Qur'an has instructed the believers, again and again, to have faith and perform good deeds. The two injunctions are inseparable and always go together. Implicit in these commands is the fact that the fruits of true faith in the heart are good deeds pleasing to Allah. Thus, by being truthful to the shahâdah, one can escape the torment of hellfire:

Anas ibn Mâlik (رضي الله عنه) narrated:

«Once Mu'âdh (رضي الله عنه) was with Allah's Messenger (ﷺ) as a companion rider. Allah's Messenger (ﷺ) said: O Mu'âdh ibn Jabal!

Mu'âdh (رضي الله عنه) replied: I respond to your call. How can I help you, O Allah's Messenger?

Again the Prophet (ﷺ) said: O Mu'âdh!

Mu'âdh (رضي الله عنه) responded thrice with the same expression.

Allah's Messenger (ﷺ) went on to say: Those who testify sincerely that none has the right to be worshipped but Allah and Muhammad is his Messenger, will be saved by Allah from the hellfire.

Mu'âdh (رضي الله عنه) said: O Allah's Messenger! Should I not inform the people about it so that they may have glad tidings?

He replied: When people hear about it, they will solely depend on it.

Mu'âdh (رضي الله عنه) narrated this hadith just before his death, being afraid of committing a sin (through withholding his knowledge of it).» (Bukhari)

Chapter Eight

The Fourth Condition: Compliance

Compliance entails complete submission to what the shahâdah entails. Consider the following verses:

﴿ يَٰٓأَيُّهَا ٱلَّذِينَ ءَامَنُواْ ٱدۡخُلُواْ فِي ٱلسِّلۡمِ كَآفَّةٗ وَلَا تَتَّبِعُواْ خُطُوَٰتِ ٱلشَّيۡطَٰنِۚ إِنَّهُۥ لَكُمۡ عَدُوّٞ مُّبِينٞ ٢٠٨ ﴾ (سورة البقرة: ٢٠٨)

﴿O you who have believed, enter into Islam completely [and perfectly] and do not follow the footsteps of Satan. Indeed, he is to you a clear enemy.﴾ *(Qur'an 2: 208)*

﴿وَمَا كَانَ لِمُؤۡمِنٖ وَلَا مُؤۡمِنَةٍ إِذَا قَضَى ٱللَّهُ وَرَسُولُهُۥٓ أَمۡرًا أَن يَكُونَ لَهُمُ ٱلۡخِيَرَةُ مِنۡ أَمۡرِهِمۡۗ وَمَن يَعۡصِ ٱللَّهَ وَرَسُولَهُۥ فَقَدۡ ضَلَّ ضَلَٰلٗا مُّبِينٗا ٣٦﴾ (سورة الأحزاب: ٣٦)

﴿It is not for a believing man or a believing woman, when Allah and His Messenger have decided a matter, that they should [thereafter] have any choice about their affair. Whoever disobeys Allah and His Messenger has certainly strayed into clear error.﴾ *(Qur'an 33: 36)*

﴿ وَمَنۡ أَحۡسَنُ دِينٗا مِّمَّنۡ أَسۡلَمَ وَجۡهَهُۥ لِلَّهِ وَهُوَ مُحۡسِنٞ وَٱتَّبَعَ مِلَّةَ إِبۡرَٰهِيمَ حَنِيفٗاۗ وَٱتَّخَذَ ٱللَّهُ إِبۡرَٰهِيمَ خَلِيلٗا ١٢٥ ﴾ (سورة النساء: ١٢٥)

﴿And who is better in religion than one who submits himself to Allah while being a doer of good and follows the religion of Abraham, inclining toward truth? And Allah took Abraham as an intimate friend.﴿ *(Qur'an 4: 125)*

Absolute and total compliance with the *shahâdah*

Compliance, the fourth condition of the shahâdah, necessitates a complete and wholehearted submission to 'lâ ilâha illâ Allâh, Muḥammadun rasool Ullâh'. In other words, it means absolute obedience to Allah and His Prophet (ﷺ) in all matters and affairs. Any word or deed to the contrary can lead to disbelief, as per the following hadith.

It was narrated on the authority of Abu Hurayrah (رضي الله عنه) that the Messenger of Allah (ﷺ) observed:

> «Be prompt in doing good deeds (before you are overtaken) by turbulence (trial), which would be like a part of the dark night. During (that stormy period), a man would be a Muslim in the morning and a disbeliever in the evening; or he would be a believer in the evening and a disbeliever in the morning. This would be because he had sold his faith (religion) for a miserable price of worldly goods.» (Muslim)

In other words, it is not necessarily true that those who pronounce the shahâdah remain Muslims until they die. This is because they may say things that nullify their shahâdah, in which case, they cease to be a Muslim until they repent and renew it. There are many things that can nullify a person's shahâdah, such as:[51]

- Shirk in the worship of Allah;

---

[51] Darussalam, *The Concise Collection on Creed and Tauhid* (Riyadh: Darussalam Publishers and Distributors, 2002), 207-209.

- Setting up intermediaries between some people and Allah, supplicating to them, trusting them, and asking them to intercede on one's behalf with Allah;
- Not considering the polytheists to be disbelievers, failing to doubt their infidelity, or accepting their beliefs to be valid;
- Believing that the guidance of others is more perfect than that of Prophet Muhammad (ﷺ), considering the laws of others to be better than his, or preferring the rule of false gods to that of Allah;
- Hating anything that was brought by the Prophet (ﷺ), though one may be acting upon it;
- Ridiculing the religion of Islam by accepting one part and rejecting another;
- Practicing sorcery, or going to a sorcerer and believing in whatever he or she does;
- Supporting polytheists and aiding them against the Muslims;
- Believing that some people are exempt from obeying the Sharia of Prophet Muhammad (ﷺ);
- Disregarding Allah's religion by neither learning it nor acting upon it.

Abu Bakr aṣ-Ṣiddeeq (رضي الله عنه) and the apostates

Some of the Companions of the Prophet (ﷺ) were renowned for their conviction: their total and complete submission to Allah and His Prophet (ﷺ). It was this particular characteristic that enabled them to make the right decisions during times of great trials and difficulty. For instance, Abu Bakr aṣ-Ṣiddeeq's stance towards a group of apostates was uncompromising and inexorable, despite the opposition of the majority that included 'Umar ibn al-Khaṭṭâb (ﷺ).

After the demise of the Prophet (ﷺ), during the Caliphate of Abu Bakr (ﷺ), a group of people refused to pay zakâh while agreeing to comply with the other obligatory pillars of Islam. Since the instructions to establish ṣalâh and to pay zakâh are often found together in the Qur'an, refusing the latter was a clear denial of the basic fundamental principles of Islam. Furthermore, the rejection of any one of the five compulsory religious commitments makes an individual an apostate, subject to the penalty of death as prescribed in the Qur'an.

However, the apostates continued to deny the obligation of zakâh, choosing to fight to assert their right of refusal. When he consulted with the other Companions, Abu Bakr (ﷺ) was quoted as swearing, "By Allah, I will fight anyone who separates the two [prayer and zakâh]."[52]

Others felt they could not execute the mandatory death penalty on fellow Muslims — that is, those who had pronounced the shahâdah. Surprisingly, 'Umar ibn al-Khaṭṭâb (ﷺ), reputedly inflexible and harsh in his adherence to Islam, was among those who opposed Abu Bakr. However, Abu Bakr recognized that wholehearted submission requires the execution of Allah's commands without any compromise; he remained determined to fight the apostates. His decision finally prevailed. 'Umar and some of the other Companions joined Abu Bakr and, in the ensuing combat, the apostates were killed. Thus, the evils of apostasy were nipped in the bud.

While acknowledging the wisdom of Abu Bakr in this matter, 'Umar said:

---

[52] Muhammad ibn Ismâ'eel Bukhari, *Sahih Al-Bukhari* (Arabic–English), trans. Dr. Muhammad Muhsin Khan (Riyadh: Darussalam Publishers and Distributors, 2007).

By Allah! Nothing happened that day except that Allah opened the heart of Abu Bakr to the truth. The people were disbelievers; they had denied a pillar of Islam after taking the shahâdah. If one denies one pillar of Islam, one is guilty of rejecting the whole of Islam.[53]

This incident clearly illustrates that observance of and obedience to all five pillars of Islam are absolutely essential and obligatory if one is to fully submit as a Muslim. In effect, the fourth condition of the shahâdah stipulates that for belief to be acceptable and beneficial, one has to enter Islam wholeheartedly. One cannot have one foot in Islam with the other foot stuck fast in any kind of ignorance. Embracing Islam means leaving all habits, ideas, and cultural practices that are contradictory to it.

Total submission to the Qur'an and the Sunnah

It is regrettable that lack of conviction is rife amongst Muslims today. For instance, non-compliance with the Sunnah is quite common. One finds Muslims celebrating the birthday of Prophet Muhammad (ﷺ) when clearly this was neither an established practice during his lifetime nor a practice observed by the Companions or the followers of the Companions. What is even more deplorable is the commemoration of occasions that are clearly linked with a false deity or ideology, such as Christmas, Easter, Valentine's Day, and others. It is interesting that when those who celebrate these occasions are informed that it is not allowed for Muslims to take part in these celebrations and that Muslims have their own celebrations permissible under the Sharia, they choose

[53] Bukhari, *Sahih Al-Bukhari*.

to follow their own opinions and desires in opposition to Allah and his Messenger (ﷺ).

We also find some Muslim men wearing gold rings and silk clothing during these celebrations or even during congregational prayers on Eids[54] or Fridays. Muslim women have no qualms about applying perfume whilst going out of their houses. When they are informed that such acts are prohibited in Islam, and the hadiths of the Prophet (ﷺ) are recited to them, they raise their voices above the words of the Prophet (ﷺ) by arguing. Allah has clearly warned:

﴿وَمَا كَانَ لِمُؤْمِنٍ وَلَا مُؤْمِنَةٍ إِذَا قَضَى ٱللَّهُ وَرَسُولُهُۥٓ أَمْرًا أَن يَكُونَ لَهُمُ ٱلْخِيَرَةُ مِنْ أَمْرِهِمْ ۗ
وَمَن يَعْصِ ٱللَّهَ وَرَسُولَهُۥ فَقَدْ ضَلَّ ضَلَٰلًا مُّبِينًا ﴿٣٦﴾﴾ (سورة الأحزاب: ٣٦)

﴿It is not for a believing man or a believing woman, when Allah and His Messenger have decided a matter, that they should [thereafter] have any choice about their affair. Whoever disobeys Allah and His Messenger has certainly strayed into clear error.﴾

(Qur'an 33: 36)

In his exegesis of this verse, Syed Abul A'lâ Mawdoodi quotes several hadiths attributed to Ibn 'Abbâs, Qatâdah, 'Ikrimah, and Muqâtil ibn Hayyân and mentions the story of the marriage of Zaynab bint Jaḥsh (رضي الله عنها) to Zayd ibn Ḥarith (رضي الله عنه) as a reason for its revelation.

When Prophet Muhammad (ﷺ) proposed marriage to Zaynab (his cousin and the daughter of his paternal aunt, Umaymah bint 'Abdul-Muṭṭalib) on behalf of Zayd, her family expressed their disapproval. They felt that Zayd, a freed slave, was not a suitable match for Zaynab, a noble woman of the Quraysh. However, it

---

54 Eid: *lit.* festival; the two celebrations: one at the end of Ramadan and the other at the culmination of the Hajj.

was precisely to erase such mistaken notions of superiority and to promote the equality of all those who utter the shahâdah that the Prophet (ﷺ) had made this proposition in the first place. After the revelation of this verse, therefore, Zaynab and her relatives immediately yielded to the proposal and the marriage took place. The Prophet (ﷺ) himself contributed to the bridal gift on behalf of Zayd.

Notwithstanding the particular reason for the revelation of this verse, Mawdoodi explains that according to the main principle of Sharia, no Muslim person, institution, or nation may rely on his or her own opinion regarding a matter which has already been decided by Allah and His Messenger (ﷺ). He writes:

> To be a Muslim means to surrender one's freedom of opinion and action before Allah and His Messenger. It would be a contradiction in terms if a person or a nation claimed to be Muslim and then reserved for itself the freedom of choice and action. No sensible person can think of combining the two contradictory attitudes together. The one who desires to remain a Muslim will inevitably have to bow down to the Command of Allah and His Prophet, and the one who is not inclined to bow will have to admit that he is not a Muslim. If he does not admit he will be regarded as a hypocrite both by God and by the people even though he might proclaim to be a Muslim at the top of his voice.[55]

The commands to take heed of and respect Prophet Muhammad (ﷺ) have been mentioned a number of times in the Qur'an. For instance, Allah has admonished:

﴿يَٰٓأَيُّهَا ٱلَّذِينَ ءَامَنُواْ لَا تُقَدِّمُواْ بَيۡنَ يَدَيِ ٱللَّهِ وَرَسُولِهِۦۖ وَٱتَّقُواْ ٱللَّهَۚ إِنَّ ٱللَّهَ سَمِيعٌ عَلِيمٞ
١ يَٰٓأَيُّهَا ٱلَّذِينَ ءَامَنُواْ لَا تَرۡفَعُوٓاْ أَصۡوَٰتَكُمۡ فَوۡقَ صَوۡتِ ٱلنَّبِيِّ وَلَا تَجۡهَرُواْ لَهُۥ بِٱلۡقَوۡلِ

[55] Abul A'lâ Mawdoodi, *The Meaning of the Qur'an* (Nairobi, Kenya: The Islamic Foundation, 1989), 10:113, footnotes 65 and 66.

﴿كَجَهْرِ بَعْضِكُمْ لِبَعْضٍ أَن تَحْبَطَ أَعْمَالُكُمْ وَأَنتُمْ لَا تَشْعُرُونَ ۝٢﴾

(سورة الحُجُرات: ١-٢)

﴿O you who have believed, do not put [yourselves] before Allah and His Messenger but fear Allah. Indeed, Allah is Hearing and Knowing. O you who have believed, do not raise your voices above the voice of the Prophet or be loud to him in speech like the loudness of some of you to others, lest your deeds become worthless while you perceive not.﴾ *(Qur'an 49: 1-2)*

Prophet Muhammad's words, deeds, and actions were all exemplary, in accordance with the Qur'an, and sanctioned by Allah for His prophet and messenger. For this reason, according to a narration related by 'Amr ibn al-'Âṣ (رضي الله عنه), the Messenger of Allah (ﷺ) said:

«None of you (truly) believes until his desires are in accordance with what I have brought.» (An authentic hadith related by al-Maqdidsi in his *Ḥujjah*)[56]

Anas (رضي الله عنه) narrated that the Prophet (ﷺ) said:

«Whoever possesses the following three qualities will taste the sweetness (delight) of faith:

i. To love Allah and His Messenger (ﷺ) so much that they become dearer to him than anything else;
ii. To love a person solely for Allah's sake;
iii. To regard reverting to disbelief as akin to being thrown into the fire.» (Bukhari)

The implication of conviction, the fourth condition of the shahâdah, is that one abandons any whims and desires that are contrary to the Qur'an and the Sunnah, surrendering wholeheart-

---

[56] Ibrahim and Johnson-Davies, *An-Nawawi's Forty Hadith*, 124, hadith no. 41.

edly to the dictates of Allah and His Messenger (ﷺ). Only under these circumstances is one's submission complete and true.

Moreover, if the laws and instructions had been according to human desires, the heavens and the earth would have been totally corrupted and destroyed, as per the following verses:

﴿ وَلَوِ ٱتَّبَعَ ٱلۡحَقُّ أَهۡوَآءَهُمۡ لَفَسَدَتِ ٱلسَّمَٰوَٰتُ وَٱلۡأَرۡضُ وَمَن فِيهِنَّۚ بَلۡ أَتَيۡنَٰهُم بِذِكۡرِهِمۡ فَهُمۡ عَن ذِكۡرِهِم مُّعۡرِضُونَ ﴿٧١﴾ ﴾ (سورة المؤمنون: ٧١)

﴿But if the truth had followed their inclinations, the heavens and the earth and whoever is in them would have been ruined. Rather, We have brought them their message, but they, from their message, are turning away.﴾ *(Qur'an 23: 71)*

﴿ فَلَا وَرَبِّكَ لَا يُؤۡمِنُونَ حَتَّىٰ يُحَكِّمُوكَ فِيمَا شَجَرَ بَيۡنَهُمۡ ثُمَّ لَا يَجِدُواْ فِيٓ أَنفُسِهِمۡ حَرَجٗا مِّمَّا قَضَيۡتَ وَيُسَلِّمُواْ تَسۡلِيمٗا ﴿٦٥﴾ ﴾ (سورة النساء: ٦٥)

﴿But no, by your Lord, they will not [truly] believe until they make you [O Muhammad] judge concerning that over which they dispute among themselves and then find within themselves no discomfort from what you have judged and submit in [full, willing] submission.﴾ *(Qur'an 4: 65)*

The importance of observing the Sunnah cannot be overstressed. It is clear from the verses above that abiding by and respecting the Sunnah to the utmost is essential for one's faith.

The following hadith from the collection of *Ṣaḥeeḥ al-Bukhâri* narrated by 'Urwah describes the cause of the revelation of the latter verse:

«Zubayr (ﷺ) quarrelled with a man of the *Anṣâr*[57] over a natural mountainous stream at al-Harra. The Prophet (ﷺ)

---

[57] Anṣâr: 'helpers': the Muslim citizens of Madinah who gave refuge to the Prophet (ﷺ) and the other Muslim emigrants from Makkah.

said: O Zubayr! Irrigate (your lands) and then let the water flow to your neighbour.

The Anṣâri (displeased with this decision) asked: O Allah's Messenger, (is this because) he is your cousin?

At that, the Prophet's face became red (with anger) and he said: O Zubayr! Irrigate (your land) and then withhold the water until it fills (and overflows) the walls and then let it flow to your neighbour.

The Prophet (ﷺ) had initially given an order in favour of both of the parties. After the Anṣâri provoked the Prophet (ﷺ) (by his accusation of unfairness), the Prophet (ﷺ) permitted Zubayr (رضي الله عنه) to take his full right.

Zubayr (رضي الله عنه) said: I feel the verse was revealed in this connection:

﴿ فَلَا وَرَبِّكَ لَا يُؤْمِنُونَ حَتَّىٰ يُحَكِّمُوكَ فِيمَا شَجَرَ بَيْنَهُمْ ... ﴿٦٥﴾ ﴾

(سورة النساء: ٦٥)

﴿But no, by your Lord, they will not [truly] believe until they make you [O Muhammad] judge concerning that over which they dispute among themselves…﴾

(Qur'an 4: 65)» (Bukhari)

In fact, there are very many verses in the Qur'an in which Allah commands us to submit fully to whatever the Prophet (ﷺ) gave us. We should obey and emulate him in every aspect of our lives in order to conform to the fourth condition of the shahâdah. Indeed, complete and total compliance to the Sunnah is obligatory because if we fail to do so, we will be hit by tribulations that afflict the disobedient:

﴿ ... وَمَآ ءَاتَىٰكُمُ ٱلرَّسُولُ فَخُذُوهُ وَمَا نَهَىٰكُمْ عَنْهُ فَٱنتَهُوا۟ ... ﴿٧﴾ ﴾

(سورة الحشر: ٧)

﴾...And whatever the Messenger has given you — take; and what he has forbidden you — refrain from [it]...﴿ *(Qur'an 59: 7)*

﴿ وَمَن يُشَاقِقِ ٱلرَّسُولَ مِنۢ بَعْدِ مَا تَبَيَّنَ لَهُ ٱلْهُدَىٰ وَيَتَّبِعْ غَيْرَ سَبِيلِ ٱلْمُؤْمِنِينَ نُوَلِّهِۦ مَا تَوَلَّىٰ وَنُصْلِهِۦ جَهَنَّمَ ۖ وَسَآءَتْ مَصِيرًا ﴿١١٥﴾ ﴾ (سورة النساء: ١١٥)

﴾And whoever opposes the Messenger after guidance has become clear to him and follows other than the way of the believers — We will give him what he has taken and drive him into hell, and evil it is as a destination.﴿ *(Qur'an 4: 115)*

For this reason, those who claim to believe, but who follow only the Qur'an and reject the Sunnah of Prophet Muhammad (ﷺ), calling themselves the people of the Qur'an, have in reality failed to fulfil the fourth condition of the shahâdah. In reality, one cannot do without the Sunnah. The Hadith and Sunnah clarify all five pillars and enable the practical implementation of Islam. The Qur'an is revelation; so are the hadiths:

﴿ مَا ضَلَّ صَاحِبُكُمْ وَمَا غَوَىٰ ﴿٢﴾ وَمَا يَنطِقُ عَنِ ٱلْهَوَىٰٓ ﴿٣﴾ إِنْ هُوَ إِلَّا وَحْىٌ يُوحَىٰ ﴿٤﴾ ﴾

(سورة النجم: ٢-٤)

﴾Your companion [Muhammad] has not strayed, nor has he erred. Nor does he speak from [his own] inclination. It is not but a revelation revealed.﴿ *(Qur'an 53: 2-4)*

Thus, if we abstain from practicing the Sunnah of Prophet Muhammad (ﷺ), we become guilty of mocking Allah's revelations. Moreover, we have been warned of the repercussions of not implementing the Sunnah:

﴿ ... فَلْيَحْذَرِ ٱلَّذِينَ يُخَالِفُونَ عَنْ أَمْرِهِۦٓ أَن تُصِيبَهُمْ فِتْنَةٌ أَوْ يُصِيبَهُمْ عَذَابٌ أَلِيمٌ ﴿٦٣﴾ ﴾

(سورة النور: ٦٣)

﴾...So let those beware who dissent from the Prophet's order, lest fitnah strike them or a painful punishment.﴿ *(Qur'an 24: 63)*

﴿وَمَن يَعْصِ ٱللَّهَ وَرَسُولَهُۥ وَيَتَعَدَّ حُدُودَهُۥ يُدْخِلْهُ نَارًا خَٰلِدًا فِيهَا وَلَهُۥ عَذَابٌ مُّهِينٌ ١٤﴾ (سورة النساء: ١٤)

﴾And whoever disobeys Allah and His Messenger and transgresses His limits — He will put him into the fire to abide eternally therein, and he will have a humiliating punishment.﴿

(Qur'an 4: 14)

The companions' implementation of the *shahâdah*

The Companions of the Prophet (ﷺ) consciously practiced all the conditions of the shahâdah. We can draw many lessons from their exemplary behaviour. In fact, a number of noteworthy incidents occurred during the lifetime of the Prophet (ﷺ) that demonstrated the Companions' absolute commitment to the shahâdah.

A case in point is the man who sought the opinion of Prophet Muhammad (ﷺ) on a certain matter. Dissatisfied with the outcome, he went to Abu Bakr (رضي الله عنه) and asked for his opinion. Abu Bakr's views disgruntled him as well, so he approached 'Umar ibn al-Khaṭṭâb (رضي الله عنه), who dealt with him summarily and violently for having doubted Prophet Muhammad's advice. 'Umar ibn al-Khaṭṭâb's justification for his action was the contention that since the Prophet (ﷺ) was guided entirely by Allah's revelation, only his verdict was valid. Seeking an alternative was a sign of hypocrisy and disbelief and, for this reason, deserved the severest punishment.

﴿ أَلَمْ يَعْلَمُوٓا۟ أَنَّهُۥ مَن يُحَادِدِ ٱللَّهَ وَرَسُولَهُۥ فَأَنَّ لَهُۥ نَارَ جَهَنَّمَ خَٰلِدًا فِيهَا ۚ
ذَٰلِكَ ٱلْخِزْىُ ٱلْعَظِيمُ (٦٣) يَحْذَرُ ٱلْمُنَٰفِقُونَ أَن تُنَزَّلَ عَلَيْهِمْ سُورَةٌ
تُنَبِّئُهُم بِمَا فِى قُلُوبِهِمْ ۚ قُلِ ٱسْتَهْزِءُوٓا۟ إِنَّ ٱللَّهَ مُخْرِجٌ مَّا تَحْذَرُونَ (٦٤) وَلَئِن
سَأَلْتَهُمْ لَيَقُولُنَّ إِنَّمَا كُنَّا نَخُوضُ وَنَلْعَبُ ۚ قُلْ أَبِٱللَّهِ وَءَايَٰتِهِۦ وَرَسُولِهِۦ
كُنتُمْ تَسْتَهْزِءُونَ (٦٥) لَا تَعْتَذِرُوا۟ قَدْ كَفَرْتُم بَعْدَ إِيمَٰنِكُمْ ۚ إِن نَّعْفُ عَن طَآئِفَةٍ
مِّنكُمْ نُعَذِّبْ طَآئِفَةًۢ بِأَنَّهُمْ كَانُوا۟ مُجْرِمِينَ (٦٦) ﴾ (سورة التوبة: ٦٣-٦٦)

﴿Do they not know that whoever opposes Allah and His Messenger — that for him is the fire of hell, wherein he will abide eternally? That is the great disgrace. The hypocrites are apprehensive lest a chapter be revealed about them, informing them of what is in their hearts. Say: Mock [as you wish]; indeed, Allah will expose that which you fear. And if you ask them, they will surely say: We were only conversing and playing. Say: Is it Allah and His verses and His Messenger that you were mocking? Make no excuse; you have disbelieved after your belief. If We pardon one faction of you — We will punish another faction because they were criminals.﴾ *(Qur'an 9: 63-66)*

Abu Dharr's understanding and implementation of the *shahâdah*

Abu Dharr al-Ghifâri (ﷺ) was renowned among the Companions of Prophet Muhammad (ﷺ) for his piety and knowledge. 'Ali ibn Abi Ṭâlib (ﷺ) has been quoted as saying, "Abu Dharr is the custodian of knowledge that other people are incapable of acquiring."

The story of his reversion is a testament to his forthright character and a remarkable demonstration of conviction. Abu Jamra narrated this story in a hadith recorded by Bukhari. When Abu Dharr first received news of the Prophet's mission, he sent his brother to

Makkah to investigate this person who had claimed to be a recipient of divine revelation. In due course, his brother returned and informed Abu Dharr that he had found Muhammad (ﷺ) to be a man of praiseworthy habits and excellent conduct. As for his wonderful revelations, they were neither poetry nor soothsaying, despite the allegations of those opposed to his mission.

This aroused Abu Dharr's curiosity, and in order to satisfy himself further, he set out for Makkah. Upon his arrival in Makkah, he went straight to the Kaaba without seeking Muhammad (ﷺ), who was completely unknown to him. Towards nightfall, 'Ali ibn Abi Ṭâlib (رضي الله عنه) noticed the silent stranger and took him home. Hospitality and care for the travellers, the poor, and the strangers were second nature to the Companions. 'Ali did not even question Abu Dharr about his business; rather, he continued to extend his hospitality to him. However, on the third night, he finally asked Abu Dharr (رضي الله عنه) why he had come to Makkah. It should be remembered that these were the early days of Prophet Muhammad's mission in Makkah and persecution of the few early Muslims was rife. For this reason, Abu Dharr (رضي الله عنه) was reluctant to disclose his intention of meeting Muhammad (ﷺ) until he had ascertained the reliability of his host.

However, when 'Ali (رضي الله عنه) discovered Abu Dharr's objective, he said:

> You have reached your goal; I am going to him just now, so follow me; wherever I enter, enter after me. If I see someone who may cause you trouble, I will stand near a wall pretending to spill water (as a warning), and you should go away then.[58]

Thus, Abu Dharr met the Prophet (ﷺ) and, in this very first meeting, he embraced Islam after the Prophet (ﷺ) explained its principles to him.

---

[58] Bukhari, *Sahih Al-Bukhari.*

The Prophet (ﷺ), fearing that the Quraysh might harm Abu Dharr, enjoined upon him to keep his conversion secret. He told him to return to his clan and come back once the Muslims were victorious. However, Abu Dharr responded, "By Him Who has sent you with the truth, I will announce my conversion to Islam publicly amongst them (the disbelievers)."

Abu Dharr (رضي الله عنه) went to the Kaaba, where some of the people from the Quraysh were present. There he bore witness that there is no deity worthy of worship but Allah and that Muhammad (ﷺ) is the Messenger of Allah.

The disbelievers fell upon him from all sides and would have beaten him to death had 'Abbâs ibn 'Abdul-Muṭṭalib (رضي الله عنه) not intervened, restraining the mob by saying:

> Woe to you! You want to kill a man from the tribe of Ghifâr, although your trade and your communications are through the territory of Ghifâr?[59]

Notwithstanding the beating he had suffered, Abu Dharr's commitment to Islam was absolute and wholehearted. He chose to go to the Kaaba the very next day and pronounce the shahâdah yet again to show his true allegiance. He would surely have been beaten to death if 'Abbâs (رضي الله عنه) had not interfered a second time to save him.

The zeal, enthusiasm, and fortitude of the early Muslims were without parallel. There are many accounts of the hardships and persecution they suffered for their belief. It was the spirit of their commitment and implementation of the shahâdah that took the Companions of Prophet Muhammad (ﷺ) to great heights of material and spiritual progress. No power on earth, nor any form of oppression or tyranny, could turn them away from their dedication to Islam.

---

[59] Bukhari, *Sahih Al-Bukhari.*

For instance, Bilâl ibn Rabâḥ (ﷺ), the former slave from Abyssinia, underwent all kinds of persecution and torture at the hands of his master, Ummayyah ibn Khalaf, yet he refused to relinquish his faith. Similarly, Sumayyah (ﷺ) and Yâsir (ﷺ), the parents of 'Ammâr ibn Yâsir (ﷺ), suffered the severest afflictions, which included the torment of the scorching sands. Their refusal to abandon the shahâdah incensed their tormentor, Abu Jahl, so much that he killed Sumayyah by running a spear through her private parts; she thus became the first martyr in the cause of Islam.

Chapter Nine

The Fifth Condition: Acceptance

Acceptance entails acknowledgement of the ultimate truth and renunciation of all falsehood. Consider the following verses:

﴿ فَإِنَّهُمْ يَوْمَئِذٍ فِي ٱلْعَذَابِ مُشْتَرِكُونَ ﴿٣٣﴾ إِنَّا كَذَٰلِكَ نَفْعَلُ بِٱلْمُجْرِمِينَ ﴿٣٤﴾ إِنَّهُمْ كَانُوٓا۟ إِذَا
قِيلَ لَهُمْ لَآ إِلَٰهَ إِلَّا ٱللَّهُ يَسْتَكْبِرُونَ ﴿٣٥﴾ وَيَقُولُونَ أَئِنَّا لَتَارِكُوٓا۟ ءَالِهَتِنَا لِشَاعِرٍ مَّجْنُونٍۭ
﴿٣٦﴾ بَلْ جَآءَ بِٱلْحَقِّ وَصَدَّقَ ٱلْمُرْسَلِينَ ﴿٣٧﴾ ﴾ (سورة الصافات: ٣٣-٣٧)

﴾So indeed they, that day, will be sharing in the punishment. Indeed, that is how We deal with the criminals. Indeed they, when it was said to them: There is no deity but Allah, were arrogant, and were saying: Are we to leave our gods for a mad poet? Rather, he [the Prophet] has come with the truth and confirmed the [previous] messengers.﴿ *(Qur'an 37: 33-37)*

﴿ وَكَذَٰلِكَ مَآ أَرْسَلْنَا مِن قَبْلِكَ فِى قَرْيَةٍ مِّن نَّذِيرٍ إِلَّا قَالَ مُتْرَفُوهَآ إِنَّا وَجَدْنَآ ءَابَآءَنَا عَلَىٰٓ
أُمَّةٍ وَإِنَّا عَلَىٰٓ ءَاثَٰرِهِم مُّقْتَدُونَ ﴿٢٣﴾ ۞ قَٰلَ أَوَلَوْ جِئْتُكُم بِأَهْدَىٰ مِمَّا وَجَدتُّمْ عَلَيْهِ
ءَابَآءَكُمْ ۖ قَالُوٓا۟ إِنَّا بِمَآ أُرْسِلْتُم بِهِۦ كَٰفِرُونَ ﴿٢٤﴾ فَٱنتَقَمْنَا مِنْهُمْ ۖ فَٱنظُرْ كَيْفَ كَانَ عَٰقِبَةُ
ٱلْمُكَذِّبِينَ ﴿٢٥﴾ ﴾ (سورة الزُّخرُف: ٢٣-٢٥)

﴾And similarly, We did not send before you any warner into a city except that its affluent said: Indeed, we found our fathers upon a religion and we are following in their footsteps. [Each warner] said:

Even if I brought you better guidance than that [religion] upon which you found your fathers? They said: Indeed we, in that with which you were sent, are disbelievers. So we took retribution from them; then see how was the end of the deniers.﴾ *(Qur'an 43: 23-25)*

﴿ٱلَّذِينَ كَفَرُوا۟ وَصَدُّوا۟ عَن سَبِيلِ ٱللَّهِ أَضَلَّ أَعْمَـٰلَهُمْ ۝١ وَٱلَّذِينَ ءَامَنُوا۟ وَعَمِلُوا۟ ٱلصَّـٰلِحَـٰتِ
وَءَامَنُوا۟ بِمَا نُزِّلَ عَلَىٰ مُحَمَّدٍ وَهُوَ ٱلْحَقُّ مِن رَّبِّهِمْ ۙ كَفَّرَ عَنْهُمْ سَيِّـَٔاتِهِمْ وَأَصْلَحَ بَالَهُمْ ۝٢ ذَٰلِكَ
بِأَنَّ ٱلَّذِينَ كَفَرُوا۟ ٱتَّبَعُوا۟ ٱلْبَـٰطِلَ وَأَنَّ ٱلَّذِينَ ءَامَنُوا۟ ٱتَّبَعُوا۟ ٱلْحَقَّ مِن رَّبِّهِمْ ۚ كَذَٰلِكَ يَضْرِبُ ٱللَّهُ لِلنَّاسِ
أَمْثَـٰلَهُمْ ۝٣﴾ (سورة محمد: ١-٣)

﴾Those who disbelieve and avert [people] from the way of Allah — He will waste their deeds. And those who believe and do righteous deeds and believe in what has been sent down upon Muhammad — and it is the truth from their Lord — He will remove from them their misdeeds and amend their condition. That is because those who disbelieve follow falsehood, and those who believe follow the truth from their Lord. Thus does Allah present to the people their comparisons.﴾ *(Qur'an 47: 1-3)*

Condemning all forms of falsehood

Acceptance is the fifth condition of the shahâdah; it stipulates the acceptance of Allah alone as one's Lord and of all that emanates from Him: His prophets, His messengers, and His guidance. An essential corollary to acceptance is the renunciation of all types of falsehood. In essence, acceptance necessitates compliance with the Qur'an and the Sunnah as a whole. In other words, one cannot selectively obey certain religious regulations and reject others as per one's whim. Simultaneously, one must repulse and repudiate disbelief, associating partners with Allah, and hypocrisy, as these are fabrications and lies.

The implication of acceptance, the fifth condition of the shahâdah, is that Muslims cannot have double standards; they cannot choose to condemn certain types of falsehood and sanction others. For example, sometimes when the weak, the poor, or the elderly commit the shirk of worshipping the graves of righteous scholars, they are condemned by others instantly. On the other hand, those who have power, wealth, weapons, influence, and so forth and are even guiltier of associating partners with Allah are not censured by the public at all; rather, they themselves are feared. One has to remember that Allah alone deserves to be feared:

﴿... فَلَا تَخَافُوهُمْ وَخَافُونِ إِن كُنتُم مُّؤْمِنِينَ ﴿١٧٥﴾﴾ (سورة آل عمران: ١٧٥)

﴿...So fear them not, but fear Me, if you are [indeed] believers.﴾ *(Qur'an 3: 175)*

Thus, acceptance means not only to acknowledge the ultimate truth, Islam, but also to stand firm, undaunted, and fearless in the face of all falsehood.

> Indeed, the Prophet (ﷺ) said: «The best (form) of jihad is a just word in the presence of a tyrannical ruler.» (Abu Dâwood; a sound hadith according to al-Albâni)[60]

Sa'eed ibn Jubayr's implementation of the fifth condition

Sa'eed ibn Jubayr was one of the famous *tâbi'oon* (those who knew or met any of the Companions and transmitted hadiths from them). He lived during the time of Ḥajjâj ibn Yoosuf, the notorious bloodshedder.

Ḥajjâj's rule of harshness and tyranny is well known in human history. However, the rulers in those days, despite their shortcomings, never lagged behind in propagating Islam and waging jihad

---

60 As quoted in Abu Ameenah Bilal Philips, *The Best in Islam* (Sharjah: Dar Al Fatah Printing, Publishing & Distribution Co., 1996), 51.

against the enemies of Islam and Muslims. Nevertheless, we consider them to be among the worst of rulers when compared to the just and God-fearing rulers such as Abu Bakr, 'Umar, 'Uthmân, 'Ali, and 'Umar ibn 'Abdul-'Azeez.

Ḥajjâj was the viceroy of the caliph and king, 'Abdul-Malik ibn Marwân, for the Hijaz and Iraq. The king lived in Damascus, and Ḥajjâj had his headquarters in Kufa.

Sa'eed ibn Jubayr had fought against Ḥajjâj and taken the side of the opposition. After being defeated, Sa'eed ran away and took asylum in Makkah. The government posted a very stern individual as the governor of Makkah with instructions to arrest him. The governor assembled all the people of Makkah and read before them the order of 'Abdul-Malik ibn Marwân, which warned that anyone who gave shelter to Sa'eed ibn Jubayr would meet the same fate as Sa'eed himself. He then announced to the people:

> By Allah, I must kill the person who gives shelter to Sa'eed ibn Jubayr. His and his neighbours' houses shall be razed to the ground.

Yet, even in the face of all these threats, it was with great difficulty that Sa'eed ibn Jubayr was arrested and sent to Kufa. There, he was taken before Ḥajjâj ibn Yoosuf and the following conversation ensued:

Ḥajjâj: What is your name?

Sa'eed: My name is Sa'eed (*lit.* auspicious, happy).

Ḥajjâj: What is your father's name?

Sa'eed: Jubayr (*lit.* trimmed).

Ḥajjâj: No! You are, in fact, a wretched son of Kusayr (*lit.* a broken thing).

Sa'eed: My mother knew my name better than you.

Ḥajjâj: You are wretched and your mother is also wretched.

Sa'eed: The Knower of the unseen is someone else.

Ḥajjâj: Look! I am putting you to the sword.

Sa'eed: Then my mother was right in giving me this name.

Ḥajjâj: I shall send you to hell.

Sa'eed: If I was sure that you had that power, I would have taken you as my God.

Ḥajjâj: What is your belief about the Prophet (ﷺ)?

Sa'eed: He was a Messenger of mercy and a Prophet of Allah, sent with the best guidance for the whole creation.

Ḥajjâj: What do you say about the (Rightly-Guided) Caliphs?

Sa'eed: I am not a warden over them. Everybody is responsible for his own actions.

Ḥajjâj: Who is the most exalted of the four Caliphs?

Sa'eed: The one who has been able to please Allah more than the rest.

Ḥajjâj: Which of them had been able to please Allah more than the rest?

Sa'eed: This is known to Him Who knows what is hidden in the bosoms and what the hearts conceal.

Ḥajjâj: Is 'Ali in paradise or in hell?

Sa'eed: I can answer only when I visit the two places and meet their dwellers.

Ḥajjâj: How shall I fare on the Day of Judgement?

Sa'eed: I am not fit to receive the knowledge of the unseen.

Ḥajjâj: You do not intend to tell me the truth.

Sa'eed: I did not tell a lie either.

Ḥajjâj: Why do you never laugh?

Sa'eed: I do not see anything to laugh at and indeed, why should the one who is created from dust, has to appear on the Day of Judgement, and is always surrounded with tribulations laugh?

Ḥajjâj: I laugh.

Sa'eed: Allah has created us with different temperaments.

Ḥajjâj: I am now going to kill you.

Sa'eed: The time and mode of my death has already been decreed.

Ḥajjâj: Allah has preferred me over you.

Sa'eed: Nobody can be proud of his relation with Allah, unless he knows his position; only Allah is the Knower of the unseen.

Ḥajjâj: Why should I not be proud of my relation with Allah, when I am with the leader of the believers and you are with the rebels?

Sa'eed: I am with the other Muslims. I myself shun mischief, but nobody can change the decree of Allah.

Ḥajjâj: What do you say about what we collect for the leader of the believers?

Sa'eed: I do not know what you collect for him.

Ḥajjâj sent for gold, silver, and dresses from the state treasury and showed these to Sa'eed.

Sa'eed: These are useful, provided you are able to obtain with them the things that may provide you peace on the day when every nursing mother will forget her nursling and every pregnant one will deliver her burden and when nothing but good will be of any avail.

Ḥajjâj: Are our collections not good?

Sa'eed: You have collected them and you are the best judge.

Ḥajjâj: Would you like any of these things for yourself?

Sa'eed: I only like the things which Allah likes.

Ḥajjâj: Woe to you!

Sa'eed: Woe is for the person who is deprived of paradise and forced to enter hell.

Ḥajjâj (annoyed): Say, how should I kill you?

Sa'eed: As you would like to be killed.

Ḥajjâj: Should I forgive you?

Sa'eed: Allah's forgiveness is real. Your forgiveness is of no value.

Ḥajjâj (to the executioner): Kill this man.

Sa'eed laughed as he was taken for execution. Ḥajjâj was informed of this. He called him back.

Ḥajjâj: What made you laugh?

Sa'eed: Your audacity with Allah and His clemency to you.

Ḥajjâj: I am killing a person who has caused dissent among Muslims. (To the executioner:) Kill him in front of me.

Sa'eed: Let me say a prayer of two units. (After finishing his prayer, still facing the qibla, he recited:)

﴿إِنِّي وَجَّهْتُ وَجْهِيَ لِلَّذِي فَطَرَ السَّمَاوَاتِ وَالْأَرْضَ حَنِيفًا وَمَا أَنَا مِنَ الْمُشْرِكِينَ ﴿٧٩﴾﴾ (سورة الأنعام: ٧٩)

﴾Indeed, I have turned my face toward He who created the heavens and the earth, inclining toward truth, and I am not of those who associate others with Allah.﴿ *(Qur'an 6: 79)*

Ḥajjâj: Turn him away from our qibla and let him face the qibla of the Christians, who have also caused dissension and dispute among their community. (His face was immediately turned to the other direction.)

Sa'eed: Allah has said:

﴿وَلِلَّهِ الْمَشْرِقُ وَالْمَغْرِبُ ۚ فَأَيْنَمَا تُوَلُّوا فَثَمَّ وَجْهُ اللَّهِ ۚ إِنَّ اللَّهَ وَاسِعٌ عَلِيمٌ ﴿١١٥﴾﴾

(سورة البقرة: ١١٥)

﴾And to Allah belongs the east and the west. So wherever you [might] turn, there is the Face of Allah. Indeed, Allah is All-Encompassing and Knowing.﴿ *(Qur'an 2: 115)*

Ḥajjâj: Make him lie on his face. We are only responsible for appearance.

Sa'eed was made to lie on his face and he said:

﴿ ۞ مِنۡهَا خَلَقۡنَٰكُمۡ وَفِيهَا نُعِيدُكُمۡ وَمِنۡهَا نُخۡرِجُكُمۡ تَارَةً أُخۡرَىٰ ﴿٥٥﴾ ﴾ (سورة طه: ٥٥)

﴾From it [the earth] We created you, and into it We will return you, and from it We will extract you another time.﴿ *(Qur'an 20: 55)*

Ḥajjâj: Kill him.

Sa'eed: I call you to witness what I recite:

I bear witness that there is no god worthy of worship except Allah alone, who has no associates, and I bear witness that Muhammad (ﷺ) is his servant and Messenger.

He was beheaded — indeed, to Allah we belong and to Him is our return. After the execution, blood gushed out from Sa'eed ibn Jubayr's body. Ḥajjâj ibn Yoosuf himself marvelled at it. He inquired from his doctors about the reason for the overflow of blood; they said that his tranquillity and composure at the time of death had kept his blood in its original form. Generally, people who are going to be executed are so scared and afraid of death that their blood curdles and does not flow profusely.

Allah has mentioned such examples of steadfastness in the face of tyranny in the following verses:

﴿إِنَّ ٱلَّذِينَ قَالُواْ رَبُّنَا ٱللَّهُ ثُمَّ ٱسۡتَقَٰمُواْ تَتَنَزَّلُ عَلَيۡهِمُ ٱلۡمَلَٰٓئِكَةُ أَلَّا تَخَافُواْ وَلَا تَحۡزَنُواْ وَأَبۡشِرُواْ بِٱلۡجَنَّةِ ٱلَّتِي كُنتُمۡ تُوعَدُونَ ﴿٣٠﴾ نَحۡنُ أَوۡلِيَآؤُكُمۡ فِي ٱلۡحَيَوٰةِ ٱلدُّنۡيَا وَفِي ٱلۡأٓخِرَةِۖ وَلَكُمۡ فِيهَا مَا تَشۡتَهِيٓ أَنفُسُكُمۡ وَلَكُمۡ فِيهَا مَا تَدَّعُونَ ﴿٣١﴾ نُزُلًا مِّنۡ غَفُورٖ رَّحِيمٖ ﴿٣٢﴾ ﴾ (سورة فُصِّلَت: ٣٠-٣٢)

﴾Indeed, those who have said: Our Lord is Allah, and then remained on a right course — the angels will descend upon them, [saying]: Do not fear and do not grieve but receive good tidings of paradise, which you were promised. We [angels] were your allies in worldly life and [are so] in the hereafter. You will have therein whatever your souls desire, and you will have therein whatever you request [or wish] as accommodation from a [Lord who is] Forgiving and Merciful.﴿ *(Qur'an 41: 30-32)*

The polytheists of Makkah knew the implications of the *shahâdah*

As mentioned previously, achievement of the fifth condition is bilateral. This requires the acceptance of Islam on unconditional terms, with the concurrent rejection of all types and forms of falsehoods. Therefore, it becomes incumbent on the believers to act upon whatever Allah has commanded, while abandoning whatever He has prohibited. The polytheists of Makkah clearly understood the implications of the shahâdah, for when Allah's Messenger (ﷺ) called them to affirm it, their answer was:

﴿ أَجَعَلَ الْآلِهَةَ إِلَٰهًا وَاحِدًا ۖ إِنَّ هَٰذَا لَشَيْءٌ عُجَابٌ ﴿٥﴾ ﴾ (سورة ص: ٥)

﴾Has he made the gods [only] one God? Indeed, this is a curious thing.﴿ *(Qur'an 38: 5)*

Clarifying the real impact of the shahâdah, Imam Ibn Rajab (may Allah rest his soul) states:

> To explain this meaning and to clarify it: When a person says 'lâ ilâha illâ Allâh', it means, according to him, that none has the right to be deified and worshipped except Allah. Al-ilâh is the One Who is obeyed and not disobeyed, due to [one's] awe and veneration of Him, due to [one's] love, fear, hope and reliance upon Him, as well as being the One Who is asked from and is supplicated to. None of this is applicable except to Allah the Mighty and the Majestic.[61]

[61] Ibn Rajab, *Kalimatul-Ikhlâṣ*, 25.

The hostility of the polytheistic disbelievers among the Quraysh, aroused by Prophet Muhammad's mission, stemmed primarily from the fact that they were unwilling to abandon the worship of their idols and restrict worship to Allah alone. The idols in the Kaaba were central to their social practices as well as a major source of their economic prosperity and prestige. Acceptance of Islam signified a cut at the root of all types and forms of their pre-Islamic practices. It also meant that they could no longer bury female infants alive, discriminate against women, drink alcohol, conduct unfair business transactions, or indulge in usury, fornication, or adultery. They could neither circumambulate naked around the Kaaba nor wage tribal wars and vendettas, as Islam denounced indecency and notions of tribal superiority. In short, embracing Islam necessitated a revolutionary change in their social, moral, economic, and political systems; this was an objectionable and completely unacceptable outlook for the leaders of the Quraysh.

For this reason, 'lâ ilâha illâ Allâh' is a radical concept in terms of its implications. Not only does it signify that Allah alone should be singled out for worship, but that the worship of all other deities should be abandoned. Worship is a very comprehensive word that encompasses speech, actions, intentions, and emotions, all of which are undertaken solely for Allah's sake, to please Him and earn His rewards. Since no act of a human being is excluded from the laws of Allah, the proclamation of 'lâ ilâha illâ Allâh' effectively liberates one from the subservience of all false gods as well as ideologies such as democracy, capitalism, tribalism, nationalism, and all other '-isms' and schisms. One's complete and total allegiance is to Allah.

Clearly, acceptance — the fifth condition of the shahâdah — implies an absolute commitment to the Qur'an and the Sunnah. Furthermore, since acceptance also compels the rejection of all other deities, creeds, and systems, it becomes incumbent upon true believers to stand up for their beliefs. What this means is that there will invariably be conflict between the believers and those in authority when the latter defy Allah's guidance. In reality, adherence to this prerequisite of the shahâdah demands exceptional courage in the face of tyranny and oppression. Parables in the Qur'an and stories from the Sunnah mention several examples of steadfastness and fortitude on the part of individuals and earlier prophets against cruelty and repression.

The King of Yemen and the Pharaoh slaughtered the believers

The following verses from the Qur'an refer to the story of the brutality of the King of Yemen against those who rejected him as a false deity and chose to worship the one true God — Allah.

﴿وَالسَّمَاءِ ذَاتِ الْبُرُوجِ ﴿١﴾ وَالْيَوْمِ الْمَوْعُودِ ﴿٢﴾ وَشَاهِدٍ وَمَشْهُودٍ ﴿٣﴾ قُتِلَ أَصْحَابُ الْأُخْدُودِ
﴿٤﴾ النَّارِ ذَاتِ الْوَقُودِ ﴿٥﴾ إِذْ هُمْ عَلَيْهَا قُعُودٌ ﴿٦﴾ وَهُمْ عَلَىٰ مَا يَفْعَلُونَ بِالْمُؤْمِنِينَ شُهُودٌ
﴿٧﴾ وَمَا نَقَمُوا مِنْهُمْ إِلَّا أَن يُؤْمِنُوا بِاللَّهِ الْعَزِيزِ الْحَمِيدِ ﴿٨﴾ الَّذِي لَهُ مُلْكُ السَّمَاوَاتِ
وَالْأَرْضِ ۚ وَاللَّهُ عَلَىٰ كُلِّ شَيْءٍ شَهِيدٌ ﴿٩﴾ إِنَّ الَّذِينَ فَتَنُوا الْمُؤْمِنِينَ وَالْمُؤْمِنَاتِ ثُمَّ لَمْ يَتُوبُوا
فَلَهُمْ عَذَابُ جَهَنَّمَ وَلَهُمْ عَذَابُ الْحَرِيقِ ﴿١٠﴾ إِنَّ الَّذِينَ آمَنُوا وَعَمِلُوا الصَّالِحَاتِ لَهُمْ
جَنَّاتٌ تَجْرِي مِن تَحْتِهَا الْأَنْهَارُ ۚ ذَٰلِكَ الْفَوْزُ الْكَبِيرُ ﴿١١﴾﴾ (سورة البروج: ١-١١)

﴿By the sky containing great stars, and [by] the promised day, and [by] the witness and what is witnessed, cursed were the companions of the trench [containing] the fire full of fuel, when they were sitting near it. They were witnesses to what they were doing against the believers, and they only resented them because they believed in Allah, the Exalted in Might, the Praiseworthy, to whom belongs the dominion of the heavens and the earth. And

Allah, over all things, is Witness. Indeed, those who have tortured the believing men and believing women and then have not repented will have the punishment of hell, and they will have the punishment of the burning fire. Indeed, those who have believed and done righteous deeds will have gardens beneath which rivers flow. That is the great attainment.› *(Qur'an 85: 1-11)*

The background of the story associated with these verses has been narrated in a hadith recorded by Imam Muslim in his collection; it is titled, "The story of the people of the ditch, the magician, the monk, and the slave."

> Ṣuhayb (رضي الله عنه) reported that Allah's Messenger (ﷺ) said:
>
> «There lived a king before your time, and he had a court magician. As the magician grew old, he said to the king: I have grown old; send some young boy to me so that I can teach him magic. The king sent to him a young boy to be trained as a magician.
>
> On his way to the magician, the young boy encountered a monk, who befriended him and taught him the concept of the Oneness of Allah. The boy listened to the monk's talk and was impressed by it. It became his habit to stop by and converse with the monk on his way to the magician. Since this made him late for his lesson in magic, the magician beat him. The boy complained to the monk, who advised him: When you feel afraid of the magician, say: Members of my family detained me. When you feel afraid of your family, say: The magician detained me.
>
> It so happened that there came a huge beast of prey and it blocked the way of the people. The young boy thought: I will come to know today whether the magician is superior or the monk is superior. He picked up a stone and said: O Allah, if the affair of the monk is dearer to you than the affair of the magician, cause this animal to die so that the people are able to move about freely.

He threw that stone towards the beast and it killed it; thus, people began to move about freely. The young boy then came to the monk and informed him of what he had done.

The monk said: O my son! Today, you are my superior. Your affair has come to a stage where I conjecture that you will soon be put to a trial. In case you are put to a trial, do not give any clue of my influence on you.

As the young boy's faith in Allah grew stronger, he became the means to treat the blind and those suffering from leprosy; in fact, he began to cure people from all kinds of illnesses.

A companion of the king, who had gone blind, heard about him and came to him with numerous gifts, saying: If you cure me, all these gifts will be yours.

The boy replied: I myself do not cure anyone. It is Allah who cures, so if you affirm faith in Allah, I shall also supplicate to Him to cure you.

The king's courtier affirmed his faith in Allah and was cured. When the king saw that his companion's affliction was cured, he asked: Who restored your eyesight?

The man replied: My Lord!

The king responded: Am I not your Lord, or do you have another Lord besides me?

The man replied: My Lord and your Lord is Allah!

The king seized him and tormented him until he revealed the boy's identity. The young man was summoned and the king said to him: Young man, it has been conveyed to me that you have become so proficient in your magic that you cure the blind and those suffering from diseases such as leprosy and leucoderma,[62] and you do such-and-such things.

---

[62] Leucoderma, or vitiligo, is a skin disease, incurable by modern medicine, characterized by white or light patches on the skin. [Editor]

The young boy said: I do not cure anyone; it is Allah Who cures.

The king seized him and began to torment him. Hence, he had no choice but to reveal the source of his guidance: the monk. The monk was summoned and it was said to him: You should turn back from your religion.

When he refused to do so, the king ordered that his head be hacked into two. Then the courtier of the king was brought forward and it was said to him: Turn back from your religion. When he, too, refused to do so, his head was cut into two pieces. Then the young boy was brought and it was said to him: Turn back from your religion. He refused to do so, and he was handed over to a group of the king's courtiers.

The king ordered his men: Take him to such-and-such mountain and make him climb it. When he reaches its top, if he continues to defy my order to renounce his faith, throw him off the peak of the mountain. Thus, they took him and made him climb the mountain.

He said: O Allah, save me from them (in any way) you like. The mountain began to quake, and they all fell down. The young man came walking back to the king.

The king asked: What has happened to your companions?

He replied: Allah has saved me from them.

He was again handed over to courtiers of the king, who were ordered: Take him and carry him in a small boat; when you reach the middle of the ocean, if he still refuses to renounce his religion, throw him into the sea.

They took him into the middle of the sea, and he supplicated: O Allah, save me from them and what they want to do.

Soon the boat turned over and the courtiers were drowned; the boy returned, safe and sound, to the king, who asked: What has happened to your companions?

Again, the boy replied: Allah has saved me from them.

The young boy said to the king: You cannot kill me until you do what I ask you to do.

The king enquired: What is that?

He answered: You should gather the people on a plain and fasten me to the trunk of a tree. Then take an arrow from the quiver and say: In the name of Allah, the Lord of this young man. Then shoot the arrow. If you do that in the name of Allah, you will be able to kill me.

The king did as the young boy had proposed. After tying the young boy to the tree, with the people gathered as his audience, he placed the arrow in the bow, saying: In the name of Allah, the Lord of the young boy. He shot the arrow and it hit the temporal region of the skull of the boy, who placed his hands where the arrow had pierced him and died.

The people, having witnessed the effect of the faith in the young boy's heart, all proclaimed: We affirm our faith in the Lord of this young man! Yes, we affirm our faith in the Lord of this young man. For a third time we repeat: we affirm our faith in the Lord of this young man!

The courtiers came to the king and said to him: Do you see that Allah has actually done what you aimed at averting? People have attested to their faith in Allah.

Upon hearing this, the king ordered ditches to be dug along important points in the path. When these ditches were dug, fires were lit in them. People were asked to reject their faith in the young boy's religion. If they refused, they would be consigned to the fires. However, people chose death by jumping into the fire rather than abandoning their belief in Allah. Indeed, there was no dithering or uncertainty, for the people were truly steadfast of faith, except for a woman with her young child. When she hesitated before jumping into the fire, the child said to her: O mother, endure (this ordeal), for you are on the truth. Thus, she threw herself into the ditch of fire along with her child to join the ranks of martyrs in paradise.» (Muslim)

Thus, despite the unspeakable torture of being burnt alive, the true believers upheld their commitment to 'lâ ilâha illâ Allâh' — the shahâdah.

Another significant example is the story of the Pharaoh ruling Egypt during the time of Prophet Moses (عليه السلام). The Pharaoh instigated a public contest between his court magicians and Moses, intending to refute the latter's belief in the one true God. Allah has very vividly portrayed this incident in the Qur'an:

﴿وَقَالَ مُوسَىٰ يَٰفِرۡعَوۡنُ إِنِّي رَسُولٞ مِّن رَّبِّ ٱلۡعَٰلَمِينَ (١٠٤) حَقِيقٌ عَلَىٰٓ أَن لَّآ أَقُولَ
عَلَى ٱللَّهِ إِلَّا ٱلۡحَقَّۚ قَدۡ جِئۡتُكُم بِبَيِّنَةٖ مِّن رَّبِّكُمۡ فَأَرۡسِلۡ مَعِيَ بَنِيٓ إِسۡرَٰٓءِيلَ
(١٠٥) قَالَ إِن كُنتَ جِئۡتَ بِـَٔايَةٖ فَأۡتِ بِهَآ إِن كُنتَ مِنَ ٱلصَّٰدِقِينَ (١٠٦) فَأَلۡقَىٰ
عَصَاهُ فَإِذَا هِيَ ثُعۡبَانٞ مُّبِينٞ (١٠٧) وَنَزَعَ يَدَهُۥ فَإِذَا هِيَ بَيۡضَآءُ لِلنَّٰظِرِينَ (١٠٨) قَالَ
ٱلۡمَلَأُ مِن قَوۡمِ فِرۡعَوۡنَ إِنَّ هَٰذَا لَسَٰحِرٌ عَلِيمٞ (١٠٩) يُرِيدُ أَن يُخۡرِجَكُم مِّنۡ أَرۡضِكُمۡۖ
فَمَاذَا تَأۡمُرُونَ (١١٠) قَالُوٓاْ أَرۡجِهۡ وَأَخَاهُ وَأَرۡسِلۡ فِي ٱلۡمَدَآئِنِ حَٰشِرِينَ (١١١) يَأۡتُوكَ
بِكُلِّ سَٰحِرٍ عَلِيمٖ (١١٢) وَجَآءَ ٱلسَّحَرَةُ فِرۡعَوۡنَ قَالُوٓاْ إِنَّ لَنَا لَأَجۡرًا إِن كُنَّا
نَحۡنُ ٱلۡغَٰلِبِينَ (١١٣) قَالَ نَعَمۡ وَإِنَّكُمۡ لَمِنَ ٱلۡمُقَرَّبِينَ (١١٤) قَالُواْ يَٰمُوسَىٰٓ إِمَّآ
أَن تُلۡقِيَ وَإِمَّآ أَن نَّكُونَ نَحۡنُ ٱلۡمُلۡقِينَ (١١٥) قَالَ أَلۡقُواْۖ فَلَمَّآ أَلۡقَوۡاْ سَحَرُوٓاْ
أَعۡيُنَ ٱلنَّاسِ وَٱسۡتَرۡهَبُوهُمۡ وَجَآءُو بِسِحۡرٍ عَظِيمٖ (١١٦) ۞ وَأَوۡحَيۡنَآ إِلَىٰ مُوسَىٰٓ
أَنۡ أَلۡقِ عَصَاكَۖ فَإِذَا هِيَ تَلۡقَفُ مَا يَأۡفِكُونَ (١١٧) فَوَقَعَ ٱلۡحَقُّ وَبَطَلَ مَا كَانُواْ يَعۡمَلُونَ
(١١٨) فَغُلِبُواْ هُنَالِكَ وَٱنقَلَبُواْ صَٰغِرِينَ (١١٩) وَأُلۡقِيَ ٱلسَّحَرَةُ سَٰجِدِينَ (١٢٠) قَالُوٓاْ ءَامَنَّا
بِرَبِّ ٱلۡعَٰلَمِينَ (١٢١) رَبِّ مُوسَىٰ وَهَٰرُونَ (١٢٢) قَالَ فِرۡعَوۡنُ ءَامَنتُم بِهِۦ قَبۡلَ أَنۡ ءَاذَنَ لَكُمۡۖ

إِنَّ هَٰذَا لَمَكْرٌ مَّكَرْتُمُوهُ فِي ٱلْمَدِينَةِ لِتُخْرِجُوا۟ مِنْهَآ أَهْلَهَا ۖ فَسَوْفَ تَعْلَمُونَ ﴿١٢٣﴾ لَأُقَطِّعَنَّ
أَيْدِيَكُمْ وَأَرْجُلَكُم مِّنْ خِلَٰفٍ ثُمَّ لَأُصَلِّبَنَّكُمْ أَجْمَعِينَ ﴿١٢٤﴾ قَالُوٓا۟ إِنَّآ إِلَىٰ رَبِّنَا مُنقَلِبُونَ
﴿١٢٥﴾ وَمَا تَنقِمُ مِنَّآ إِلَّآ أَنْ ءَامَنَّا بِـَٔايَٰتِ رَبِّنَا لَمَّا جَآءَتْنَا ۚ رَبَّنَآ أَفْرِغْ عَلَيْنَا صَبْرًا وَتَوَفَّنَا
مُسْلِمِينَ ﴿١٢٦﴾ وَقَالَ ٱلْمَلَأُ مِن قَوْمِ فِرْعَوْنَ أَتَذَرُ مُوسَىٰ وَقَوْمَهُۥ لِيُفْسِدُوا۟ فِي ٱلْأَرْضِ
وَيَذَرَكَ وَءَالِهَتَكَ ۚ قَالَ سَنُقَتِّلُ أَبْنَآءَهُمْ وَنَسْتَحْيِۦ نِسَآءَهُمْ وَإِنَّا فَوْقَهُمْ قَٰهِرُونَ
﴿١٢٧﴾ قَالَ مُوسَىٰ لِقَوْمِهِ ٱسْتَعِينُوا۟ بِٱللَّهِ وَٱصْبِرُوٓا۟ ۖ إِنَّ ٱلْأَرْضَ لِلَّهِ يُورِثُهَا مَن
يَشَآءُ مِنْ عِبَادِهِۦ ۖ وَٱلْعَٰقِبَةُ لِلْمُتَّقِينَ ﴿١٢٨﴾ (سورة الأعراف: ١٠٤-١٢٨)

﴿And Moses said: O Pharaoh, I am a messenger from the Lord of the worlds [who is] obligated to say nothing about Allah except the truth. I have come to you with clear evidence from your Lord, so send with me the Children of Israel. [Pharaoh] said: If you have come with a sign, then bring it forth, if you should be of the truthful. So Moses threw his staff, and suddenly it was a serpent, manifest. He drew out his hand; thereupon it was white [with radiance] for the observers. Said the eminent among the people of Pharaoh: Indeed, this is a learned magician who wants to expel you from your land [through magic], so what do you instruct? They said: Postpone [the matter of] him and his brother and send among the cities gatherers — who will bring you every learned magician. The magicians came to Pharaoh and said: Indeed for us is a reward if we are the predominant. He said: Yes, and [moreover] you will be among those made near [to me]. They said: O Moses, either you throw [your staff], or we will be the ones to throw [first]. He said: Throw. When they threw, they bewitched the eyes of the people and struck terror into them, and they presented a great [feat of] magic. We inspired to Moses: Throw your staff. At once it devoured what they were falsifying. So the truth was established, and abolished was what they were doing. Pharaoh and his people were overcome right there and became debased, and the magicians fell down in prostration [to Allah]. They said: We have believed in the Lord of the worlds, the Lord of Moses and Aaron. Said Pharaoh: You believed in him before I gave you permission. Indeed, this is a conspiracy which you conspired in the city to expel therefrom its people. But you are going to know. I will surely cut off your hands and your feet on opposite sides; then I will surely crucify you all. They said: Indeed, to our Lord we will return. You only resent us because we believed in the signs of our Lord when they came to us. Our Lord, pour upon us patience and let us die as Muslims [in submission to You]. The eminent among the people of Pharaoh said: Will you leave Moses and his people to cause corruption in the land and abandon you and your gods? [Pharaoh] said: We will kill their sons and keep their women alive; indeed, we are subjugators over them. Said Moses to his people: Seek help through Allah and be patient. Indeed, the earth belongs to Allah. He causes to inherit it whom He wills of His servants, and the [best] outcome is for the righteous.》 *(Qur'an 7: 104-128)*

Believers at all times have upheld their faith as a requirement of acceptance — the fifth condition of the shahâdah. They have suffered at the hands of tyrants, as exemplified in the narratives of the king in Yemen and the Pharaoh in Egypt. Their allegiance to Allah, and their absolute and total commitment to His laws and commands, imbued them with the fortitude and endurance necessary to withstand all the trials and tribulations meted out by their cruel oppressors. Indeed, theirs will be the final and eternal victory, as per Allah's promise to the God-fearing, the patient, and the steadfast.

Chapter Ten

The Sixth Condition: Sincerity

The sixth condition of the shahâdah is sincerity and devotion that negates shirk. Consider the following verses and hadiths:

﴿قُلْ إِنَّ صَلَاتِي وَنُسُكِي وَمَحْيَايَ وَمَمَاتِي لِلَّهِ رَبِّ الْعَالَمِينَ ﴿١٦٢﴾ لَا شَرِيكَ لَهُ ۖ وَبِذَٰلِكَ أُمِرْتُ وَأَنَا أَوَّلُ الْمُسْلِمِينَ ﴿١٦٣﴾ قُلْ أَغَيْرَ اللَّهِ أَبْغِي رَبًّا وَهُوَ رَبُّ كُلِّ شَيْءٍ ۚ وَلَا تَكْسِبُ كُلُّ نَفْسٍ إِلَّا عَلَيْهَا ۚ وَلَا تَزِرُ وَازِرَةٌ وِزْرَ أُخْرَىٰ ۚ ثُمَّ إِلَىٰ رَبِّكُم مَّرْجِعُكُمْ فَيُنَبِّئُكُم بِمَا كُنتُمْ فِيهِ تَخْتَلِفُونَ ﴿١٦٤﴾﴾ (سورة الأنعام: ١٦٢-١٦٤)

﴾Say: Indeed, my prayer, my rites of sacrifice, my living and my dying are for Allah, Lord of the worlds. No partner has He. This I have been commanded, and I am the first [among you] of the Muslims. Say: Is it other than Allah I should desire as a lord, while He is the Lord of all things? Every soul earns not [blame] except against itself, and no bearer of burdens will bear the burden of another. Then to your Lord is your return, and He will inform you concerning that over which you used to differ.﴿ *(Qur'an 6: 162-164)*

﴿أَلَا لِلَّهِ الدِّينُ الْخَالِصُ ۚ وَالَّذِينَ اتَّخَذُوا مِن دُونِهِ أَوْلِيَاءَ مَا نَعْبُدُهُمْ إِلَّا لِيُقَرِّبُونَا إِلَى اللَّهِ زُلْفَىٰ إِنَّ اللَّهَ يَحْكُمُ بَيْنَهُمْ فِي مَا هُمْ فِيهِ يَخْتَلِفُونَ ۗ إِنَّ اللَّهَ لَا يَهْدِي مَنْ هُوَ كَاذِبٌ كَفَّارٌ ﴿٣﴾﴾ (سورة الزُّمَر: ٣)

﴿Unquestionably, for Allah is the pure religion. Those who take protectors besides Him [say]: We only worship them that they may bring us nearer to Allah in position. Indeed, Allah will judge between them concerning that over which they differ. Indeed, Allah does not guide one who is a liar and [confirmed] disbeliever.﴾

(Qur'an 39: 3)

﴿وَمَآ أُمِرُوٓاْ إِلَّا لِيَعْبُدُواْ ٱللَّهَ مُخْلِصِينَ لَهُ ٱلدِّينَ حُنَفَآءَ وَيُقِيمُواْ ٱلصَّلَوٰةَ وَيُؤْتُواْ ٱلزَّكَوٰةَ وَذَٰلِكَ دِينُ ٱلْقَيِّمَةِ ۝٥﴾ (سورة البيّنة: ٥)

﴿And they were not commanded except to worship Allah, [being] sincere to Him in religion, inclining to truth, and to establish and prayer and to give zakâh. And that is the correct religion.﴾

(Qur'an 98: 5)

«Abu Hurayrah (رضي الله عنه) narrated that he asked: O Allah's Messenger! Who will be the happiest person to gain your intercession on the Day of Resurrection?

Allah's Messenger (ﷺ) replied: O Abu Hurayrah! I knew none would ask me about this before you, because I have witnessed your eagerness for the (learning of) Hadith. The happiest person who will have my intercession on the Day of Resurrection will be the one who proclaimed sincerely from the bottom of his heart: None has the right to be worshipped except Allah.» (Bukhari)

«Abu Hurayrah (رضي الله عنه) reported that the Prophet said: Whoever says: *Lâ ilâha illâ Allâhu waḥdahu lâ shareeka lahu, lahul-mulku wa lahul-ḥamdu, wa huwa 'alâ kulli shay'in qadeer* (There is no God but Allah, alone, without partner. His is the sovereignty and His is the praise, and He has power over everything) one hundred times a day will have a reward equivalent to the reward for freeing ten slaves. In addition, one hundred good deeds will be recorded for him and one hundred bad deeds will be wiped off; it will be a safeguard for him from Satan that day until evening, and no one will be better in deeds than this person except the one who does more than that.» (Bukhari, Muslim, at-Tirmidhi, an-Nasâ'i, and Ibn Mâjah)

The aforementioned verses and hadiths emphasize the importance of sincerity and honesty in worship and devotion. Moreover, they clarify the virtues of this characteristic in one's testimony of faith — 'lâ ilâha illâ Allâh'. Without doubt, sincerity in one's utterances and actions is vitally significant. For this reason, Imam an-Nawawi (may Allah rest his soul) has devoted the first chapter of his book, *Riyâḍ aṣ-Ṣâliḥeen* (*Gardens of the Righteous*), to this topic. Titled *al-Ikhlâṣ* (purity of intentions), it constitutes twelve hadiths, beginning with the well-known hadith attributed to 'Umar ibn al-Khaṭṭâb (رضي الله عنه), in which the Prophet (ﷺ) said:

«Verily, deeds are judged according to the intention behind them, and everyone will be rewarded according to what he intended.» (Bukhari)

The association of partners with Allah (سبحانه وتعالى) nullifies all good deeds

The sixth condition of the shahâdah, sincerity, requires that all forms of worship should be purely for Allah alone. Given that worship covers all our thoughts, actions, and intentions, it signifies that everything — big or small — should be done solely for Allah's sake. In other words, all our religious observances as well as our other activities should be free of shirk: association of partners with Allah. This is because shirk is a direct contradiction of our sincerity, honesty, and purity of belief. Shirk also negates our purpose of creation and makes all our deeds worthless in the sight of Allah.

﴿ وَٱعۡبُدُواْ ٱللَّهَ وَلَا تُشۡرِكُواْ بِهِۦ شَيۡـٔٗاۖ ... ﴿٣٦﴾ ﴾ (سورة النساء: ٣٦)

﴾Worship Allah and associate nothing with Him...﴿ *(Qur'an 4: 36)*

Indeed, we have been commanded to worship Allah and ordered to refrain from shirk. Shirk is the greatest sin; in fact, it is the only sin that will not be forgiven if one does not sincerely repent:

﴿ إِنَّ ٱللَّهَ لَا يَغۡفِرُ أَن يُشۡرَكَ بِهِۦ وَيَغۡفِرُ مَا دُونَ ذَٰلِكَ لِمَن يَشَآءُۚ وَمَن يُشۡرِكۡ بِٱللَّهِ فَقَدِ ٱفۡتَرَىٰٓ إِثۡمًا عَظِيمًا ﴿٤٨﴾ ﴾ (سورة النساء: ٤٨)

﴾Indeed, Allah does not forgive association with Him, but He forgives what is less than that for whom He wills. He who associates others with Allah has certainly fabricated a tremendous sin.﴿ *(Qur'an 4: 48)*

﴿ إِنَّ ٱللَّهَ لَا يَغۡفِرُ أَن يُشۡرَكَ بِهِۦ وَيَغۡفِرُ مَا دُونَ ذَٰلِكَ لِمَن يَشَآءُۚ وَمَن يُشۡرِكۡ بِٱللَّهِ فَقَدۡ ضَلَّ ضَلَٰلَۢا بَعِيدًا ﴿١١٦﴾ ﴾ (سورة النساء: ١١٦)

﴾Indeed, Allah does not forgive association with Him, but He forgives what is less than that for whom He wills. He who associates others with Allah has certainly gone far astray.﴿ *(Qur'an 4: 116)*

Not only is shirk an unforgiveable sin, but it also deprives us of the rewards of our righteous deeds. Whenever Satan fails to convince us to commit any major or minor sins, he approaches us in a deceptive way in order to ensure that our good deeds are not done truly for the sake of Allah. Due to this lack of sincerity, we become guilty of associating partners with Allah in our righteous deeds. We end up losing all the blessings of our good deeds; moreover, if we do not repent, we end up perpetrating the worst and unpardonable sin: shirk. For this reason, Allah has warned us repeatedly:

﴿ ذَٰلِكَ هُدَى ٱللَّهِ يَهۡدِي بِهِۦ مَن يَشَآءُ مِنۡ عِبَادِهِۦۚ وَلَوۡ أَشۡرَكُواْ لَحَبِطَ عَنۡهُم مَّا كَانُواْ يَعۡمَلُونَ ﴿٨٨﴾ ﴾ (سورة الأنعام: ٨٨)

﴾That is the guidance of Allah by which He guides whomever He wills of His servants. But if they had associated others with Allah, then worthless for them would be whatever they were doing.﴿

(Qur'an 6: 88)

﴿ وَلَقَدْ أُوحِيَ إِلَيْكَ وَإِلَى ٱلَّذِينَ مِن قَبْلِكَ لَئِنْ أَشْرَكْتَ لَيَحْبَطَنَّ عَمَلُكَ وَلَتَكُونَنَّ مِنَ ٱلْخَٰسِرِينَ ﴿٦٥﴾ بَلِ ٱللَّهَ فَٱعْبُدْ وَكُن مِّنَ ٱلشَّٰكِرِينَ ﴿٦٦﴾ ﴾ (سورة الزُّمَر: ٦٥-٦٦)

﴾And it was already revealed to you and to those before you that if you should associate [anything] with Allah, your work would surely become worthless, and you would surely be among the losers. Rather, worship [only] Allah and be among the grateful.﴿

(Qur'an 39: 65-66)

﴿ ... فَمَن كَانَ يَرْجُوا۟ لِقَآءَ رَبِّهِۦ فَلْيَعْمَلْ عَمَلًا صَٰلِحًا وَلَا يُشْرِكْ بِعِبَادَةِ رَبِّهِۦٓ أَحَدًۢا ﴿١١٠﴾ ﴾

(سورة الكهف: ١١٠)

﴾...So whoever would hope for the meeting with his Lord — let him do righteous work and not associate in the worship of his Lord anyone.﴿ *(Qur'an 18: 110)*

﴿ وَقَدِمْنَآ إِلَىٰ مَا عَمِلُوا۟ مِنْ عَمَلٍ فَجَعَلْنَٰهُ هَبَآءً مَّنثُورًا ﴿٢٣﴾ ﴾ (سورة الفرقان: ٢٣)

﴾And We will regard what they have done of deeds and make them as dust dispersed.﴿ *(Qur'an 25: 23)*

Likewise, Prophet Muhammad (ﷺ) cautioned us against the penalties of shirk. Abu Hurayrah (رضي الله عنه) reported Allah's Messenger (ﷺ) as saying:

> «Allah, the Most High and Exalted, has said: I am the One, the One Who does not stand in need of a partner. If anyone does anything in which he associates anyone else with Me, I shall abandon him with the one whom he associates with Me.» (Muslim)

Unfortunately, the Muslim community today appears to be ignorant of the sixth condition of the shahâdah. Due to deficient sincerity, shirk in various forms has become prevalent. Belief in Allah, which should be absolute and unconditional, is negated and flawed.

﴿ وَمَا يُؤْمِنُ أَكْثَرُهُم بِٱللَّهِ إِلَّا وَهُم مُّشْرِكُونَ ۝١٠٦ ﴾ (سورة يوسف: ١٠٦)

﴿And most of them believe not in Allah except while they associate others with Him.﴾ *(Qur'an 12: 106)*

Shirk is a direct contradiction of the shahâdah. Worshipping others alongside Allah is termed *shirk al-'ibâdah*. Some of the common forms of shirk are:

Worshipping others besides or alongside Allah (ﷻ) is *shirk*

This involves the worship of deities other than Allah. Whether or not one prays directly to an idol, if one seeks a reward or a benefit from a creature other than the Creator, Allah, then this is the most obvious form of idolatry.[63] This form of shirk is considered to be the greatest act of rebellion against Allah; it is the ultimate sin, cancelling out all the good that a person may do. It guarantees its perpetrator eternal damnation in hell. All false religions and man-made systems primarily base their worship on this form of shirk, calling people to the worship of Allah's creation. All the prophets and messengers were entrusted with and propagated the same message: the message of tawḥeed — the Oneness of Allah. Furthermore, in order to safeguard themselves from shirk, the unpardonable sin, they were very insistent in clarifying their position as Allah's servants and messengers. For instance, Prophet Jesus (ﷺ) explicitly invited his people to worship Allah alone, warning them of the consequences of shirk:

---

[63] Abu Ameenah Bilal Philips, *The Fundamentals of Tawheed* (Riyadh: International Islamic Publishing House, 2006), 36.

﴿لَقَدْ كَفَرَ ٱلَّذِينَ قَالُوٓاْ إِنَّ ٱللَّهَ هُوَ ٱلْمَسِيحُ ٱبْنُ مَرْيَمَ ۖ وَقَالَ ٱلْمَسِيحُ يَٰبَنِىٓ
إِسْرَٰٓءِيلَ ٱعْبُدُواْ ٱللَّهَ رَبِّى وَرَبَّكُمْ ۖ إِنَّهُۥ مَن يُشْرِكْ بِٱللَّهِ فَقَدْ حَرَّمَ ٱللَّهُ عَلَيْهِ ٱلْجَنَّةَ
وَمَأْوَىٰهُ ٱلنَّارُ ۖ وَمَا لِلظَّٰلِمِينَ مِنْ أَنصَارٍ ﴿٧٢﴾﴾ (سورة المائدة: ٧٢)

﴾They have certainly disbelieved who say: Allah is the Messiah, the son of Mary, while the Messiah has said: O Children of Israel, worship Allah, my Lord and your Lord. Indeed, he who associates others with Allah — Allah has forbidden him paradise, and his refuge is the fire. There are not for the wrongdoers any helpers.﴿ *(Qur'an 5: 72)*

The Muslims whose acts of worship fall into this form of shirk pray to Prophet Muhammad (ﷺ) as an intermediary to Allah. Alternatively, they pray to mystics in the Sufi hierarchy of saints as mediators or go-betweens to Allah, with the view that the intercession of a pious person (albeit deceased) will merit an answer to their prayers. In contrast, Allah has unambiguously established the futility of any kind of mediation:

﴿قُلْ أَرَءَيْتَكُمْ إِنْ أَتَىٰكُمْ عَذَابُ ٱللَّهِ أَوْ أَتَتْكُمُ ٱلسَّاعَةُ أَغَيْرَ ٱللَّهِ تَدْعُونَ إِن كُنتُمْ
صَٰدِقِينَ ﴿٤٠﴾﴾ (سورة الأنعام: ٤٠)

﴾Say: Have you considered: if there came to you the punishment of Allah or there came to you the hour — is it other than Allah you would invoke, if you should be truthful?﴿ *(Qur'an 6: 40)*

Shirk aṭ-ṭâ'ah: Obeying the creation in unlawful matters

This form of shirk involves obeying the creation rather than the Creator; that is, abiding by the authority of other human beings in opposition to Allah's authority. For instance, this would involve making lawful and permissible what Allah has declared unlawful, or vice versa. Submission and obedience in such matters must be exclusive to Allah. As the following verse illustrates, sons and daughters (who are otherwise enjoined repeatedly in the Qur'an to respect, defer to, and be gentle and kind towards their parents) can and should disobey them if they are asked to do anything against the commandments of Allah:

﴿ وَإِن جَٰهَدَاكَ عَلَىٰٓ أَن تُشْرِكَ بِى مَا لَيْسَ لَكَ بِهِۦ عِلْمٌ فَلَا تُطِعْهُمَا ۖ وَصَاحِبْهُمَا فِى ٱلدُّنْيَا مَعْرُوفًا ۖ وَٱتَّبِعْ سَبِيلَ مَنْ أَنَابَ إِلَىَّ ۚ ثُمَّ إِلَىَّ مَرْجِعُكُمْ فَأُنَبِّئُكُم بِمَا كُنتُمْ تَعْمَلُونَ ﴿١٥﴾ ﴾ (سورة لقمان: ١٥)

﴿But if they endeavour to make you associate with Me that of which you have no knowledge, do not obey them, but accompany them in [this] world with appropriate kindness and follow the way of those who turn back to Me [in repentance]. To Me will be your return, and I will inform you about what you used to do.﴾

(Qur'an 31: 15)

«On one occasion, the Prophet's Companion 'Adiyy ibn Ḥâtim (ﷺ), who was a revert from Christianity, heard the Prophet (ﷺ) reciting the following Qur'anic verse:

﴿ ٱتَّخَذُوٓا۟ أَحْبَارَهُمْ وَرُهْبَٰنَهُمْ أَرْبَابًا مِّن دُونِ ٱللَّهِ وَٱلْمَسِيحَ ٱبْنَ مَرْيَمَ وَمَآ أُمِرُوٓا۟ إِلَّا لِيَعْبُدُوٓا۟ إِلَٰهًا وَٰحِدًا ۖ لَّآ إِلَٰهَ إِلَّا هُوَ ۚ سُبْحَٰنَهُۥ عَمَّا يُشْرِكُونَ ﴿٣١﴾ ﴾ (سورة التوبة: ٣١)

﴿They have taken their scholars and monks as lords besides Allah, and [also] the Messiah, the son of Mary. They were not commanded except to worship one God; there is no deity except Him. Exalted is He above whatever they associate with Him.﴾ *(Qur'an 9: 31)*

Upon hearing this, 'Adiyy (ﷺ) said: Surely we did not worship them?

The Prophet (ﷺ) turned to him and said: Did they not forbid what Allah had allowed,[64] and you took it as forbidden? Did they not allow what Allah had prohibited,[65] and you all treated it as allowed?

He replied: We certainly did.

The Prophet (ﷺ) explained: That is how you worshipped them.» (at-Tirmidhi; a reliable hadith according to al-Albâni)[66]

The Prophet (ﷺ) also said:

«There should not be any obedience to the creature when it involves the disobedience of the Creator: obedience is obligatory only in what is good (and reasonable).» (Muslim)

The consequences of shirk aṭ-ṭâ'ah are terrifying and frightening. Disobedience to Allah and His Prophet (ﷺ) will assuredly lead people to hellfire.

﴿ إِنَّ ٱللَّهَ لَعَنَ ٱلْكَٰفِرِينَ وَأَعَدَّ لَهُمْ سَعِيرًا ﴿٦٤﴾ خَٰلِدِينَ فِيهَآ أَبَدًا ۖ لَّا يَجِدُونَ وَلِيًّا وَلَا
نَصِيرًا ﴿٦٥﴾ يَوْمَ تُقَلَّبُ وُجُوهُهُمْ فِى ٱلنَّارِ يَقُولُونَ يَٰلَيْتَنَآ أَطَعْنَا ٱللَّهَ وَأَطَعْنَا ٱلرَّسُولَا۠
﴿٦٦﴾ وَقَالُوا۟ رَبَّنَآ إِنَّآ أَطَعْنَا سَادَتَنَا وَكُبَرَآءَنَا فَأَضَلُّونَا ٱلسَّبِيلَا۠ ﴿٦٧﴾ رَبَّنَآ ءَاتِهِمْ
ضِعْفَيْنِ مِنَ ٱلْعَذَابِ وَٱلْعَنْهُمْ لَعْنًا كَبِيرًا ﴿٦٨﴾ ﴾ (سورة الأحزاب: ٦٤-٦٨)

﴿Indeed, Allah has cursed the disbelievers and prepared for them a blaze. Abiding therein forever, they will not find a protector or

---

[64] Christian clergy forbade polygamy and the marriage of first cousins. Roman Catholics forbade priests from marrying and forbade divorce in general. This is being disputed today by many priests who want such restrictions lifted so that they can marry. In 2004, there was a heated debate about this issue among priests in the U.S..

[65] The Christian Church permitted the consumption of pork, blood, and alcohol. Others also allowed painting and sculpting statues depicting God as a human.

[66] Philips, *The Fundamentals of Tawheed*, 25.

a helper. The day their faces will be turned about in the fire, they will say: How we wish we had obeyed Allah and obeyed the Messenger. And they will say: Our Lord, indeed we obeyed our masters and our dignitaries, and they led us astray from the [right] way. Our Lord, give them double the punishment and curse them with a great curse.﴿ *(Qur'an 33: 64-68)*

Shirk al-maḥabbah: Loving a creature more than Allah (ﷻ)

Love is a form of worship which, in its perfection, should be directed to Allah alone. According to Islam, love of Allah is expressed by total obedience to Him. This love is not the type of love that a human instinctively feels for other creatures. For instance, love for one's parents, children, certain foods, and so on is very different. To direct such love to Allah means to lower Him to the level of His creation and perpetrate the shirk of love. Love, which is worship, is the total surrender of one's will to Allah. Consequently, Allah commanded the Prophet (ﷺ) to tell the believers to take heed:[67]

﴿قُلْ إِن كُنتُمْ تُحِبُّونَ اللَّهَ فَاتَّبِعُونِي يُحْبِبْكُمُ اللَّهُ وَيَغْفِرْ لَكُمْ ذُنُوبَكُمْ ۗ وَاللَّهُ غَفُورٌ رَّحِيمٌ ﴿٣١﴾﴾ (سورة آل عمران: ٣١)

﴾Say [O Muhammad]: If you should love Allah, then follow me, [so] Allah will love you and forgive you your sins. Allah is Forgiving and Merciful.﴿ *(Qur'an 3: 31)*

One can also become guilty of *shirk al-maḥabbah* by allowing the love of anything or anyone to come in between oneself and Allah. If one loves something or someone as much as or more than Allah, one stands culpable of worshipping it. It is in this manner

---

[67] Philips, *The Fundamentals of Tawheed*, 37.

that money can become one's false god; even one's desires could become a god. In this context, the Prophet (ﷺ) said:

> «The worshipper of the dirham will always be miserable.» (Bukhari)

Allah has enquired:

﴿أَرَءَيْتَ مَنِ ٱتَّخَذَ إِلَٰهَهُۥ هَوَىٰهُ أَفَأَنتَ تَكُونُ عَلَيْهِ وَكِيلًا ﴿٤٣﴾﴾

(سورة الفرقان: ٤٣)

﴿Have you seen the one who takes as his god his own desire? Then would you be responsible for him?﴾ *(Qur'an 25: 43)*

Shirk al-maḥabbah will be the cause of humiliation for its perpetrators on the Day of Judgement. The individuals or things that were treated as 'false gods', with a love that should have been exclusively for Allah, will abandon their worshippers on that day as they will be driven into hellfire. Hence, the culprits of shirk al-maḥabbah will have nothing but regret and a strong desire to disown their false idols who had seemed ever so powerful! They will beg for an opportunity in this world again, in order to efface their sin, but alas — all power on that day will belong to Allah, who will consign them to the everlasting hell.

This eventful scene has been vividly portrayed in the Qur'an as a reminder and a warning in order for people to abstain from shirk al-maḥabbah:

﴿وَمِنَ ٱلنَّاسِ مَن يَتَّخِذُ مِن دُونِ ٱللَّهِ أَندَادًا يُحِبُّونَهُمْ كَحُبِّ ٱللَّهِ ۖ وَٱلَّذِينَ ءَامَنُوٓا۟
أَشَدُّ حُبًّا لِّلَّهِ ۗ وَلَوْ يَرَى ٱلَّذِينَ ظَلَمُوٓا۟ إِذْ يَرَوْنَ ٱلْعَذَابَ أَنَّ ٱلْقُوَّةَ لِلَّهِ جَمِيعًا وَأَنَّ ٱللَّهَ
شَدِيدُ ٱلْعَذَابِ ﴿١٦٥﴾ إِذْ تَبَرَّأَ ٱلَّذِينَ ٱتُّبِعُوا۟ مِنَ ٱلَّذِينَ ٱتَّبَعُوا۟ وَرَأَوُا۟ ٱلْعَذَابَ
وَتَقَطَّعَتْ بِهِمُ ٱلْأَسْبَابُ ﴿١٦٦﴾ وَقَالَ ٱلَّذِينَ ٱتَّبَعُوا۟ لَوْ أَنَّ لَنَا كَرَّةً فَنَتَبَرَّأَ مِنْهُمْ كَمَا
تَبَرَّءُوا۟ مِنَّا ۗ كَذَٰلِكَ يُرِيهِمُ ٱللَّهُ أَعْمَٰلَهُمْ حَسَرَٰتٍ عَلَيْهِمْ ۖ وَمَا هُم بِخَٰرِجِينَ مِنَ ٱلنَّارِ
﴿١٦٧﴾﴾

(سورة البقرة: ١٦٥-١٦٧)

﴾And [yet] among the people are those who take other than Allah as equals [to Him]. They love them as they [should] love Allah. But those who believe are stronger in love for Allah. If only they who have wronged would consider [that] when they see the punishment, [they will be certain] that all power belongs to Allah and that Allah is severe in punishment. [They should consider that] when those who have been followed disassociate themselves from those who followed [them], and they [all] see the punishment, and cut off from them are the ties [of relationship]. Those who followed will say: If only we had another turn [at worldly life] so we could disassociate ourselves from them as they have disassociated themselves from us. Thus will Allah show them their deeds as regrets upon them, and they are never to emerge from the fire.﴿

(Qur'an 2: 165-167)

Shirk ad-du'â': Supplicating to deities other than Allah (سبحانه وتعالى)

Shirk ad-du'â' means invocation and supplication to a false deity besides Allah. This can take one of two forms:

a. Praying to idols or deceased righteous individuals, saints, and others as intercessors in one's prayers to Allah;
b. Directly invoking false gods, saints, or others for help and relief.

The role of Catholic priests is the former; they act as middlemen between people and God, as they hear confessions and absolve people on behalf of God. The latter form includes direct supplication to Mary, mother of Jesus, or to Jesus himself as God.

Unfortunately, Muslims who are ignorant of sincerity, the sixth condition of the shahâdah, commit shirk ad-du'â' without realizing that this is exactly what the pre-Islamic Arabs used to do.

They used their idols as intermediaries, claiming that they were not worshipping the idols but that their idols only brought them closer to Allah, the Creator. He has quoted them as saying:

﴿... مَا نَعۡبُدُهُمۡ إِلَّا لِيُقَرِّبُونَآ إِلَى ٱللَّهِ زُلۡفَىٰٓ ... ﴿٣﴾﴾ (سورة الزُّمَر: ٣)

﴾...We only worship them that they may bring us nearer to Allah in position...﴿ *(Qur'an 39: 3)*

In *The Fundamentals of Tawheed*, Abu Ameenah Bilal Philips explains that Muslims who visit the graves of pious people, intending to seek their help to intercede with Allah on their behalf, are also guilty of shirk ad-du'â'. It is an even greater transgression when those in their graves are begged and implored directly for forgiveness of sins. This is a very offensive contradiction of tawḥeed, as if the deceased humans are given Allah's attributes of being *at-Tawwâb* (the Accepting of repentance) and *al-Ghafoor* (the One Who forgives).

This practice is similar to the tradition of Catholics who invoke specific saints for particular purposes. Bilal Philips has given a number of examples in his book. For instance, St. Jude of Thaddaeus is the patron saint for impossible causes, so people pray to him for intercession in the case of incurable diseases or unlikely marriages.

Another case in point is St. Christopher, the patron saint of travellers; misguided followers supplicate to him for protection during journeys. In addition, almost all denominations of Christians, including Catholics, pray directly to Jesus, whom they consider to be God incarnate, in a gross manifestation of shirk ad-du'â'. Muslims who pray to Prophet Muhammad (ﷺ) either directly or for his intercession are similarly guilty of this form of shirk.

The intercession of the dead, whether prophets or pious people, is completely futile, since according to Islamic doctrine, the dead are in the intermediate state termed *barzakh*, wherein their deeds have terminated. They are unable to do anything for the living. Indeed, the dead can only benefit themselves by certain good deeds performed while they were alive, according to the following hadith reported by Abu Hurayrah (ﷺ), in which the Prophet (ﷺ) said:

> «When a man dies, all his (good) deeds are cut off except three: charity of continuing benefit, knowledge that is beneficial to people, and a righteous child who supplicates for him.» (Muslim)

For this reason, the Prophet (ﷺ) was quite emphatic and took great pains to explain that he could not benefit anyone in this life, regardless of his or her closeness to him, as Allah commanded him to say to his followers:

﴿قُل لَّآ أَمۡلِكُ لِنَفۡسِي نَفۡعٗا وَلَا ضَرًّا إِلَّا مَا شَآءَ ٱللَّهُۚ وَلَوۡ كُنتُ أَعۡلَمُ ٱلۡغَيۡبَ لَٱسۡتَكۡثَرۡتُ مِنَ ٱلۡخَيۡرِ وَمَا مَسَّنِيَ ٱلسُّوٓءُۚ إِنۡ أَنَا۠ إِلَّا نَذِيرٞ وَبَشِيرٞ لِّقَوۡمٖ يُؤۡمِنُونَ ١٨٨﴾ (سورة الأعراف: ١٨٨)

﴿Say: I hold not for myself [the power of] benefit or harm, except what Allah has willed. If I knew the unseen, I could have acquired much wealth, and no harm would have touched me. I am only a warner and a bringer of good tidings to a people who believe.﴾

(Qur'an 7: 188)

> «One of his Companions, Abu Hurayrah (ﷺ) reported that when the verse:
>
> ﴿وَأَنذِرۡ عَشِيرَتَكَ ٱلۡأَقۡرَبِينَ ٢١٤﴾ (سورة الشعراء: ٢١٤)
>
> ﴿And warn [O Muhammad] your closest kindred.﴾
>
> *(Qur'an 26: 214)*
>
> — was revealed to the Prophet (ﷺ), he said: O people of Quraysh, secure deliverance from Allah (by doing good deeds). I cannot avail you at all against Allah; O sons of 'Abdul-Muṭṭalib, I cannot avail you at all against Allah;

O (my uncle) 'Abbâs ibn 'Abdul-Muṭṭalib, O (my aunt) Ṣafiyah, I cannot avail you at all against Allah; O Fâṭimah, daughter of Muhammad, ask me whatever you like, but I have nothing which can avail you against Allah.» (Bukhari)

«On another occasion, one of the Prophet's Companions concluded his statement to the Prophet (ﷺ) with the phrase: It is what Allah wills and you will.

The Prophet (ﷺ) immediately corrected him saying: You have put me as an equal with Allah. It is what Allah alone wills.» (Bukhari and Aḥmad)

Unfortunately, in spite of all the Prophet's exhortations, those who remain in a state of ignorance about the conditions of the shahâdah continue to pray to the Prophet (ﷺ) and to a hierarchy of saints. This heretical practice is based on the claim of mystics (Sufis) that the cosmic order is preserved by a fixed number of saints called 'the men of the unseen world'. When a holy man among them dies, his place is immediately filled by a substitute. At the peak of the hierarchy is the *quṭb* (the pole or mystic axis of the world), or the *ghawth* (succour). 'Abdul-Qâdir al-Jeelâni (d. 1166 CE) is popularly referred to as 'the greatest source of help'. During times of calamity, many turn to him for help, crying out, "O 'Abdul-Qâdir, save me!"

Such unmistakable pronouncements of shirk ad-du'â' are common even though practicing Muslims recite Soorat *al-Fâtiḥah* at least seventeen times daily in their ṣalâh and this chapter includes the following phrase (translated as):

﴿إِيَّاكَ نَعْبُدُ وَإِيَّاكَ نَسْتَعِينُ ۝٥﴾ (سورة الفاتحة: ٥)

«It is You [alone] we worship and You [alone] we ask for help.»

(Qur'an 1: 5)

Any form of supplication that constitutes shirk ad-du'â', in particular the aforementioned practices that have crept into Muslim religious observances, have to be vigorously eradicated. Our allegiance to Allah must be sincere, whole, and not compromised in any way. To Him belongs the dominion over the entire universe and He is the Almighty, the All-Powerful.

In a hadith narrated by Ibn 'Abbâs (رضي الله عنه), the Prophet (ﷺ) elucidated the helplessness and vulnerability of human beings as well as their utter dependence on Allah:

> «One day I was (mounted) behind the Prophet (ﷺ) and he said to me: Young man, I shall give you some words (of advice):
>
> Be mindful of Allah, and Allah will protect you. Be mindful of Allah, and you will find Him in front of you.
>
> If you ask, ask Allah; if you seek help, seek help from Allah.
>
> Know that if the whole nation gathers to benefit you with something, it will not benefit you with anything except what Allah has already prescribed for you; and if they gather to harm you with anything, they will not be able to harm you except to the extent that Allah has already prescribed for you. The pens have already been lifted and the pages have dried.» (An authentic hadith recorded by at-Tirmidhi)

Invoking or supplicating to other than Allah is a gross and monstrous violation of tawḥeed. For this reason, there are many passages in the Qur'an that warn us against this outrageous practice, illustrating the powerlessness and ineffectuality of these false gods:

﴿قُلِ ٱدْعُواْ ٱلَّذِينَ زَعَمْتُم مِّن دُونِ ٱللَّهِ لَا يَمْلِكُونَ مِثْقَالَ ذَرَّةٍ فِى ٱلسَّمَٰوَٰتِ وَلَا فِى ٱلْأَرْضِ وَمَا لَهُمْ فِيهِمَا مِن شِرْكٍ وَمَا لَهُۥ مِنْهُم مِّن ظَهِيرٍ ﴿٢٢﴾﴾

(سورة سبأ: ٢٢)

﴾Say [O Muhammad]: Invoke those you claim [as deities] besides Allah. They do not possess an atom's weight [of ability] in the heavens or on the earth, and they do not have therein any partnership [with Him], nor is there for Him from among them any assistant.﴾ *(Qur'an 34: 22)*

﴿إِن تَدْعُوهُمْ لَا يَسْمَعُوا دُعَاءَكُمْ وَلَوْ سَمِعُوا مَا اسْتَجَابُوا لَكُمْ وَيَوْمَ الْقِيَامَةِ يَكْفُرُونَ بِشِرْكِكُمْ وَلَا يُنَبِّئُكَ مِثْلُ خَبِيرٍ ﴿١٤﴾﴾ (سورة فاطر: ١٤)

﴾If you invoke them, they do not hear your supplication; and if they heard, they would not respond to you. On the Day of Resurrection, they will deny your association. None can inform you like [One] Acquainted [with all matters].﴿ *(Qur'an 35: 14)*

﴿إِنَّمَا تَعْبُدُونَ مِن دُونِ اللَّهِ أَوْثَانًا وَتَخْلُقُونَ إِفْكًا إِنَّ الَّذِينَ تَعْبُدُونَ مِن دُونِ اللَّهِ لَا يَمْلِكُونَ لَكُمْ رِزْقًا فَابْتَغُوا عِندَ اللَّهِ الرِّزْقَ وَاعْبُدُوهُ وَاشْكُرُوا لَهُ إِلَيْهِ تُرْجَعُونَ ﴿١٧﴾﴾ (سورة العنكبوت: ١٧)

﴾You only worship, besides Allah, idols, and you produce a falsehood. Indeed, those you worship besides Allah do not possess for you [the power of] provision. So seek from Allah provision and worship Him and be grateful to Him. To Him you will be returned.﴿ *(Qur'an 29: 17)*

﴿وَلَا تَدْعُ مِن دُونِ اللَّهِ مَا لَا يَنفَعُكَ وَلَا يَضُرُّكَ فَإِن فَعَلْتَ فَإِنَّكَ إِذًا مِّنَ الظَّالِمِينَ ﴿١٠٦﴾ وَإِن يَمْسَسْكَ اللَّهُ بِضُرٍّ فَلَا كَاشِفَ لَهُ إِلَّا هُوَ وَإِن يُرِدْكَ بِخَيْرٍ فَلَا رَادَّ لِفَضْلِهِ يُصِيبُ بِهِ مَن يَشَاءُ مِنْ عِبَادِهِ وَهُوَ الْغَفُورُ الرَّحِيمُ ﴿١٠٧﴾﴾

(سورة يونس: ١٠٦-١٠٧)

﴾And do not invoke besides Allah that which neither benefits you nor harms you, for if you did, then indeed you would be of the wrongdoers. If Allah should touch you with adversity, there is no remover of it except Him; and if He intends for you good, then there is no repeller of His bounty. He causes it to reach whom He wills of His servants, and He is the Forgiving, the Merciful.﴿ *(Qur'an 10: 106-107)*

﴿ وَمَنْ أَضَلُّ مِمَّن يَدْعُوا مِن دُونِ اللَّهِ مَن لَّا يَسْتَجِيبُ لَهُ إِلَىٰ يَوْمِ الْقِيَامَةِ وَهُمْ عَن
دُعَائِهِمْ غَافِلُونَ ﴿٥﴾ وَإِذَا حُشِرَ النَّاسُ كَانُوا لَهُمْ أَعْدَاءً وَكَانُوا بِعِبَادَتِهِمْ كَافِرِينَ ﴿٦﴾ ﴾

(سورة الأحقاف: ٥-٦)

﴿And who is more astray than he who invokes besides Allah those who will not respond to him until the Day of Resurrection, and they, of their invocation, are unaware. When the people are gathered [that day], they [who were invoked] will be enemies to them, and they will be deniers of their worship.﴾ *(Qur'an 46: 5-6)*

Allah has commanded us to supplicate directly to Him instead. Indeed, Allah will answer our prayers and provide us with all that we need, as well as solve all our problems. However, Allah's response to our supplications is conditional upon the fact that we must obey Him, abstain from the unlawful, pray to Him alone without associating any partners, and be absolutely certain that He will answer our call. Allah has promised:

﴿ وَقَالَ رَبُّكُمُ ادْعُونِي أَسْتَجِبْ لَكُمْ ۚ إِنَّ الَّذِينَ يَسْتَكْبِرُونَ عَنْ عِبَادَتِي
سَيَدْخُلُونَ جَهَنَّمَ دَاخِرِينَ ﴿٦٠﴾ ﴾ (سورة غافر: ٦٠)

﴿And your Lord says: Call upon Me; I will respond to you. Indeed, those who disdain My worship will enter hell [rendered] contemptible.﴾ *(Qur'an 40: 60)*

﴿ وَإِذَا سَأَلَكَ عِبَادِي عَنِّي فَإِنِّي قَرِيبٌ ۖ أُجِيبُ دَعْوَةَ الدَّاعِ إِذَا دَعَانِ ۖ
فَلْيَسْتَجِيبُوا لِي وَلْيُؤْمِنُوا بِي لَعَلَّهُمْ يَرْشُدُونَ ﴿١٨٦﴾ ﴾ (سورة البقرة: ١٨٦)

﴿And when My servants ask you [O Muhammad] concerning Me — indeed I am near. I respond to the invocation of the supplicant when he calls upon Me. So let them respond to Me [by obedience] and believe in Me that they may be [rightly] guided.﴾ *(Qur'an 2: 186)*

﴿ أَمَّن يُجِيبُ الْمُضْطَرَّ إِذَا دَعَاهُ وَيَكْشِفُ السُّوءَ وَيَجْعَلُكُمْ خُلَفَاءَ الْأَرْضِ ۗ
أَإِلَٰهٌ مَّعَ اللَّهِ ۚ قَلِيلًا مَّا تَذَكَّرُونَ ﴿٦٢﴾ ﴾ (سورة النمل: ٦٢)

﴾Is He [not best] who responds to the desperate one when he calls upon Him and removes evil and makes you inheritors of the earth? Is there a deity with Allah? Little do you remember.﴿

(Qur'an 27: 62)

Shirk al-ḥâkimiyah: Ruling with other than Allah's laws

This is yet another form of shirk that comes under shirk al-'ibâdah, which negates the sixth condition of the shahâdah. In Islam, the term 'ibâdah, as mentioned previously, means total obedience, where Allah is considered the ultimate lawgiver. Therefore, the implementation of any laws that contradict the Sharia, such as secular legal systems or cultural or man-made regulations, are acts of disbelief and fall under *shirk al-ḥâkimiyah*. Association of partners with Allah in His divine law — that is, ruling by a mixture of Allah's laws and man-made laws or considering the two to be equal or even preferring secular laws over Allah's laws — all constitute shirk al-ḥâkimiyah. The penalty for this form of shirk is very severe and strongly condemned by Allah. Undeniably, lack of sincerity in one's shahâdah renders one a disbeliever:

﴿... وَمَن لَّمْ يَحْكُم بِمَآ أَنزَلَ ٱللَّهُ فَأُو۟لَـٰٓئِكَ هُمُ ٱلْكَـٰفِرُونَ ﴿٤٤﴾﴾

(سورة المائدة: ٤٤)

﴾...And whoever does not judge by what Allah has revealed — then it is those who are the disbelievers.﴿ *(Qur'an 5: 44)*

The sixth condition of the shahâdah, sincerity, stipulates that all aspects of our lives should be governed according to Allah's commands and injunctions — His divine laws. For this reason, those who profess their belief yet ignore or evade His laws and commandments are considered to be hypocrites. This is because they have acted in opposition to the sincerity and devotion due to their shahâdah. Several verses in the Qur'an stress this obligation and warn against the consequences of the ensuing shirk al-ḥâkimiyah:

﴿... مَا لَهُم مِّن دُونِهِۦ مِن وَلِيٍّ وَلَا يُشْرِكُ فِي حُكْمِهِۦٓ أَحَدًا ﴿٢٦﴾﴾

(سورة الكهف: ٢٦)

﴿...They have not besides Him any protector, and He shares not His legislation with anyone.﴾ *(Qur'an 18: 26)*

﴿... وَٱللَّهُ يَحْكُمُ لَا مُعَقِّبَ لِحُكْمِهِۦ ۚ وَهُوَ سَرِيعُ ٱلْحِسَابِ ﴿٤١﴾﴾

(سورة الرعد: ٤١)

﴿...And Allah decides; there is no adjuster of His decision, and He is swift in account.﴾ *(Qur'an 13: 41)*

﴿أَلَمْ تَرَ إِلَى ٱلَّذِينَ يَزْعُمُونَ أَنَّهُمْ ءَامَنُوا۟ بِمَآ أُنزِلَ إِلَيْكَ وَمَآ أُنزِلَ مِن قَبْلِكَ
يُرِيدُونَ أَن يَتَحَاكَمُوٓا۟ إِلَى ٱلطَّٰغُوتِ وَقَدْ أُمِرُوٓا۟ أَن يَكْفُرُوا۟ بِهِۦ وَيُرِيدُ ٱلشَّيْطَٰنُ
أَن يُضِلَّهُمْ ضَلَٰلًۢا بَعِيدًا ﴿٦٠﴾ وَإِذَا قِيلَ لَهُمْ تَعَالَوْا۟ إِلَىٰ مَآ أَنزَلَ ٱللَّهُ وَإِلَى
ٱلرَّسُولِ رَأَيْتَ ٱلْمُنَٰفِقِينَ يَصُدُّونَ عَنكَ صُدُودًا ﴿٦١﴾﴾

(سورة النساء: ٦٠-٦١)

﴿Have you not seen those who claim to have believed in what was revealed to you [O Muhammad] and what was revealed before you? They wish to refer legislation to ṭâghoot, while they were commanded to reject it; Satan wishes to lead them far astray. When it is said to them: Come to what Allah has revealed and to the Messenger, you see the hypocrites turning away from you in aversion.﴾ *(Qur'an 4: 60-61)*

According to ash-Sha'bi (and the same explanation is given by aṭ-Ṭabari), the aforementioned verses were revealed in connection with a hypocrite claiming to be a Muslim who had a dispute with a Jew. The Jew suggested, "Let us seek a judgement from Muhammad", for he knew that he did not accept bribes. The hypocrite said, "Let us get a judgement from the Jews", because he knew that they did accept bribes. Thus, both of them agreed to take their case to a soothsayer in Juhaynah. It was on this occasion that the verse: ﴿Have you not seen those who claim …﴾ was revealed.

Other commentators have explained that there was a dispute between two men. One of them said, "Let us take the dispute to the Prophet (ﷺ) for his judgement", but the other said, "No, let us take it to Ka'b ibn al-Ashraf." They both went to 'Umar ibn al-Khaṭṭâb (رضي الله عنه), and one of them told 'Umar (رضي الله عنه) the story. 'Umar (رضي الله عنه) asked the other (who had not been willing to take the case to Prophet [ﷺ]), "Is that so (as the first man said)?" He replied, "Yes." 'Umar (رضي الله عنه) struck him with his sword and killed him.[68]

Allah has placed a rhetorical question before the people who prefer the inferior judgement of other men over His ruling, in order to reinforce the transgression and error of such practices:

﴿أَفَحُكْمَ ٱلْجَٰهِلِيَّةِ يَبْغُونَ ۚ وَمَنْ أَحْسَنُ مِنَ ٱللَّهِ حُكْمًا لِّقَوْمٍ يُوقِنُونَ ﴿٥٠﴾﴾

(سورة المائدة: ٥٠)

﴿Then is it the judgement of [the time of] ignorance they desire? But who is better than Allah in judgement for a people who are certain [in faith]?﴾ *(Qur'an 5: 50)*

Hence, due to a lack of understanding and implementation of the sixth condition of shahâdah in many Muslim countries, shirk al-ḥâkimiyah has become quite rampant, and this is a source of Muslim humiliation in the twenty-first century. Bilal Philips, in his book on tawḥeed, has given some words of advice on how to ameliorate this situation:

---

68 Darussalam, *The Concise Collection on Creed and Tauhid*, 135-136.

Divine law has yet to be re-introduced in many so-called Muslim countries where governments now rule according to imported capitalist or communist constitutions, and the Islamic law is either totally extinct or relegated to a few areas of minor importance. Likewise, Muslim countries, where Islamic law is on the books but secular laws are in force, have also to be brought in line with the Shari'ah as it pertains to all aspects of life. The acceptance of non-Islamic rule in place of Shari'ah in Muslim lands is Shirk and an act of Kufr [disbelief]. Those in a position to change it must do so, while those unable to do so must speak against the rule of Kufr and call for the implementation of Shari'ah. If even this becomes impossible, un-Islamic government must be sincerely hated and despised for the pleasure of Allah and the upholding of Tawheed.[69]

[69] Philips, *The Fundamentals of Tawheed*, 25-26.

Chapter Eleven

The Seventh Condition: Love and Hate for the Sake of Allah

﴿لَّا تَجِدُ قَوْمًا يُؤْمِنُونَ بِٱللَّهِ وَٱلْيَوْمِ ٱلْآخِرِ يُوَآدُّونَ مَنْ حَآدَّ ٱللَّهَ وَرَسُولَهُۥ وَلَوْ كَانُوٓا۟ ءَابَآءَهُمْ أَوْ أَبْنَآءَهُمْ أَوْ إِخْوَٰنَهُمْ أَوْ عَشِيرَتَهُمْ ۚ أُو۟لَٰٓئِكَ كَتَبَ فِى قُلُوبِهِمُ ٱلْإِيمَٰنَ وَأَيَّدَهُم بِرُوحٍ مِّنْهُ ۖ وَيُدْخِلُهُمْ جَنَّٰتٍ تَجْرِى مِن تَحْتِهَا ٱلْأَنْهَٰرُ خَٰلِدِينَ فِيهَا ۚ رَضِىَ ٱللَّهُ عَنْهُمْ وَرَضُوا۟ عَنْهُ ۚ أُو۟لَٰٓئِكَ حِزْبُ ٱللَّهِ ۚ أَلَآ إِنَّ حِزْبَ ٱللَّهِ هُمُ ٱلْمُفْلِحُونَ ﴿٢٢﴾﴾ (سورة المجادلة: ٢٢)

﴾You will not find a people who believe in Allah and the last day having affection for those who oppose Allah and His Messenger, even if they are their fathers or their sons or their brothers or their kindred. Those — He has decreed within their hearts faith and supported them with spirit[70] from Him. We will admit them to gardens beneath which rivers flow, wherein they abide eternally. Allah is pleased with them, and they are pleased with Him — those are the party of Allah. Unquestionably, the party of Allah — they are the successful.﴿ *(Qur'an 58: 22)*

---

[70] That is, 'that which gives life': explained as the guidance of the Qur'an or victory over their opponents.

﴿ يَٰٓأَيُّهَا ٱلَّذِينَ ءَامَنُوا۟ لَا تَتَّخِذُوٓا۟ ءَابَآءَكُمْ وَإِخْوَٰنَكُمْ أَوْلِيَآءَ إِنِ ٱسْتَحَبُّوا۟
ٱلْكُفْرَ عَلَى ٱلْإِيمَٰنِ ۚ وَمَن يَتَوَلَّهُم مِّنكُمْ فَأُو۟لَٰٓئِكَ هُمُ ٱلظَّٰلِمُونَ ﴿٢٣﴾ ﴾

(سورة التوبة: ٢٣)

﴿O you who have believed, do not take your fathers or your brothers as allies if they have preferred disbelief over belief. Whoever does so among you — it is those who are the wrongdoers.﴾

(Qur'an 9: 23)

﴿ يَٰٓأَيُّهَا ٱلَّذِينَ ءَامَنُوا۟ لَا تَتَّخِذُوا۟ عَدُوِّى وَعَدُوَّكُمْ أَوْلِيَآءَ تُلْقُونَ إِلَيْهِم بِٱلْمَوَدَّةِ وَقَدْ
كَفَرُوا۟ بِمَا جَآءَكُم مِّنَ ٱلْحَقِّ يُخْرِجُونَ ٱلرَّسُولَ وَإِيَّاكُمْ ۙ أَن تُؤْمِنُوا۟ بِٱللَّهِ رَبِّكُمْ إِن كُنتُمْ
خَرَجْتُمْ جِهَٰدًا فِى سَبِيلِى وَٱبْتِغَآءَ مَرْضَاتِى ۚ تُسِرُّونَ إِلَيْهِم بِٱلْمَوَدَّةِ وَأَنَا۠ أَعْلَمُ بِمَآ
أَخْفَيْتُمْ وَمَآ أَعْلَنتُمْ ۚ وَمَن يَفْعَلْهُ مِنكُمْ فَقَدْ ضَلَّ سَوَآءَ ٱلسَّبِيلِ ﴿١﴾ ﴾

(سورة الممتحنة: ١)

﴿O you who have believed, do not take My enemies and your enemies as allies,[71] extending to them affection while they have disbelieved in what came to you of the truth, having driven out the Prophet and yourselves [only] because you believe in Allah, your Lord. If you have come out for jihad in My cause and seeking means to My approval [take them not as friends]. You confide to them affection, but I am most knowing of what you have concealed and what you have declared. Whoever does it among you has certainly strayed from the soundness of the way.﴾

(Qur'an 60: 1)

﴿ إِنَّمَا وَلِيُّكُمُ ٱللَّهُ وَرَسُولُهُۥ وَٱلَّذِينَ ءَامَنُوا۟ ٱلَّذِينَ يُقِيمُونَ ٱلصَّلَوٰةَ وَيُؤْتُونَ ٱلزَّكَوٰةَ وَهُمْ
رَٰكِعُونَ ﴿٥٥﴾ وَمَن يَتَوَلَّ ٱللَّهَ وَرَسُولَهُۥ وَٱلَّذِينَ ءَامَنُوا۟ فَإِنَّ حِزْبَ ٱللَّهِ هُمُ ٱلْغَٰلِبُونَ ﴿٥٦﴾ ﴾

(سورة المائدة: ٥٥-٥٦)

---

[71] That is, close associates and friends.

﴿Your ally is none but Allah and [therefore] His Messenger and those who have believed — those who establish prayer and give zakâh, and they bow [in worship]. Whoever is an ally of Allah and His Messenger and those who have believed — indeed, the party of Allah — they will be the predominant.﴾ *(Qur'an 5: 55-56)*

Anas (ﷺ) narrated that the Prophet (ﷺ) said:

«Whoever possesses the following three qualities will taste the sweetness (delight) of faith:

- To love Allah and His Messenger (ﷺ) so much that they become dearer to him than anything else
- To love a person solely for Allah's sake
- For him, to revert to disbelief is akin to being thrown into the fire.» (Bukhari)

Meaning of *al-walâ' wal-barâ'*

The seventh condition of the shahâdah, *al-walâ' wal-barâ'*, requires that we love Allah and act according to our testimony of faith; likewise, we hate, oppose, and fight anyone or anything that contradicts the shahâdah. It is for this reason that this condition is translated as 'loving and hating for the sake of Allah'.

Literally, the term *al-walâ'* means loyalty, and *al-barâ'* means distance from, freedom of, or disownment. However, in Islamic legal terminology, al-walâ' signifies loyalty to Allah and all that is pleasing to Him, as well as friendship with and closeness to the believers. On the other hand, al-barâ' means freeing oneself (keeping away) from all that is displeasing to Allah and disowning or disassociating oneself from the disbelievers, polytheists, hypocrites, and all the enemies of Allah and His Messenger (ﷺ) along with the enemies of sincere believers.

Signs of those who have *al-walâ' wal-barâ'*

In order to fulfil all the criteria of the shahâdah, one has to strive to seek the pleasure of Allah in all thoughts, words, deeds, and actions. Such are the characteristics of those who truly love Allah, His Messenger Muhammad (ﷺ), and all true, sincere Muslims. Ibn Taymiyah, in his book *Al-'Ubudiyyah,*[72] has described the signs of people who love Allah as follows:

a. Following the example of the Messenger (ﷺ)

b. Striving in the path of Allah

Unquestionably, in order to practically implement the love of Allah in one's life, one has to strictly adhere to the Sunnah of Prophet Muhammad (ﷺ). As for the second sign, Ibn Taymiyah elaborates in the following words the reason why this is a distinguishing feature for the love of Allah:

> That is because the reality of jihad is the striving to accomplish that which Allah loves of faith and righteous deeds and repulsion of that which Allah hates of disbelief, rebellion against Allah and disobedience.

The shaykh (may Allah have mercy on him) further states:

> The reality of loving someone is never complete except by having loyalty to him [the beloved one] that is by complying with him in loving what he loves and hating what he hates. For Allah loves faith and God-consciousness, while He hates disbelief, rebellion and disobedience.

---

[72] Shaykh al-Islam Ibn Taymiyyah, *Al-'Ubudiyyah, Being a True Slave of Allah,* trans. Nasiruddin al-Khattab (Birmingham: Al-Hidaayah Publishing and Distribution Ltd., 1999), 117-119.

Therefore, it is not enough just to claim love for the shahâdah and consequently the love of Allah and His Messenger (ﷺ), without having these established signs. Moreover, love for the sake of Allah must be accompanied by hate for the sake of Allah in order for it to be true love. In other words, one must love the thoughts, actions, and deeds that please Allah, and one must despise those that invoke His wrath.

For example, there are individuals among the Christians who claim to love Allah; they spend huge sums in charity, build houses of worship, and care for the orphans and the poor all over the world. However, to begin with, their belief in Allah is tainted with shirk: an unforgivable sin. Secondly, they are ignorant of His injunctions to refrain from the consumption of alcohol, pork, and usury. For this reason, their love of Allah cannot be sincere or complete, and their generous acts of charity cannot be regarded as being solely for Allah's sake.

Through their behaviour, many Muslims today demonstrate their ignorance of the seventh condition of the shahâdah. They appear to be weak and confused, loving false religions and ideologies while expressing their dislike of the adherents of Islam. This is completely contrary to our Islamic creed, wherein a Muslim is obliged to love those who conform to tawḥeed and hate those who associate partners with Allah. Given that all the prophets of Allah, over the centuries, were given the same message of tawḥeed, this article of Islamic doctrine is often referred to as the creed of Abraham (عليه السلام):

﴿وَجَٰهِدُواْ فِي ٱللَّهِ حَقَّ جِهَادِهِۦۚ هُوَ ٱجۡتَبَىٰكُمۡ وَمَا جَعَلَ عَلَيۡكُمۡ فِي ٱلدِّينِ مِنۡ حَرَجٖۚ
مِّلَّةَ أَبِيكُمۡ إِبۡرَٰهِيمَۚ هُوَ سَمَّىٰكُمُ ٱلۡمُسۡلِمِينَ مِن قَبۡلُ وَفِي هَٰذَا لِيَكُونَ ٱلرَّسُولُ شَهِيدًا
عَلَيۡكُمۡ وَتَكُونُواْ شُهَدَآءَ عَلَى ٱلنَّاسِۚ فَأَقِيمُواْ ٱلصَّلَوٰةَ وَءَاتُواْ ٱلزَّكَوٰةَ وَٱعۡتَصِمُواْ بِٱللَّهِ هُوَ
مَوۡلَىٰكُمۡۖ فَنِعۡمَ ٱلۡمَوۡلَىٰ وَنِعۡمَ ٱلنَّصِيرُ ٧٨﴾ (سورة الحج: ٧٨)

﴾And strive for Allah with the striving due to Him. He has chosen you and has not placed upon you in the religion any difficulty. [It is] the religion of your father, Abraham. Allah named you Muslims before [in former scriptures] and in this [revelation] so that the Messenger may be a witness over you and you may be witnesses over the people. So establish prayer and give zakâh and hold fast to Allah. He is your Protector; excellent is the Protector, and excellent is the Helper.﴿ *(Qur'an 22: 78)*

﴿قَدْ كَانَتْ لَكُمْ أُسْوَةٌ حَسَنَةٌ فِىٓ إِبْرَٰهِيمَ وَٱلَّذِينَ مَعَهُۥٓ إِذْ قَالُوا۟ لِقَوْمِهِمْ إِنَّا بُرَءَٰٓؤُا۟
مِنكُمْ وَمِمَّا تَعْبُدُونَ مِن دُونِ ٱللَّهِ كَفَرْنَا بِكُمْ وَبَدَا بَيْنَنَا وَبَيْنَكُمُ ٱلْعَدَٰوَةُ وَٱلْبَغْضَآءُ
أَبَدًا حَتَّىٰ تُؤْمِنُوا۟ بِٱللَّهِ وَحْدَهُۥٓ إِلَّا قَوْلَ إِبْرَٰهِيمَ لِأَبِيهِ لَأَسْتَغْفِرَنَّ لَكَ وَمَآ أَمْلِكُ لَكَ مِنَ
ٱللَّهِ مِن شَىْءٍ ۖ رَّبَّنَا عَلَيْكَ تَوَكَّلْنَا وَإِلَيْكَ أَنَبْنَا وَإِلَيْكَ ٱلْمَصِيرُ ﴿٤﴾﴾ (سورة الممتحنة: ٤)

﴾There has already been for you an excellent pattern in Abraham and those with him, when they said to their people: Indeed, we are disassociated from you and from whatever you worship other than Allah. We have denied you, and there has appeared between you and us animosity and hatred forever until you believe in Allah alone, except for the saying of Abraham to his father: I will surely ask forgiveness for you, but I have not [power to do] for you anything against Allah. Our Lord, upon You we have relied, and to You we have returned, and to You is the destination.﴿

(Qur'an 60: 4)

The stipulation to detest and hate those who go against the creed of tawḥeed (Abraham's creed), in accordance with the seventh condition of the shahâdah, has been very clearly enunciated as a command from Allah to the believers:

﴿يَٰٓأَيُّهَا ٱلَّذِينَ ءَامَنُوا۟ لَا تَتَّخِذُوا۟ ٱلْيَهُودَ وَٱلنَّصَٰرَىٰٓ أَوْلِيَآءَ ۘ بَعْضُهُمْ أَوْلِيَآءُ بَعْضٍ ۚ وَمَن
يَتَوَلَّهُم مِّنكُمْ فَإِنَّهُۥ مِنْهُمْ ۗ إِنَّ ٱللَّهَ لَا يَهْدِى ٱلْقَوْمَ ٱلظَّٰلِمِينَ ﴿٥١﴾﴾ (سورة المائدة: ٥١)

﴿O you who have believed, do not take the Jews and the Christians as allies. They are [in fact] allies of one another. Whoever is an ally to them among you — then indeed, he is [one] of them. Indeed, Allah guides not the wrongdoing people.﴾ *(Qur'an 5: 51)*

﴿وَلَن تَرۡضَىٰ عَنكَ ٱلۡيَهُودُ وَلَا ٱلنَّصَٰرَىٰ حَتَّىٰ تَتَّبِعَ مِلَّتَهُمۡۗ قُلۡ إِنَّ هُدَى ٱللَّهِ هُوَ ٱلۡهُدَىٰۗ
وَلَئِنِ ٱتَّبَعۡتَ أَهۡوَآءَهُم بَعۡدَ ٱلَّذِي جَآءَكَ مِنَ ٱلۡعِلۡمِ مَا لَكَ مِنَ ٱللَّهِ مِن وَلِيّٖ وَلَا نَصِيرٍ ١٢٠﴾

(سورة البقرة: ١٢٠)

﴿And never will the Jews or the Christians approve of you until you follow their religion. Say: Indeed, the guidance of Allah is the [only] guidance. If you were to follow their desires after what has come to you of knowledge, you would have against Allah no protector or helper.﴾ *(Qur'an 2: 120)*

Indeed, the order to desist from supporting and helping disbelievers or taking them as protectors and friends extends even to close blood relatives:

﴿يَٰٓأَيُّهَا ٱلَّذِينَ ءَامَنُواْ لَا تَتَّخِذُوٓاْ ءَابَآءَكُمۡ وَإِخۡوَٰنَكُمۡ أَوۡلِيَآءَ إِنِ ٱسۡتَحَبُّواْ
ٱلۡكُفۡرَ عَلَى ٱلۡإِيمَٰنِۚ وَمَن يَتَوَلَّهُم مِّنكُمۡ فَأُوْلَٰٓئِكَ هُمُ ٱلظَّٰلِمُونَ ٢٣﴾

(سورة التوبة: ٢٣)

﴿O you who have believed, do not take your fathers or your brothers as allies if they have preferred disbelief over belief. Whoever does so among you — it is those who are the wrongdoers.﴾

(Qur'an 9: 23)

Thus, according to the seventh criterion of the shahâdah, love, support, and protection should be based on the brotherhood of Islam rather than along blood lines. Hence, all Muslims — irrespective of their colour, language, geographical origin, and lineage — deserve our love, help, and protection. In contrast, we should hate, oppose, and fight the enemies of Islam; that is, those who wage war against 'lâ ilâha illâ Allâh', those who ridicule Prophet Muhammad (ﷺ) and his Companions, or those who oppress other Muslims. The believers are brothers in faith and creed; this tie transcends blood ties and warrants special consideration as Allah has stated:

﴿مُّحَمَّدٌ رَّسُولُ ٱللَّهِ ۚ وَٱلَّذِينَ مَعَهُۥٓ أَشِدَّآءُ عَلَى ٱلْكُفَّارِ رُحَمَآءُ بَيْنَهُمْ ۖ تَرَىٰهُمْ رُكَّعًا سُجَّدًا
يَبْتَغُونَ فَضْلًا مِّنَ ٱللَّهِ وَرِضْوَٰنًا ۖ سِيمَاهُمْ فِى وُجُوهِهِم مِّنْ أَثَرِ ٱلسُّجُودِ ۚ ذَٰلِكَ مَثَلُهُمْ فِى
ٱلتَّوْرَىٰةِ ۚ وَمَثَلُهُمْ فِى ٱلْإِنجِيلِ كَزَرْعٍ أَخْرَجَ شَطْـَٔهُۥ فَـَٔازَرَهُۥ فَٱسْتَغْلَظَ فَٱسْتَوَىٰ عَلَىٰ سُوقِهِۦ
يُعْجِبُ ٱلزُّرَّاعَ لِيَغِيظَ بِهِمُ ٱلْكُفَّارَ ۗ وَعَدَ ٱللَّهُ ٱلَّذِينَ ءَامَنُوا۟ وَعَمِلُوا۟ ٱلصَّـٰلِحَـٰتِ مِنْهُم مَّغْفِرَةً
وَأَجْرًا عَظِيمًۢا ﴿٢٩﴾﴾ (سورة الفتح: ٢٩)

﴿Muhammad is the Messenger of Allah, and those with him are forceful against the disbelievers, merciful among themselves. You see them bowing and prostrating [in prayer], seeking bounty from Allah and [His] pleasure. Their mark is on their faces from the trace of prostration. That is their description in the Torah, and their description in the Gospel is as a plant which produces its offshoots and strengthens them so they grow firm and stand upon their stalks, delighting the sowers — so that Allah may enrage by them the disbelievers. Allah has promised forgiveness and a great reward to those among them who believe and do righteous deeds.﴾ *(Qur'an 48: 29)*

﴿يَـٰٓأَيُّهَا ٱلَّذِينَ ءَامَنُوا۟ مَن يَرْتَدَّ مِنكُمْ عَن دِينِهِۦ فَسَوْفَ يَأْتِى ٱللَّهُ بِقَوْمٍ يُحِبُّهُمْ وَيُحِبُّونَهُۥٓ
أَذِلَّةٍ عَلَى ٱلْمُؤْمِنِينَ أَعِزَّةٍ عَلَى ٱلْكَـٰفِرِينَ يُجَـٰهِدُونَ فِى سَبِيلِ ٱللَّهِ وَلَا يَخَافُونَ لَوْمَةَ لَآئِمٍ ۚ
ذَٰلِكَ فَضْلُ ٱللَّهِ يُؤْتِيهِ مَن يَشَآءُ ۚ وَٱللَّهُ وَٰسِعٌ عَلِيمٌ ﴿٥٤﴾﴾ (سورة المائدة: ٥٤)

﴿O you who have believed, whoever of you should revert from his religion — Allah will bring forth [in place of them] a people He will love and who will love Him, [who are] humble toward the believers, powerful against the disbelievers; they strive in the cause of Allah and do not fear the blame of a critic. That is the favour of Allah; He bestows it upon whom He wills. Allah is All-Encompassing and Knowing.﴿ *(Qur'an 5: 54)*

Indeed the believers, from the first generation of humankind to the last, are brothers and supporters of each other. They command each other to what is good and forbid them from evil. They obey Allah and His Messenger (ﷺ). They establish prayer regularly and give zakâh; thus, the descendants follow the good examples of the ancestors while asking Allah's forgiveness for them as exemplified in the following verses:

﴿إِنَّمَا ٱلْمُؤْمِنُونَ إِخْوَةٌ فَأَصْلِحُوا۟ بَيْنَ أَخَوَيْكُمْ ۚ وَٱتَّقُوا۟ ٱللَّهَ لَعَلَّكُمْ تُرْحَمُونَ ﴿١٠﴾﴾

(سورة الحُجُرات: ١٠)

﴾The believers are but brothers, so make settlement between your brothers, and fear Allah that you may receive mercy.﴿

(Qur'an 49: 10)

﴿وَٱلْمُؤْمِنُونَ وَٱلْمُؤْمِنَٰتُ بَعْضُهُمْ أَوْلِيَآءُ بَعْضٍ ۚ يَأْمُرُونَ بِٱلْمَعْرُوفِ وَيَنْهَوْنَ عَنِ
ٱلْمُنكَرِ وَيُقِيمُونَ ٱلصَّلَوٰةَ وَيُؤْتُونَ ٱلزَّكَوٰةَ وَيُطِيعُونَ ٱللَّهَ وَرَسُولَهُۥٓ ۚ أُو۟لَٰٓئِكَ
سَيَرْحَمُهُمُ ٱللَّهُ ۗ إِنَّ ٱللَّهَ عَزِيزٌ حَكِيمٌ ﴿٧١﴾﴾ (سورة التوبة: ٧١)

﴾The believing men and believing women are allies of one another. They enjoin what is right and forbid what is wrong and establish prayer and give zakâh and obey Allah and His Messenger. Those — Allah will have mercy upon them. Indeed, Allah is Exalted in Might and Wise.﴿ *(Qur'an 9: 71)*

﴿وَٱلَّذِينَ جَآءُو مِنۢ بَعْدِهِمْ يَقُولُونَ رَبَّنَا ٱغْفِرْ لَنَا وَلِإِخْوَٰنِنَا ٱلَّذِينَ
سَبَقُونَا بِٱلْإِيمَٰنِ وَلَا تَجْعَلْ فِى قُلُوبِنَا غِلًّا لِّلَّذِينَ ءَامَنُوا۟ رَبَّنَآ إِنَّكَ رَءُوفٌ رَّحِيمٌ ﴿١٠﴾﴾

(سورة الحشر: ١٠)

﴾And [there is a share for] those who came after them, saying: Our Lord, forgive us and our brothers who preceded us in faith and put not in our hearts [any] resentment toward those who have believed. Our Lord, indeed You are Kind and Merciful.﴿

(Qur'an 59: 10)

Signs of those who take the disbelievers as friends and allies

(a) Imitating the disbelievers' way of life

Imitating the disbelievers' way of life indicates love for them. Thus, Allah has specifically prohibited the imitation of their:

- ways and objects of worship;
- traditions and cultures;
- celebrations and holidays;
- habits of eating and drinking; and
- appearances and immorality.

The Prophet (ﷺ) said:

«Whoever imitates a people is one of them.» (Recorded by Abu Dâwood and Aḥmad, and authenticated by al-Albâni)

(b) Residing in the land of the disbelievers and refusing to immigrate to Muslim countries in order to safeguard one's religion and faith

The concise meaning of Hijrah is migration. In other words, one should not live in the lands of the disbelievers except out of necessity or temporarily: for instance, for the purpose of education. Continuing to reside in the lands of the disbelievers at the peril of one's faith is a sign of friendship and love for them. Consider the following verse:

﴿إِنَّ ٱلَّذِينَ تَوَفَّىٰهُمُ ٱلْمَلَـٰٓئِكَةُ ظَالِمِىٓ أَنفُسِهِمْ قَالُوا۟ فِيمَ كُنتُمْ ۖ قَالُوا۟ كُنَّا مُسْتَضْعَفِينَ فِى
ٱلْأَرْضِ ۚ قَالُوٓا۟ أَلَمْ تَكُنْ أَرْضُ ٱللَّهِ وَٰسِعَةً فَتُهَاجِرُوا۟ فِيهَا ۚ فَأُو۟لَـٰٓئِكَ مَأْوَىٰهُمْ جَهَنَّمُ ۖ وَسَآءَتْ
مَصِيرًا ﴿٩٧﴾ إِلَّا ٱلْمُسْتَضْعَفِينَ مِنَ ٱلرِّجَالِ وَٱلنِّسَآءِ وَٱلْوِلْدَٰنِ لَا يَسْتَطِيعُونَ حِيلَةً وَلَا
يَهْتَدُونَ سَبِيلًا ﴿٩٨﴾ فَأُو۟لَـٰٓئِكَ عَسَى ٱللَّهُ أَن يَعْفُوَ عَنْهُمْ ۚ وَكَانَ ٱللَّهُ عَفُوًّا غَفُورًا ﴿٩٩﴾ ۞
وَمَن يُهَاجِرْ فِى سَبِيلِ ٱللَّهِ يَجِدْ فِى ٱلْأَرْضِ مُرَٰغَمًا كَثِيرًا وَسَعَةً ۚ ... ﴿١٠٠﴾﴾

(سورة النساء: ٩٧-١٠٠)

﴿Indeed, those whom the angels take [in death] while wronging themselves — [the angels] will say: In what [condition] were you? They will say: We were oppressed in the land. The angels will say: Was not the earth of Allah spacious [enough] for you to emigrate therein? For those, their refuge is hell — and evil it is as a destination. Except for the oppressed among men, women, and children who cannot devise a plan nor are they directed to a way — for those it is expected that Allah will pardon them, and Allah is ever Pardoning and Forgiving. Whoever emigrates for the cause of Allah will find on the earth many [alternative] locations and abundance...﴾ *(Qur'an 4: 97-100)*

In the aforementioned verse, those who have wronged themselves are the Muslims who, out of choice rather than lack of means, remain amongst the disbelievers in an environment that is hostile to the practice of Islam. In essence, the implication of this verse is that Muslims are forbidden from residing in countries where they cannot freely practice their religion; those who are able are obliged to immigrate to Muslim lands in order to secure their faith.

(c) Seeking the help, support, and protection of the disbelievers

Another indicator of friendship and love of disbelievers is to take them as allies, helpers, and supporters rather than trusting Allah's protection and seeking help and assistance from fellow Muslims. Such Muslims are very vulnerable indeed and are likened to a spider that takes its web as a protection from other animals, not realizing it is the weakest and flimsiest of protections:

﴿مَثَلُ ٱلَّذِينَ ٱتَّخَذُوا۟ مِن دُونِ ٱللَّهِ أَوْلِيَآءَ كَمَثَلِ ٱلْعَنكَبُوتِ ٱتَّخَذَتْ بَيْتًا ۖ وَإِنَّ أَوْهَنَ ٱلْبُيُوتِ لَبَيْتُ ٱلْعَنكَبُوتِ ۖ لَوْ كَانُوا۟ يَعْلَمُونَ ﴿٤١﴾ إِنَّ ٱللَّهَ يَعْلَمُ مَا يَدْعُونَ مِن دُونِهِۦ مِن شَىْءٍ ۚ وَهُوَ ٱلْعَزِيزُ ٱلْحَكِيمُ ﴿٤٢﴾ وَتِلْكَ ٱلْأَمْثَٰلُ نَضْرِبُهَا لِلنَّاسِ ۖ وَمَا يَعْقِلُهَآ إِلَّا ٱلْعَٰلِمُونَ ﴿٤٣﴾﴾

(سورة العنكبوت: ٤١-٤٣)

﴿The example of those who take allies other than Allah is like that of the spider who takes a home. Indeed, the weakest of homes is the home of the spider, if they only knew. Indeed, Allah knows whatever thing they call upon other than Him, and He is the Exalted in Might, the Wise. These examples We present to the people, but none will understand them except those of knowledge.﴾

(Qur'an 29: 41-43)

The Islamic ruling about ties with non-Muslims

As mentioned previously, Muslims are prohibited from residing in lands where the free practice of Islam is restricted. However, Islamic law does permit Muslims to live in these countries for the purpose of propagating Islam. Furthermore, the Sharia stipulates varying obligations on Muslims towards non-Muslims, depending upon the position and behaviour of the disbelievers. In this context, disbelievers are divided into three groups.

For obvious reasons, the approach and attitude of Islam and the Muslims will differ depending on the category of the disbelievers.

i. Those who fight against Islam and the Muslims

Those who fight against Islam and the Muslims, with a view to usurping or controlling Islamic principles or Muslim lands, should be fought and opposed — since they are the aggressors and invaders — until there is no more turmoil. However, in the process of defending themselves as well as their lands, religion, and properties, Muslims should not transgress the limits. These have been clearly specified: no killing of innocent children, women, people working on farm lands, and so forth. Neither should trees be cut down nor domestic animals be slaughtered. In effect, Islamic law stipulates that there should be no wanton destruction; rather, Muslims should only fight those who fight them.

﴿وَقَٰتِلُوا۟ فِى سَبِيلِ ٱللَّهِ ٱلَّذِينَ يُقَٰتِلُونَكُمْ وَلَا تَعْتَدُوٓا۟ ۚ إِنَّ ٱللَّهَ لَا يُحِبُّ
ٱلْمُعْتَدِينَ ﴿١٩٠﴾ وَٱقْتُلُوهُمْ حَيْثُ ثَقِفْتُمُوهُمْ وَأَخْرِجُوهُم مِّنْ حَيْثُ أَخْرَجُوكُمْ ۚ وَٱلْفِتْنَةُ أَشَدُّ مِنَ
ٱلْقَتْلِ ۚ وَلَا تُقَٰتِلُوهُمْ عِندَ ٱلْمَسْجِدِ ٱلْحَرَامِ حَتَّىٰ يُقَٰتِلُوكُمْ فِيهِ ۖ فَإِن قَٰتَلُوكُمْ فَٱقْتُلُوهُمْ ۗ كَذَٰلِكَ
جَزَآءُ ٱلْكَٰفِرِينَ ﴿١٩١﴾ فَإِنِ ٱنتَهَوْا۟ فَإِنَّ ٱللَّهَ غَفُورٌ رَّحِيمٌ ﴿١٩٢﴾ وَقَٰتِلُوهُمْ حَتَّىٰ لَا تَكُونَ فِتْنَةٌ وَيَكُونَ
ٱلدِّينُ لِلَّهِ ۖ فَإِنِ ٱنتَهَوْا۟ فَلَا عُدْوَٰنَ إِلَّا عَلَى ٱلظَّٰلِمِينَ ﴿١٩٣﴾﴾ (سورة البقرة: ١٩٠-١٩٣)

﴿Fight in the way of Allah those who fight you, but do not transgress. Indeed, Allah does not like transgressors. Kill them wherever you overtake them and expel them from wherever they have expelled you, and fitnah is worse than killing. Do not fight them at *al-Masjid al-Ḥarâm* [the Sacred Mosque in Makkah] until they fight you there. But if they fight you, then kill them. Such is the recompense of the disbelievers. If they cease, then indeed, Allah is Forgiving and Merciful. Fight them until there is no [more] fitnah and [until] worship is [acknowledged to be] for Allah. But if they cease, then there is to be no aggression except against the oppressors.﴾ *(Qur'an 2: 190-193)*

﴿... وَقَٰتِلُوا۟ ٱلْمُشْرِكِينَ كَآفَّةً كَمَا يُقَٰتِلُونَكُمْ كَآفَّةً ۚ وَٱعْلَمُوٓا۟ أَنَّ ٱللَّهَ مَعَ ٱلْمُتَّقِينَ ﴿٣٦﴾﴾ (سورة التوبة: ٣٦)

﴿...And fight against the disbelievers collectively as they fight against you collectively, and know that Allah is with the righteous [who fear Him].﴾ *(Qur'an 9: 36)*

Ibn 'Umar (رضي الله عنه) narrated that Allah's Messenger (ﷺ) said: «I have been ordered (by Allah) to fight against people until they testify that none has the right to be worshipped but Allah and that Muhammad is Allah's Messenger and [until they] offer the prayers perfectly and give the obligatory charity. If they perform that, then they save their lives and property from me except for Islamic laws, and then their reckoning (accounts) will be done by Allah.» (Bukhari)

In the event of a war between Muslims and non-Muslim aggressors, Islamic law stipulates clearly-defined terms of engagement. Not only is unjustifiable carnage and destruction strictly forbidden, but retaliation also should be limited to what the enemy has inflicted on the Muslims. Allah has prescribed:

﴿وَإِنْ عَاقَبْتُمْ فَعَاقِبُوا۟ بِمِثْلِ مَا عُوقِبْتُم بِهِۦ ۖ وَلَئِن صَبَرْتُمْ لَهُوَ خَيْرٌ لِّلصَّٰبِرِينَ ﴿١٢٦﴾﴾ (سورة النحل: ١٢٦)

﴿And if you punish [an enemy, O believers], punish with an equivalent of that with which you were harmed. But if you are patient — it is better for those who are patient.﴾ *(Qur'an 16: 126)*

ii. Those who are neutral, neither supporting nor fighting Islam and the Muslims

As for this second category of non-Muslims, no war should be waged against them. However, if they are guilty of oppressing other people (even non-Muslims) or causing corruption in the land by committing all sorts of evils, then Islamic law, in the interest of justice and decency, obliges the Muslim army to give them three options:

a. They are invited to accept Islam, affirm and adhere to the shahâdah, and renounce their evil and corrupt ways. Thus, they will benefit from the Islamic brotherhood and live a good life in this world and the hereafter.

b. They can adhere to their own religion and continue to reside as protected minorities (*dhimmis*) under the Islamic state. For those who are financially able, a tax called *jizyah* will be imposed. As long as they cause no mischief, they will all benefit from the facilities provided by the Islamic state, including protection of their wealth and property and protection against external enemies. Meanwhile, they are invited to Islam in the best way possible, as Allah has commanded:

﴿ ٱدْعُ إِلَىٰ سَبِيلِ رَبِّكَ بِٱلْحِكْمَةِ وَٱلْمَوْعِظَةِ ٱلْحَسَنَةِ ۖ وَجَٰدِلْهُم بِٱلَّتِى هِىَ أَحْسَنُ ۚ إِنَّ رَبَّكَ هُوَ أَعْلَمُ بِمَن ضَلَّ عَن سَبِيلِهِۦ ۖ وَهُوَ أَعْلَمُ بِٱلْمُهْتَدِينَ ﴿١٢٥﴾ ﴾

(سورة النحل: ١٢٥)

﴿Invite to the way of your Lord with wisdom and good instruction, and argue with them in a way that is best. Indeed, your Lord is most knowing of who has strayed from His way, and He is most knowing of who is [rightly] guided.﴾

(Qur'an 16: 125)

c. If they decline the first two options and continue to create mischief, oppression, and corruption in the land, then the only option is for the Islamic army to wage war against them until they are subjugated. In that event, the first two options are applicable: either they willingly accept Islam or come under the jurisdiction of the Islamic state as dhimmis and pay jizyah. Allah has stated in the Qur'an:

﴿ قَٰتِلُوا۟ ٱلَّذِينَ لَا يُؤْمِنُونَ بِٱللَّهِ وَلَا بِٱلْيَوْمِ ٱلْـَٔاخِرِ وَلَا يُحَرِّمُونَ مَا حَرَّمَ ٱللَّهُ وَرَسُولُهُۥ وَلَا يَدِينُونَ دِينَ ٱلْحَقِّ مِنَ ٱلَّذِينَ أُوتُوا۟ ٱلْكِتَٰبَ حَتَّىٰ يُعْطُوا۟ ٱلْجِزْيَةَ عَن يَدٍ وَهُمْ صَٰغِرُونَ ﴿٢٩﴾ ﴾ (سورة التوبة: ٢٩)

﴿Fight those who do not believe in Allah or in the last day and who do not consider unlawful what Allah and His Messenger have made unlawful and who do not adopt the religion of truth from those who were given the scripture — [fight] until they give the jizyah willingly while they are humbled.﴾ *(Qur'an 9: 29)*

In the Tabook expedition of 9 AH (630 CE), Prophet Muhammad (ﷺ) offered these three options to some of the pro-Roman Ghassanid tribes. Because of rumours about the dangers threatening the Muslims from the Byzantines in the north, Prophet Muhammad (ﷺ) had marched northwards with thirty thousand of his troops to fight against the Romans. When the Muslim army reached Tabook, they found no Roman army and no threat.

In order to secure themselves against any future danger, scouts and emissaries were sent out to the pro-Roman tribes in the area. Several of the local tribes gave their allegiance to Prophet Muhammad (ﷺ) and agreed to the payment of the jizyah. Yahnah ibn Rawbah, a leader of one of the tribes, also chose the option of retaining his faith and paying the jizyah. In return, Prophet Muhammad (ﷺ) gave each tribe a letter of guarantee similar to Yahnah's, guaranteeing their freedom to practice their religion.

iii. Those who are sympathetic to Islam and the Muslims

In the case of the third category of non-Muslims, Islam has made it obligatory for Muslims to treat them kindly and justly. They should be offered charity and any other assistance they might need, in order to motivate them to become Muslims. Allah has instructed:

﴿لَّا يَنْهَىٰكُمُ ٱللَّهُ عَنِ ٱلَّذِينَ لَمْ يُقَـٰتِلُوكُمْ فِى ٱلدِّينِ وَلَمْ يُخْرِجُوكُم مِّن دِيَـٰرِكُمْ أَن تَبَرُّوهُمْ وَتُقْسِطُوٓا۟
إِلَيْهِمْ ۚ إِنَّ ٱللَّهَ يُحِبُّ ٱلْمُقْسِطِينَ ﴿٨﴾ إِنَّمَا يَنْهَىٰكُمُ ٱللَّهُ عَنِ ٱلَّذِينَ قَـٰتَلُوكُمْ فِى ٱلدِّينِ وَأَخْرَجُوكُم
مِّن دِيَـٰرِكُمْ وَظَـٰهَرُوا۟ عَلَىٰٓ إِخْرَاجِكُمْ أَن تَوَلَّوْهُمْ ۚ وَمَن يَتَوَلَّهُمْ فَأُو۟لَـٰٓئِكَ هُمُ ٱلظَّـٰلِمُونَ ﴿٩﴾﴾

(سورة الممتحنة: ٨-٩)

﴿Allah does not forbid you from those who do not fight you because of religion and do not expel you from your homes — from being righteous toward them and acting justly toward them. Indeed, Allah loves those who act justly. Allah only forbids you from those who fight you because of religion and expel you from your homes and aid in your expulsion — [forbids] that you make allies of them. Whoever makes allies of them, then it is those who are the wrongdoers.﴾ *(Qur'an 60: 8-9)*

Conclusion

In conclusion, let us remind ourselves that the manifest duty incumbent on all of us who have pronounced the shahâdah is to fully comprehend its implications and practically implement its seven conditions. In reality, 'lâ ilâha illâ Allâh', the first basic and fundamental pillar of Islam, is the essential underpinning of a Muslim's commitment to and steadfastness in his or her faith. Indeed, thorough knowledge, combined with sincere and vigorous practice of the seven conditions presented in this book, will go a long way to ameliorate the prevailing ills in the Muslim community today. We pray and hope that in this small contribution, the reader finds some benefit towards a better understanding and commitment to Islam. If that happens, the time spent in preparing it would have been amply justified.

All praises are due to Allah, by whose unlimited bounties all good deeds are accomplished. May the peace, blessings, and mercy of Allah be upon our beloved Prophet Muhammad (ﷺ), his family, his noble Companions, and on all those who follow them in righteousness until the last day, âmeen.

Bibliography

al-Albaani, Shaykh Muhammad Naasiru-Deen. *The Prophet's Prayer Described*. Translated by Usama ibn Suhaib Hasan. Accessed March 27, 2012. http://www.qss.org/articles/salah/toc.html.

Ali, Abdullah Yusuf. *The Meaning of the Holy Qur'an: Text, Translation and Commentary.* Beltsville, MD: Amana Publications, 1993.

Bukhari, Muhammad ibn Ismâ'eel. *Sahih Al-Bukhari* (Arabic–English). Translated by Dr. Muhammad Muhsin Khan. Riyadh: Darussalam Publishers and Distributors, 2007.

Darussalam. *The Concise Collection on Creed and Tauhid*. Riyadh: Darussalam Publishers and Distributors, 2002.

Deedat, Ahmed. *The Choice: Islam and Christianity.* Volumes One and Two. Delhi, India: Millat Book Centre, 1997.

al-Fawzaan, Saalih ibn Fawzaan. *The Declaration of Faith.* United Kingdom: Message of Islam, 1998.

Hamid, Abdul Wahid. *Islam: The Natural Way*. London: MELS Publishing and Distributing, 1989.

Hart, Michael H. *The 100: A Ranking of the Most Influential Persons in History*. Secaucus, NJ: Carol Publishing Group, 1992.

Hassan, Ahmed. *Sunan Abu Dawood: English Translation.* Lahore: Sh. Muhammad Ashraf Publishers, 1987.

Ibn Katheer, Ismâ'eel. *Tafseer Ibn Katheer.*

Ibn Rajab, 'Abdur-Raḥmân ibn Aḥmad. *Kalimatul-Ikhlâṣ wa Taḥqeeq Ma'nâhâ.* Damascus: al-Maktab al-Islâmi, 1961.

Ibn Taymiyyah, Shaykh al-Islam. *Al-'Ubudiyyah, Being a True Slave of Allah.* Translated by Nasiruddin al-Khattab. Birmingham: Al-Hidaayah Publishing and Distribution Ltd., 1999.

Ibrahim, Ezzeddin and Denys Johnson-Davies. *An-Nawawi's Forty Hadith.* UAE: Dar el-Shorouk, 2003.

al-Jabiri, 'Obaid ibn 'Abdullah Sulaiman. *Facilitation by Allah in Explaining the Evidences of the Conditions of La ilaha illa Allaah.* UK: Jami'at Ihyaa' Minhaaj al Sunnah, 1995.

Khan, Muhammad Muhsin and Muhammad Taqi-ud-Din al-Hilali. *The Noble Qur'an: Arabic-English.* Madinah: King Fahd Complex for the Printing of the Holy Qur'an, 1998.

Lamartine, Alphonse de. *History of Turkey.* New York: D. Appleton & Co., 1857.

Masserman, Jules. "Who were history's greatest leaders?" *Time Magazine*, 15 July 1974.

Mawdoodi, Abul-A'lâ. *The Meaning of the Qur'an.* Nairobi, Kenya: The Islamic Foundation, 1989.

al-Mubarakpuri, Safi-ur-Rahman. *Ar-Raheeq Al-Makhtum (The Sealed Nectar).* Riyadh: Darussalam Publishers and Distributors, 1995.

Philips, Abu Ameenah Bilal. *The Best in Islam.* Sharjah: Dar Al Fatah Printing, Publishing & Distribution Co., 1996.

______. *The Fundamentals of Tawheed.* Riyadh: International Islamic Publishing House, 2006.

al-Qahtâni, Sa'eed ibn 'Ali ibn Wahf. *Hisnul Muslim: Arabic-English*. Gassim, Saudi Arabia: Foreign Guidance Center, 1996.

Saheeh International. *The Qur'an: Arabic Text with Corresponding English Meanings*. Jeddah: Abul-Qasim Publishing House, 1997.

Sarwari, Abdul Khâliq Khan. *Muhammad Mercy for Universe*. Uganda: Pakistan Society Uganda, 1983.

Shaw, George Bernard. *Genuine Islam*. Vol. I, No. 8. Singapore, 1936.

Siddiqui, Abdul-Hamid. *English Translation of Sahih Muslim*. Volume 1. Beirut: Dar al-Arabia, 1972.

Smith, R. Bosworth. *Mohammed and Mohammedanism*. London: Smith, Elder & Co., 1876.

Zaynoo, Muhammad ibn Jameel. *The Methodology of the Saved Sect*. London: Invitation to Islam, 2003.

______. *Al-Aqeedah al-Islamiyah*. Dubai: Masjid Ibraheem Al-Khalil, 1404 AH.

Glossary of Islamic Terms*

abu (or *abi)*	أبو، أبي	father (of)
âmeen	آمين	O Allah, accept our invocation; amen
Anṣâr	أنصار	'helpers': the Muslim citizens of Madinah who gave refuge to the Prophet (ﷺ) and the other Muslim emigrants from Makkah
'Arafah	عرفة	the plain outside of Makkah where pilgrims gather at the climax of the Hajj pilgrimage
barzakh	برزخ	an intermediate state between death and the Day of Resurrection; it is also said to be a 'place' where the souls of the deceased will remain until the blowing of the trumpet
da'wah	دعوة	disseminating the teachings of Islam and calling people to accept and embrace Islam

* The Arabic words are transliterated according to the conventions of the Transliteration Chart found in this book. If a word has become part of the English language (that is, it is found in a dictionary of Standard English), that spelling is used in this book and appears first in this Glossary, with the transliterated form in brackets after it.

dhimmi	ذمّي	protected or covenanted people; non-Muslims who must pay the jizyah in lieu of zakât
dinar *(deenâr)*	دينار	originally, a gold coin; a unit of currency
dirham	درهم	a silver coin; a unit of currency
du'â'	دعاء	supplication; invocation
eemân	إيمان	faith; belief in all the six pillars of the creed of Islam
Eid *('eed)*	عيد	*lit.* festival; the two celebrations: one at the end of Ramadan and the other at the culmination of the Hajj
fitnah	فتنة	*lit.* trial, temptation; (attempting to sow) discord between Muslims
fiṭrah	فطرة	the natural inclination (of humans) instilled by Allah
Hadith *(ḥadeeth)*	حديث	the collected statements and actions of Prophet Muhammad (ﷺ) that with the Qur'an form the basis of Islamic law
hadith *(ḥadeeth)*	حديث	a statement or action of Prophet Muhammad (ﷺ) that was remembered and recorded by his Companions and followers
hadith qudsi	حديث قدسي	'sacred hadith': a hadith communicated to Prophet Muhammad (ﷺ) by Allah but which is not part of the Qur'an
Ḥâfidh	الحافظ	'one who has memorized (the Qur'an)': an honorific title

Hajj *(ḥajj)* حج the major pilgrimage to the Sacred Mosque, site of the Ka'bah at Makkah, to be undertaken by every able Muslim once in his/her lifetime

Hijaz *(Ḥijâz)* حجاز the western region of the Arabian Peninsula that includes Makkah and Madinah

Hijrah هجرة migration: *esp.* the migration from Makkah to Madinah by Prophet Muhammad (ﷺ) and his Companions that marks the start of the Islamic calendar

*'ibâdât (*sg. *'ibâdah)* عبادات acts of worship

iḥsân إحسان goodness, perfection, excellence; to worship Allah as if you see Him, but even if you do not see Him you know that He sees you

ilâh اله god; deity

jihad *(jihâd)* جهاد struggle or striving (in Allah's cause)

*jinn (*plural of *jinni)* جن non-human, rational beings created by Allah from fire, often referred to as 'demons' or 'devils'; they have free will like humans: some are Muslims, others disbelievers; some are obedient to Allah, others disobedient. Satan is a jinni. Some people try to 'foretell' the future by contacting a jinni. Some disobedient jinn mislead people into thinking that they can tell them what will happen in the future, near or. far,

		or that the jinn can provide people with riches or some sort of power
jizyah	جزية	a tax levied on the People of the Scriptures when they are under the protection of a Muslim government; it is in lieu of the alms tax paid by Muslims
Kaaba (Ka'bah)	الكعبة	the House of Allah in Makkah, originally built by Prophets Abraham and Ishmael and which Muslims face wherever they pray
kalimah	كلمة	the content of the testimony of faith: that is, *lâ ilâha illâ Allâh*
kufr	الكفر	disbelief in Allah and/or what He has revealed
lâ ilâha illâ Allâh	لا إله إلا الله	there is none worthy of worship other than Allah
al-Masjid al-Ḥarâm	المسجد الحرام	the Sacred Mosque in Makkah, where the Kaaba is situated
mu'min (pl. *mu'mineen)*	مؤمن	true believer
prophethood		The term 'prophethood' is not in the English dictionary, but is an invented term, formed along the pattern of 'childhood' and 'motherhood', as a noun reflecting a particular state of being. It is meant to translate the meaning of the Arabic word *nubuwwah*, which has no one-word equivalent in English, but which could be translated as meaning 'the state of

		be ing a prophet', and is also used to refer to 'all things that have to do with being a prophet'. The term 'prophethood' has since become common in English-language Islamic discourse.
qibla *(qiblah)*	القبلة	the bearing to the Kaaba from any point on Earth; the direction that all Muslims must face in prayer
Ramadan *(Ramaḍân)*	رمضان	the ninth month in the Islamic calendar; the month of obligatory fasting; the month in which the first verses of the Qur'an were revealed
ṣalât or *ṣalâh*	صلاة	formal prayer: a combination of physical postures, recitation, and supplication
shahâdah	الشهادة	testimony, *usu.* the statement *Lâ ilâha illâ Allâh, Muḥammadun rasool Ullâh* (There is none worthy of worship other than God [Allah]; Muhammad is the Messenger of God)
Sharia *(sharee'ah)*	شريعة	Islamic law derived from the Qur'an and the Sunnah
shaykh	شيخ	teacher, mentor; scholar
shirk	الشرك	associating partners with Allah
ṣirâṭ	الصراط	the path leading to paradise that passes over hellfire and is found by disbelievers and sinners to be extremely sharp and narrow
soorah or *soorat*	سورة	chapter of the Qur'an

Sunnah	سنة	the practice and collected sayings of Prophet Muhammad (ﷺ) that together with the Qur'an forms the basis of Islamic law
sunnah	سُنّة	acts that are recommended but not mandatory
*tâbi'oon (*sg. *tâbi'i)*	التابعون	'successors'; those who knew or met any of the Companions and transmitted hadiths from them
ṭâghoot	طاغوت	idols; everything evil that is worshipped
tajweed	تجويد	rules of pronunciation and intonation for reciting the Qur'an
tasleem(ah)	تسليم	the act of saying *as-salâmu 'alaykum wa raḥmat Allâh* (may peace be upon you, and the mercy of Allah) to end the prayer
tawḥeed	التوحيد	the Oneness of Allah: that He alone deserves to be worshipped and that He has no partners
'umrah	عمرة	a minor, non-obligatory pilgrimage to Makkah
unseen		a term used to denote phenomena or aspects that cannot be known using ordinary human faculties
al-walâ' wal-barâ'	الولاء والبراء	the concept of friendship and renunciation or 'love and hate for Allah's sake'

witr	وتر	*lit.* an odd number: a single unit of supererogatory prayer, to be prayed any time after the evening (*'ishâ'*) prayer and before the call for the dawn prayer
zakât (zakâh or *zakât)*	زكاة	obligatory charity; an 'alms tax' on wealth payable by Muslims, to be distributed to other Muslims who qualify as recipients
zakât al-fiṭr	زكاة الفطر	obligatory charity at the end of the fast of Ramadan, payable in kind

Index

A

B

C

D

T

U

W

Y

Z